MSM

MATHEMATICS

BOOK 5^y

Geoffrey Staley
Head of Mathematics,
King Edward's School, Bath

Michael Kenwood
Formerly Senior Master
King Edward's School, Bath

MSM Mathematics Series Editor:
Dr Charles Plumpton

Nelson

Thomas Nelson and Sons Ltd
Nelson House Mayfield Road
Walton-on-Thames Surrey
KT12 5PL UK

58 Albany Street
Edinburgh
EH1 3QR UK

Nelson Blackie
Wester Cleddens Road
Bishopbriggs
Glasgow
G64 2NZ UK

Thomas Nelson (Hong Kong) Ltd
Toppan Building 10/F
22A Westlands Road
Quarry Bay Hong Kong

Thomas Nelson Australia
102 Dodds Street
South Melbourne
Victoria 3205 Australia

Nelson Canada
1120 Birchmount Road
Scarborough Ontario
MIK 5G4 Canada

First published by Thomas Nelson and Sons Ltd 1994

 Thomas Nelson is an International Thomson Publishing Company.

is used under licence.

ISBN 0–17–438481–5
NPN 9 8 7 6 5 4 3 2 1

Typeset by PanTek Arts, Maidstone, Kent.
Printed in EC

The authors and publishers wish to thank the following
for permission to use the copyright material:

The Midland Examining Group (M), Northern Examining Association (N) comprised of Associated
Lancashire Schools Examining Board, Joint Matriculation Board, North Regional Examinations
Board, North West Regional Examinations Board and Yorkshire and Humberside Regional
Examinations Board; Southern Examining Group (S), University of London Examinations and
Assessment Council (L) and Welsh Joint Education Committee   (C) for questions from past
examination papers and for sample assessment material for Key Stage 4.

HMSO for questions from 1993 Key Stage 3 mathematics tests, and for the extract from the 1991
Census.

London Regional Transport for the map on page 135.

Casio Electronics Co. Ltd for the calculator on page 117.

Photographic material:

R Harding, p.13; R Harding, p.25; R Harding, p.177; Harding, p.252; T Stone, p.15; Images, p.26;
Hutchinson, p.73.

Every effort has been made to trace all the copyright holders, but if any have been inadvertently
overlooked the publishers will be pleased to make the necessary arrangement at the first opportunity.

Cover picture copyright The Photo Source

Contents

Preface

This book forms part of the MSM Secondary Mathematics course, which has been written to correspond to the existing National Criteria for GCSE Mathematics examinations and to the 1991 National Curriculum Orders. In particular the y-stream books are for the use of pupils who are likely to take the higher level of the GCSE Mathematics examination.

Each chapter of Book 5y contains worked examples and sets of graded exercises. In addition there are many investigations. These can be used for different purposes: perhaps to prepare a topic, to extend skills learned, as mini-project work and as a further extension to the exercises. Considerable scope exists to extend work beyond level 10. The final chapter provides extensive coverage of questions from past papers, at GCSE higher levels, from sample assessment material for Key Stage 4 and from top-tier Key Stage 3 tests.

In terms of the National Curriculum the work covered in Book 5y is at levels 8 to 10. Particular emphasis is placed on providing appropriate material for students aiming for the highest grades at GCSE. Optional extension work is provided in places to introduce students who will take their mathematics further to the type of material they will encounter at A and A/S Level.

1. Number

Rational numbers

The blinding of the giant Polyphemus by Odysseus in the land of the Cyclops is a famous story from Greek mythology. After he was blinded, we are told that, on each morning and evening, the giant shepherd used to sit across the entrance of the cave with a pile of pebbles. He counted each sheep that passed by moving a pebble into a new pile and this ensured that none were lost. (Even cricket umpires today use this system to count to six!)

Many of the counting systems that people have used in the past were based on the tally system. The Egyptian, the Babylonian and the Roman number systems are all examples of using a tally system to record integers.

The counting numbers, 1, 2, 3, ..., that is the positive integers or **natural numbers**, developed eventually together with symbols like those we use today .

The subtraction of positive integers leads us into the set of negative integers, and division of integers introduces us to the set of fractions. All of these types of number form the set of **rational numbers**.

Another way of looking at these extensions to the number system is by considering the solutions of equations.

The equation $y + 5 = 2$ only has a solution when negative numbers are included in the number line; the equation $5t = 2$ only has a solution when fractional numbers are included in the number line.

The first section of the chapter is included for improvement and enhancement of your skills in handling rational numbers.

Investigation A

One way of making 1 using each of the numbers 2, 3, 4 and 5 once only and any of the four operations and brackets is $3 \times (4 - 2) - 5 = 1$. Try to find at least two other ways.

Now see if you can find one way of making all the numbers from 2 to 10. (Try to do this in 10 minutes maximum.)

Using the numbers 1, 2, 3, 4 and 5, Dave made the number 81 (from $12 \times 3 + 45$), but he couldn't make 82. Can you?

Working in pairs or in a group, set a number to make and see who can get the closest in a 2-minute interval. You could try 990 for starters.

Investigation B

This is a long-term, well-known problem, which can be done in odd moments!

See how many of the numbers from 1 to 100 you can make using at most four 4s. You may use the four operations, $+$, $-$, $\times$ and $\div$, plus $\sqrt{\ }$, the decimal point (for example .4), and 4! (i.e. $4 \times 3 \times 2 \times 1$). Be warned, there are some devious ones!

Investigation C

Are there any pairs of non-zero integers a and b (a may equal b) for which $a + b = a \times b$?

Using three integers, we find that $1 + 2 + 3 = 1 \times 2 \times 3$ is the only solution to $a + b + c = a \times b \times c$.
There is one solution for 4 numbers and three solutions for 5 numbers, one of which is

$$1 + 1 + 1 + 3 + 3 = 1 \times 1 \times 1 \times 3 \times 3.$$

Investigate and try to find the other solutions.

EXERCISE 1.1

1 1 ☐ 2 ☐ 3 ☐ 4 = ...

    (a) Without using brackets, and using different operations in the boxes, make the numbers (i) -1 (ii) 1 (iii) 1.5.

    (b) Without using brackets, but allowing repeated operations in the boxes, make the numbers (i) -13 (ii) -9 (ii) 1.5.

    (c) Using one or two brackets, and allowing repeated operations, make the numbers (i) 0 (ii) 0.5 (iii) 1.

    (d) The order of the numbers can now be changed. Using an operation only once find the smallest and largest numbers that can be made, without using brackets.

2 The sum of the factors of 38 (excluding 38) is 22 ($1 + 2 + 19$).
The sum of the factors of 22 (excluding 22) is 14 ($1 + 2 + 11$).
The following diagram completes the 'factor chain' for 38.

(a) Check through this chain.

(b) Copy and complete the factor chain for 12.

(c) Construct the factor chains for (i) 6 (ii) 50 (iii) 24.

(d) Find another number that behaves like 6.

(e) What kind of numbers have 1 as the only other number in the chain?

(f) Find a number
   (i) other than 38 for which 22 is the second number in the chain,
   (ii) other than 12 for which 16 is the second number in the chain.

3 Show that the sums of the factors of 130 and of 166, including the number itself in each case, are equal.

4 For the integer N, F is the number of factors of N including 1 and N itself.

For example, when $N = 8$, $F = 4$ because 1, 2, 4 and 8 are the factors.

(a) What can be said about any number N for which
   (i) $F = 2$, (ii) $F = 3$.

(b) Find two numbers for N, where $N \le 100$, for which $F = 9$.

5 Giving your answer as a rational number in its simplest form, evaluate the following, (i) showing all working, (ii) using your calculator.

(a) $\frac{1}{3} + \frac{1}{4} + \frac{1}{5} + \frac{1}{6}$ (b) $2\frac{1}{6} - \frac{5}{9}$ (c) $\dfrac{1}{\frac{1}{2} + \frac{1}{3}}$

(d) $\frac{3}{4} \times \frac{10}{21} \times 3\frac{1}{2}$ (e) $2\frac{1}{6} \div \frac{5}{9}$

6 Ali, Bedi, and Chris share some money so that Ali gets $\frac{4}{9}$, Bedi gets $\frac{1}{3}$ and Chris gets the rest which is £16. How much do Ali and Bedi get?

7 The integers p, q and r are all less than 8.
Find values for p, q and r in each case where

(a) $8^2 p + 8 q + r = 358$

(b) $10^2 (p + q) + 10 (q + r) + (r + p) = 358$

8 The points A, B, C, D and E are placed in order on a number line so that $AB = BC = CD = DE$.
If the points A and E are at the points $\frac{2}{7}$ and $\frac{5}{3}$, find the rational numbers at B, C and D.

9 Two girls, Michelle and Noreen, are walking at 6 km/h along a hiking track. Michelle's stride is 75 cm and Noreen's is 72 cm. How many more strides does Noreen take in an hour?

10 Let $x = \dfrac{6.12 + 3.4 \times 5.2}{11.17 - 8.29}$.

(a) Without using a calculator explain how you know that
(i) x must be greater than 7 (ii) x must be less than 13.5.
Which do you think it is nearer to, 7 or 13?

(b) Set out clearly the sequence of calculator keys you would use to find x, (i) without using the memory, (ii) using the memory.

(c) Use a calculator to find x, correct to (i) 3 (ii) 4 significant figures.

11 From the rational number $\frac{a}{b}$ the rational number $\dfrac{a + 4b}{a + b}$
is formed. This new rational number $\frac{p}{q}$, say, can then be used to form the new rational number $\dfrac{p + 4q}{p + q}$ and so on.
When $a = 3$ and $b = 2$, we form the sequence of rational numbers $\frac{3}{2}, \frac{11}{5}, \frac{31}{16}, \ldots$

(a) Continue the sequence as far as the eighth term.

(b) Convert each of these fractions into decimals.

(c) As more terms are added describe what you think happens to the sequence.

12 A number whose factors, other than the number itself, have a
sum equal to the number, such as 6, is called a perfect number.

(a) Find the perfect number that lies between 25 and 30.

(b) Any number has as many factors which are smaller than
its square root as it has larger than its square root.
Explain why this is so.

(c) Use a calculator to find the factors of 496 and 8128 and
hence show that they are perfect numbers.

(d) Show that 6, 28, 496 and 8128 can all be expressed in the
form $2^n(2^{n+1} - 1)$ and find the value of n in each case.

(e) All numbers of the form $2^n(2^{n+1} - 1)$ are perfect numbers
providing $(2^{n+1} - 1)$ is a prime number.
By substituting values for n show that 6, 28, 496 and
8128 are the first four perfect numbers and show that the
next does not occur until $n = 13$.

Investigation D

Explaining your working completely, and giving reasons for your
method of investigation, show that 9137 is a prime number. It is also
true that 137, 37 and 7 are prime. Of the five other 4-digit numbers of
the form $9 ---$, where the other three digits are 1, 3 or 7, only one
has this property. Find it and show where the others break down. Try
to find at least one other 4-digit number with this property.

Indices

You will have covered the work on indices but here we revise and use it.
The two main rules are:

$$a^m \times a^n = a^{m+n} \quad \text{and} \quad \frac{a^m}{a^n} = a^{m-n}$$

Example 1

(a) $5^3 \times 5^7 \times 5^{10} = 5^{3+7+10} = 5^{20}$

(b) $2^{12} \div 2^5 = 2^{12-5} = 2^7$

(c) $\dfrac{3^8 \times 3^4}{3^7} = 3^{8+4-7} = 3^5$

Reminders:

1. The rules only apply if the base number is the same:

$$2^3 \times 3^4 \text{ is } not \ 2^7, 3^7 \text{ or } 6^7 - \text{it is } 8 \times 81 = 648$$

2. Unlike bases can be combined, if the powers are the same, for example:

$$2^5 \times 3^5 = (2 \times 3)^5 = 6^5$$

3. A consequence of the first rule is that

$$(a^m)^n = a^{mn}$$

EXERCISE 1.2

1 Without using a calculator evaluate the following.

(a) $\dfrac{10^5 \times 10^9}{10^{12}}$ (b) $\dfrac{10^8 \times 10^6}{10^9 \times 10^3}$ (c) $\dfrac{10^{12}}{10^4 \times 10^7}$

2 State which of the following are equal to 6^{12}.

(a) $6^4 \times 6^3$ (b) $6^7 \times 6^5$ (c) $(6^3)^4$ (d) $3^8 \times 4^4$

(e) $3^{12} \times 2^{12}$ (f) $6^{11} \times 6$ (g) $\dfrac{24^{15}}{4^3}$ (h) $\dfrac{18^{12}}{3^{12}}$

(i) $6^6 + 6^6$ (j) $\dfrac{6^{13} \times 6^5}{6^6}$

3 Write the following in the form a^n.

(a) $7^4 \times 7^8 \times 7^2$ (b) $(3^4)^5$ (c) $5^2 \times 7^2$ (d) $\dfrac{2^9 \times 2^4}{2^2 \times 2^{11}}$

4 $504 = 2^3 \times 3^2 \times 7$

In this form we see 504 as the product of its prime factors.

(a) Write down 1080 as the product of its prime factors.

(b) Hence express 544 320 as the product of its prime factors.

5 (a) Given that $2^x \times 2^y = 2^{18}$ and $2^{2x} \times 2^{3y} = 2^{47}$, write down two equations in x and y and solve them.

(b) Deduce the common solutions of the equations
$2^x \times 2^y = 64^3$ and $4^x \times 8^y = 2^{47}$.

6 (a) By taking out a common factor, show that $a^{x+2} + a^x = a^x(a^2 + 1)$.
Hence write $2^{10} + 2^8$ in the form $k \times 2^8$.

(b) Similarly express $2^{10} + 2^7$ in the form $c \times 2^7$.

(c) Without using a calculator deduce the value of

$\quad$ (i) $\dfrac{2^{10} + 2^8}{2^{10} + 2^7}$ $\qquad$ (ii) $\dfrac{2^{14} + 2^{12}}{2^{15} + 2^{12}}$ $\qquad$ (iii) $\dfrac{10^{12}}{10^{11} + 10^{13}}$

7 (a) Verify that $x = 3$ is a solution of the equation $2^{2x} + 8 = 9(2^x)$.

(b) Find another value of x which satisfies the equation.

8 (a) Show, by using the substitution $X = 2^x$, that the equation
$2^{2x+3} - 33(2^x) + 4 = 0$ may be written in the form
$8X^2 - 33X + 4 = 0$.

(b) Solve the equation in X and deduce the solutions for x.

Investigation E

Written as a product of prime factors, $245\,245 = 5 \times 7^3 \times 11 \times 13$.

Take a group of 6-digit numbers whose last three are the first three repeated, like 245 245, and express them as the product of their primes. You should notice that they all have the factors 7, 11 and 13 in common. Explain why this is so.

Special results

1. $a = 1$
   Any fraction of the form $\dfrac{a^m}{a^m}$ has the value 1, but its
   answer in index form will be $a^{m-m} = a^0$; hence $a^0 = 1$.
   (Question 3(d) in the previous exercise clearly demonstrates this equivalence.)

2. $a^{-m} = \dfrac{1}{a^m}$
   As $a^m \times a^{-m} = a^0 = 1$ it follows that, if we divide both sides
   by a^m, $a^{-m} = \dfrac{1}{a^m}$.

3. $a^{\frac{m}{n}} = \sqrt[n]{(a^m)}$; in particular $a^{\frac{1}{n}} = \sqrt[n]{a}$.

Example 2

(a) $5^{-2} = \dfrac{1}{5^2} = \dfrac{1}{25}$

(b) $5^0 + 4^{-1} - 5^{-2} = 1 + \dfrac{1}{4} - \dfrac{1}{25} = 1.21$

(c) $\left(\dfrac{2}{5}\right)^{-2} = \dfrac{1}{\left(\frac{2}{5}\right)^2} = \dfrac{1}{\left(\frac{4}{25}\right)} = \dfrac{25}{4} = 6\dfrac{1}{4}$

EXERCISE 1.3

1 Without using a calculator, write the following in the form $\dfrac{a}{b}$.

    (a) 3^{-2} (b) $\left(\frac{7}{8}\right)^{-1}$ (c) 10^{-3} (d) 2^{-5}

    (e) $\left(\frac{2}{3}\right)^{-3}$ (f) $(0.6)^{-2}$ (g) $\left(1\frac{1}{4}\right)^{-1}$ (h) $2^5 \times 3^{-2}$

2 Write the following in the form a^n.

    (a) $10^7 \div 10^{-2}$ (b) $5^{-3} \div 5^{-4}$ (c) 27×2^{-9} (d) $3^{-2} \times 3^{-1}$

    (e) $(2^{-1})^2$ (f) $(4^{-2})^{-2}$ (g) $4^0 \times 3^4 \times 9^{-1}$ (h) $(2^{-1} \times 2^{-2})^{-1}$

3 Solve the following equations.

    (a) $3^x = \dfrac{1}{81}$ (b) $(x)^{-2} = \dfrac{1}{16}$ (c) $(x)^{-2} = 2\dfrac{1}{4}$ (d) $x = \left(\dfrac{3}{5}\right)^{-2}$

Example 3

(a) $4^{\frac{1}{2}} = \sqrt{4} = 2$

(b) $(-8)^{\frac{1}{3}} = \sqrt[3]{(-8)} = -2$

(c) $16^{\frac{3}{4}} = \sqrt[4]{(16^3)} = (\sqrt[4]{16})^3 = (2)^3 = 8$

Reminder:

$\sqrt{x}$ denotes only the *positive* square root of x.

(This should be familiar, as we write the two solutions of the
quadratic equation $x^2 = 7$ as $x = \pm\sqrt{7}$.)

EXERCISE 1.4

1 Without using a calculator evaluate

(a) $81^{\frac{1}{2}}$

(b) $125^{\frac{1}{3}}$

(c) $14400^{\frac{1}{2}}$

(d) $\left(\dfrac{38}{16}\right)^{\frac{1}{4}}$

(e) $27^{\frac{2}{3}}$

(f) $\sqrt[3]{10^6}$

(g) $121^{\frac{1}{2}}$

(h) $\left(4\dfrac{21}{25}\right)^{\frac{1}{2}}$

2 Evaluate the following; only use a calculator to check your answers.

(a) $(16)^{\frac{3}{4}}$

(b) $\left(\dfrac{9}{16}\right)^{\frac{3}{2}}$

(c) $(0.01)^{\frac{1}{2}}$

(d) $\left(-\dfrac{1}{64}\right)^{\frac{1}{3}}$

(e) $(25)^{-\frac{1}{2}}$

(f) $(8)^{-\frac{1}{3}}$

(g) $\left(3\dfrac{3}{8}\right)^{-\frac{1}{3}}$

(h) $32^{\frac{4}{5}}+\left(\dfrac{4}{25}\right)^{-\frac{1}{2}}$

3 Solve the following equations without using a calculator.

(a) $8^x = 2$

(b) $5^{\frac{2}{3}} = 25^x$

(c) $x^{\frac{3}{4}} = \dfrac{8}{125}$

Standard form

On a calculator 5^{20} may be displayed as 9.53674 13.
This is the calculator's way of writing 9.53674×10^{13}.
Similarly 0.18^6 may be displayed as 3.40122 −05, representing 3.40122×10^{-5}.

This way of writing numbers, in the form $A \times 10^n$, where $1 < A < 10$ and n is an integer, is called **standard form**. It is particularly useful for very large and very small numbers as the power of 10 gives a clear picture of the size of the number, without having to count the number of digits or decimal places.

Note: In each of the cases given above the answers are not exact (how do you know?) – they are given to 6 significant figures – but the first number has *14* digits (one more than the power) and the second has its first significant figure, 3, in the 5th place of decimals, i.e. 0.000 034 01 2 2…

The following set of examples, showing how numbers in standard form are manipulated, should be followed without using a calculator.

Example 4

$(6.25 \times 10^4) \times (4 \times 10^7) = 25 \times 10^{11} = 2.5 \times 10^{12}$

Example 5

$(4 \times 10^8) \div (8 \times 10^{-6}) = 0.5 \times 10^{8-(-6)} = 0.5 \times 10^{14} = 5 \times 10^{13}$

Example 6

$(4 \times 10^{12}) + (5 \times 10^{10}) = 10^{10} (4 \times 10^2 + 5) = 405 \times 10^{10} = 4.05 \times 10^{12}$

Alternatively the numbers could be converted to normal form:
$4\,000\,000\,000\,000 + 50\,000\,000\,000 = 4\,050\,000\,000\,000 = 4.05 \times 10^{12}$,
but for very large and very small numbers the advantage of the
standard form can be seen.

Example 7

$$(1.91 \times 10^{-4}) - (6.08 \times 10^{-6}) \quad = 10^{-6}(1.91 \times 10^2 - 6.08)$$
$$= 184.92 \times 10^{-6} = 1.8492 \times 10^{-4}$$

To input a number into a calculator in standard form, the EXP button
should be used.

Example 8

To evaluate $(3.18 \times 10^{18}) \times (4.47 \times 10^{23})$ the sequence is

| 3 | . | 1 | 8 | EXP | 1 | 8 | × | 4 | . | 4 | 7 | EXP | 2 | 3 | = |

The display is 1.42146 42 representing $1.421\,46 \times 10^{42}$.

To input negative powers use the +/– key.

Example 9

$(5.9 \times 10^{-7}) \div (6.4 \times 10^{-4})$ is keyed in as follows:

| 5 | . | 9 | EXP | 7 | +/– | ÷ | 6 | . | 4 | EXP | 4 | +/– | = |

The display of 9.21875 −04 signifies 9.21875×10^{-4} in standard
form, which is 0.000 921 875.

Reminder:
A negative power of $-n$ indicates that the first significant figure
occurs in the nth place of decimals.

EXERCISE 1.5

(This includes a general revision. Only use a calculator where indicated.)

1 Convert the following numbers written in standard form into their decimal equivalents.

(a) 3.5×10^5 (b) 1×10^9 (c) 7.2×10^0 (d) 6.9×10^6

(e) 2.12×10^{-4} (f) 8.9×10^{-1} (g) 5.04×10^{-8}

2 Convert the following numbers into standard form.

(a) 10 400 000   (b) 1178.20   (c) 126×10^7 (d) 6×100^{20}

(e) 0.0002   (f) $0.000\,07 \times 10^{-5}$ (g) 10

3 Express 0.062 and 0.0089 in standard form and hence find an approximate value of 0.062×0.0089.

4 (a) Write down the answer displayed on your calculator for $(6.74 \times 10^8) + (3.57 \times 10^6)$.

(b) Express your answer in (a) to 3 significant figures, (i) in standard form, (ii) in decimal form.

5 In each of the following groups of numbers, pair off any that are equal.

(a) (i) $\dfrac{4000}{0.008}$ (ii) 5×10^6 (iii) $\dfrac{1}{5 \times 10^{-6}}$

(b) (i) 0.062×10^{-3} (ii) 6.2×10^{-4} (iii) 0.000 062

(c) (i) 0.025×10^5 (ii) $\dfrac{1}{0.4 \times 10^{-3}}$ (iii) $\dfrac{3}{12 \times 10^{-6}}$

(d) (i) 4.05×10^{-2} (ii) $5 \times 10^{-4} + 4 \times 10^{-2}$ (iii) 5.04×10^{-4}

(e) (i) $\dfrac{1}{1.6 \times 10^{-5}}$ (ii) $\dfrac{0.4 \times 10^4}{2.5 \times 10^{-2}}$ (iii) 1.6×10^5

6 Evaluate the following, giving your answer in standard form.

(a) $\dfrac{(4 \times 10^8) \times (9 \times 10^5)}{1.2 \times 10^{-12}}$

(b) $(1.3 \times 10^{-3})^2$

(c) $\sqrt{(6.25 \times 10^{24})}$

(d) $1\,600\,000\,000 \times 0.000\,002\,5$

(e) $(0.000\,04)^3$

(f) $(0.2)^7 \times (0.4)^{-5}$

7 Use a calculator to evaluate the following. Give your answer in standard form, correct to 3 significant figures.

(a) $(3.14 \times 10^{12}) \times (6.94 \times 10^{-7})$

(b) $(9.7 \times 10^{-5})^3$

(c) $(0.056)^6$

(d) $\dfrac{(5.6 \times 10^6)^{-3}}{9.7 \times 10^{-2}}$

(e) $\dfrac{(3.2 \times 10^{-2}) - 8.4 \times 10^{-5}}{(6.9 \times 10^{-8})^2}$

We shall now look at problems involving work with standard form.

Example 10

Assuming that the earth rotates in a circular orbit of radius 9.30×10^7 miles about the sun in 365 days, estimate its orbital speed, in m.p.h.

$\text{Speed} = \dfrac{\text{Distance}}{\text{Time}}$ and so we need to find the distance covered.

$\text{Distance} = 2 \times \pi \times 9.30 \times 10^7 \text{ miles} = 5.84 \times 10^8 \text{ miles (3 s.f.)}$

$\text{Speed, in m.p.h.,} = \dfrac{5.84 \times 10^8}{365 \times 24} = 6.67 \times 10^4$

EXERCISE 1.6

1 Find, in standard form, the average of the numbers

(a) 1.4×10^4 and 3.9×10^7

(b) 4×10^{-5} and 6×10^{-1}

2 The geometric mean of two numbers a and b is $\sqrt{(ab)}$.
Calculate the geometric mean of 9.6×10^{-8} and 2.7×10^{-9}.

3 The length of one side of a rectangular field, of area
1.155×10^5 hectares, is 2.1×10^4 m (1 hectare $= 10^4$ m^2).
Calculate, giving your answer in standard form, the length,
in metres, of the other side.

4 2.4 litres of water are poured into a rectangular tank of base area
3.0×10^{-1} m^2. Calculate the height, in cm, of water in the tank.

5 In a survey on a sample of 2500 adults from a population of
1.25×10^8, only 275 smoked. If the sample was representative,
how many adults from this population are likely to smoke.

6 A circular biological specimen, of area 1.91×10^{-6} cm^2, is
enlarged using a microscope with magnification factor 100.
Calculate, giving your answer in standard form correct to 3
significant figures,

(*a*) the radius, in cm, of the specimen

(*b*) the area of the enlarged shape in cm^2.

7 A spacecraft, travelling at 7.36×10^3 m/s, travels a distance
of 1.1×10^6 km in its orbit.

(*a*) How long, to the nearest
minute, does one orbit
take to complete?

(*b*) Calculate its speed in
m.p.h., giving your
answer in standard form
to 3 significant figures.
(Use 1 mile $= 1.6$ km.)

(*c*) How long, to the nearest
half day, would it take
Concorde, travelling at a
speed of 1400 m.p.h., to
cover the same distance
as the spacecraft's orbit?

(*d*) Calculate, correct to
3 significant figures, the
ratio of the speeds of the
spacecraft and
Concorde.

8 A population is estimated to increase by 60% every 10 years. In 1900 the population was 5×10^6.

(a) Estimate, giving your answer in standard form, the population in the year (i) 1950 (ii) 1995 (iii) 3000.

(b) Presuming that the growth had been like this since 1750, estimate the population in 1800.

9 A new disinfectant, 'Gotchew', is under test and will only go on the market if it consistently kills over 85% of germs. Tests are done on batches of 1.1×10^8 germs. In the first test the disinfectant kills 9.4×10^7 germs.

(a) How many germs did it not kill?

(b) If results continue in this way, will it go on the market?

After the second test its cumulative score of germs killed was over 85%.

(c) Calculate the least number of germs it killed in the second test.

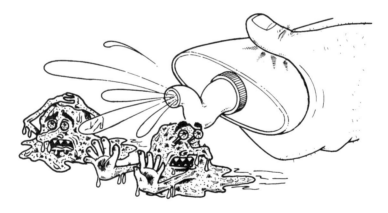

10 The mass of the Earth is 5.98×10^{24} kg and the mass of the moon is 7.35×10^{22} kg.

(a) Write down, in standard form, (i) the difference, in kg, between the two masses, and (ii) their ratio.

The densities of the Earth and the moon are in the ratio 5:3, and the diameter of the moon is 2160 miles. (Density $= \dfrac{\text{mass}}{\text{volume}}$)

(b) Using the data in this question only, calculate the diameter of the Earth.

11

Region	Population (in thousands)	Area (sq. miles)
A	56 000	9.4×10^4
B	2 070 000	3.6×10^6

(a) Which region has the larger population per square mile and by how much?

(b) If region B were to lose an area of land equal in area to that of region A, calculate how many people would need to emigrate so that its population density remains the same,

12 Tracey was asked how many times bigger, in surface area, she thought the Atlantic Ocean was than Lake Superior, the biggest lake in North America. Her guesstimate was about 1000. Do you think that this was a reasonable answer?
   Using the data given below, calculate a good estimate.
The surface areas of Lake Superior and the Atlantic Ocean are 8.23×10^4 km^2 and 3.17×10^7 square miles respectively, and 1 mile = 1.6 km.

13 Light travels at 1.86×10^5 miles per second. A **light-year** is the distance travelled by light in one year.

(a) Write, in standard form to 2 significant figures, the length of a light-year, in miles.

(b) An Astronomical Unit, AU, the mean distance between the Earth and the Sun, is 92.9×10^6 miles.
   Calculate, to the nearest integer, the number of AUs in a light-year.

14 The light from the the star, Alpha Centauri, takes about 4.35 light-years to reach Earth.

(a) Find, giving your answer in standard form, this distance in miles.

   The nearest star, Proxima Centauri, is 2.48×10^{13} miles from Earth.

(b) Write down, in standard form, the distance in light-years.

15

Planet	Average distance from sun (in 10^6 miles)	Diameter (miles)	Orbit time
Mercury	36	3032	88 days
Earth	93	7926	365.25 days
Mars	142	4217	687 days
Pluto	3674	3700	247.7 years

Using the data given above and in question 13:

(a) Show that light from the Sun takes a little over 8 minutes to reach Earth.

(b) Find an estimate for the orbital speed of Mars around the Sun, in m.p.h.

(c) Just by looking at the data Ade reckoned that Mercury travelled about twice as fast as Mars. Suggest how he could see this.

(d) Is it reasonable to suggest that Mercury travels 10 times faster in its orbit than Pluto?

(e) Calculate the distance in light-years between the orbits of Earth and Mars.

(f) Assuming the planets are spheres, calculate their surface areas and volumes, giving your answer in standard form correct to 3 significant figures. (Surface area of a sphere $= 4\pi r^2$ and volume of a sphere $= \frac{4}{3}\pi r^3$.)

(g) Given that about 70% of the Earth's surface is water, calculate the fraction of this water surface area that is covered by the Atlantic Ocean. (Use the data given in question 12.)

Investigation F

You can use your calculator to find the number of digits in the number 2^{400}. How many are there?

For a number such as $2^{756\,839}$ it is more difficult to find the number of digits. How many digits do you think there are in this number? Using the fact that 2^{10} is approximately 10^3, give an approximate conversion of $2^{756\,839}$ to standard form and hence show that it has more than 227 000 digits. (In 1992 the highest prime number was stated as $2^{756\,839} - 1$ and shown to have 227 832 digits.)

Irrational numbers

All the numbers, even very large and very small numbers, encountered in this chapter so far can be written in the form $\frac{m}{n}$ where m and n are integers, with n non-zero.

All such fractions, when written in their decimal form, are either exact or recurring, although some, as we saw in Book 3y, may not appear as recurring on your calculator display as their cycle is too long.

EXERCISE 1.7

1 Some of the fractions below have recurring decimals.

$$\frac{3}{8} \quad \frac{2}{11} \quad \frac{5}{27} \quad \frac{5}{72} \quad \frac{7}{108} \quad \frac{13}{1250}$$

   (*a*) Write down which you think they are.

   (*b*) Use your calculator to convert the fractions into decimals. For the recurring decimals add a further 4 decimal places.

2 The following fractions are all recurring decimals. Using your calculator write down the first 10 decimal places.

   (*a*) $\frac{4}{33}$ (*b*) $\frac{121}{999}$ (*c*) $\frac{4037}{33300}$ (*d*) $\frac{5}{22}$ (*e*) $\frac{11}{37}$

3 (*a*) Write down your calculator displays for $\frac{1}{17}, \frac{2}{17}, \frac{3}{17}, \frac{4}{17}$ and $\frac{5}{17}$, and try to deduce the cycle of sixteen digits that produce the recurring decimal for $\frac{1}{17}$.

   (*b*) Copy and continue the division sum shown below to check your result for (*a*).

$$\begin{array}{r} 0.\,058\,82 \\ 17\,\overline{)\,1.\,000\,000\,000\,000\,000\,000\,0} \end{array}$$

4 Write the decimals below in the form $\frac{m}{n}$, where m and n have no common factor.

   (*a*) 2   (*b*) 3.56   (*c*) 0.36   (*d*) 0.05004   (*e*) 0.33333...

5 The recurring decimal 0.5252...(0.5̇2̇) can be written as a fraction in the following way.

Let $x = 0.525\ 252...$, then $100\ x = 52.525\ 252...$
Subtracting we see that $99x = 52$ and so $x = \frac{52}{99} = \frac{14}{33}$.

Using this method, or a similar one, write the following recurring decimals as fractions in their lowest terms.

(a) 0.3636...   (b) 1.1515...   (c) 0.125 125...

(d) 0.132 32... (e) 0.153 846 153...

6 The decimals below are never ending. To each one add the next 4 decimal places that you think the pattern suggests, and state which are recurring decimals.

(a) 0.125412541...   (b) 0.125411225544111...

(c) 0.24681012...   (d) 0.73162931...

(e) 0.153846153...   (f) 0.1233212344...

(g) 0.0537405...   (h) 0.1123581321...

(i) 0.1551551...

Numbers which have a never-ending set of digits in their decimal part, but never have a recurring sequence, such as (b) in the last question, are called **irrational**. A more formal definition of an irrational number is one that is not rational, that is, it cannot be expressed in the form $\frac{m}{n}$.

When we see a square root, such as $\sqrt{5}$, on the calculator display, it is difficult to know whether it is rational or irrational. The Greeks proved that $\sqrt{2}$ is irrational over 2500 years ago, using a method of proof called 'reductio ad absurdum', or 'proof by contradiction', but, such was the feeling at the time that all numbers were derived from integers, the Pythagoreans felt that they had to suppress their discovery.

Following is a proof that $\sqrt{5}$ is irrational using this method, which starts by assuming that the statement you want to prove is false, and then showing that your assumption leads to a contradiction. Try to follow the steps in this important type of proof.

Proof that √5 is irrational

We start by assuming that $\sqrt{5}$ is rational and that it can be written as $\sqrt{5} = \frac{m}{n}$, where m and n are integers. We say further that the rational number $\frac{m}{n}$ is reduced to its simplest form, that is, m and n have no common factors.

By squaring we have $5 = \frac{m^2}{n^2}$, that is $5n^2 = m^2$.

If n is an *even* number, so is n^2 and therefore $5n^2$, showing that m must also be even; but m and n cannot both be even as this would contradict our assumption that m and n have no common factors.

If n is *odd*, then by similar reasoning m must also be odd. (Convince yourself of the truth of this statement.)

As all odd numbers can be written as 'an even number plus 1' we can write $m = 2p + 1$ and $n = 2q + 1$, where p and q are integers.

$$\text{Then} \qquad (2p + 1)^2 = 5(2q + 1)^2 \text{ as } m^2 = 5n^2$$
$$4p^2 + 4p + 1 = 20q^2 + 20q + 5$$
$$p^2 + p = 5q^2 + 5q + 1$$
$$p(p + 1) = 5q(q + 1) + 1$$

The numbers, $p(p + 1)$ and $q(q + 1)$, are the products of two consecutive integers and therefore both must be even. With the assumptions made, the conclusion requires $p(p + 1)$, which is even, to be equal to $5q(q + 1) + 1$, which is odd since it is an even number plus 1; this is clearly not possible. The assumption that $\sqrt{5}$ can be expressed as $\frac{m}{n}$ must therefore be false.

Therefore $\sqrt{5}$ is irrational.

Investigation G

Write out, in a similar way to that above, a proof that $\sqrt{2}$ is irrational. It is not quite as involved as that for $\sqrt{5}$ but, if you have difficulty, you should be able to find a proof in your school or local library.

Many square roots, cube roots and so on are irrational but there are many other familiar numbers which fall into this category. Many trigonometric functions, such as sin 40° and cos 50°, and special constants, such as π and e (seen on your calculator), are such numbers; there seems to be no pattern in these never-ending decimal numbers.

Example 11

The numbers π, $\sin 40°$, $\sqrt[3]{5}$, and the roots of the equation $x^2 - x - 1 = 0$ can be seen on your calculator display with 8 or more figures but they are infinite non-recurring decimals; they are irrational. (The first 14 decimal places of π, for example, are $3.141\ 592\ 653\ 589\ 79...$)

Care needs to be taken however; not all roots or trigonometric functions are irrational.

Example 12

The numbers (a) $\sqrt{\left(\frac{4}{9}\right)}$ (b) $\sqrt[5]{32}$ and (c) $\sin 30°$ are all rational numbers since:

(a) $\sqrt{\left(\frac{4}{9}\right)} = \frac{2}{3}$ since $\left(\frac{2}{3}\right)^2 = \frac{4}{9}$

(b) $\sqrt[5]{32} = 2$ since $2^5 = 32$

(c) $\sin 30° = 0.5$

EXERCISE 1.8

1 Using your calculator, or a computer, suggest which of the following square roots are irrational.

(a) $\sqrt{10}$ (b) $\sqrt{2250}$ (c) $\sqrt{3.0625}$

(d) $\sqrt{0.1111...}$ (e) $\sqrt{0.6}$

2 State which of the following numbers are rational and give their value. (Only use a calculator if you feel you must!)

(a) $\sqrt{221}$ (b) $\sqrt{7}$ (c) $\sqrt[3]{8}$ (d) $\sqrt[5]{243}$

(e) $\sqrt{200}$ (f) $\sqrt{1.44}$ (g) $\sqrt{2.25}$

3 Without using your calculator, write, where possible, the following numbers in the form $\frac{m}{n}$, where m and n are integers with no common factor.

(a) 5   (b) $-2\frac{1}{3}$ (c) π (d) 2.4   (e) 0.5   (f) $\sqrt{10}$

(g) $\sqrt{\left(1\frac{9}{16}\right)}$ (h) $\cos 18°$ (i) $(\sqrt{5})^2$ (j) $\sqrt{5} - 2.23$ (k) $2^3 + 2^{-2}$

4 From the following set of numbers, (i) state those that are irrational, (ii) pair off any equal numbers. Do not use your calculator.

(a) $0.1\dot{2}$ (b) $1 + \sqrt{7}$ (c) $\frac{22}{7}$ (d) 3.14 (e) $\frac{8 \times 35}{77 \times 30}$ (f) $\frac{5}{9}$

(g) π^2 (h) $9^{-\frac{1}{2}}$ (i) $10^{\frac{1}{4}}$ (j) $0.112\ 123\ 123\ 4\ldots$ (k) $\frac{1}{1\frac{4}{5}}$

5 Write down (a) two rational numbers (b) two irrational numbers between the numbers 3 and 4.

6 (a) If n is an integer, give two values of n between 1 and 10 for which $\sqrt{n}$ is (i) rational (ii) irrational.

(b) If m is a fraction (non-integral) in its lowest terms, give two values of m for which $\sqrt{m}$ is (i) rational (ii) irrational.

7 (a) Write down two pairs of integer values of m and n for which both $\sqrt{m}$ and $\sqrt{n}$ are irrational but both $\sqrt{(mn)}$ and $\sqrt{\left(\frac{m}{n}\right)}$ are not.

(b) Write down two pairs of integer values of p and q for which $\sqrt{(p^2 + q^2)}$ is (i) rational (ii) irrational.

8 Which of the following statements define an irrational number? For those that do not, prepare explanations, which could be read out to the rest of the group, of why they define rational numbers.

(a) The number of people in England.

(b) The volume, in m^2, of a cube of side 2.143 m.

(c) The length, in cm, of the hypotenuse of a right-angled triangle whose other sides are 2.5 cm and 6 cm.

(d) The number of stars in the universe.

(e) The area, in cm^2, of a circle of radius 2 cm.

(f) The length, in cm, of the diagonal of a cuboid with sides 1 cm, 2 cm and 3 cm.

(g) The number of grains of sand on Blackpool beach.

9 In the equilateral triangle ABC, AB $= 2$ m and M is the mid-point of BC.

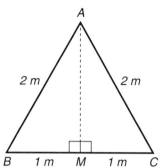

(a) Use triangle ABM to show that $\sin 60° = \dfrac{\sqrt{3}}{2}$

(b) Write down, in similar form, values for $\cos 60°$ and $\tan 60°$.

(c) Show that $\cos 60° = \sin 30°$, $\cos 30° = \sin 60°$ and

$$\tan 60° = \frac{1}{\tan 30°}$$

10 Take a square ABCD where AB $= 1$ m. Draw the diagonal AC and, by considering triangle ABC, find, using square roots, values for $\sin 45°$ and $\cos 45°$.

11 Show, without the use of a calculator, that the following expressions are all rational, and give their value.

(a) $(\sin 60°)^2$ (b) $(\sqrt{3} - \sqrt{2})(\sqrt{3} + \sqrt{2})$ (c) $\dfrac{\pi - 2}{2 - \pi}$

(d) 2.6×1.4 (e) $2.353535\ldots$

12 For each of the following equations, state (i) the number of (real) solutions, and (ii) whether these are irrational.

(a) $x^7 = 12$ (b) $4x^2 = 9$ (c) $(x^2 - 4)(x^2 - 5) = 0$

(d) $x^2 - x - 30 = 0$ (e) $x^2 + 1 = 0$ (f) $x^2 - 2x - 5 = 0$

13 Which of the following numbers are irrational? For those that are rational give their value.

(a) $2^{\frac{1}{2}} + 2^{\frac{1}{2}}$ (b) $2^{\frac{1}{2}} \times 2^{-\frac{1}{2}}$ (c) $2^0 + 2^{-2}$ (d) $9^{\frac{1}{2}} - 5^{\frac{1}{2}}$

Investigation H

Jane was asked to investigate whether the answer is necessarily irrational when two irrational numbers are (a) added and (b) multiplied. She easily found an example to show that it is not so for (b). Can you give an example? She thought it was probably true for (a). Was she right? If you think not, provide an example to show two irrational numbers adding to give a rational number.

Investigation I

Consider the infinite sum $4(1 - \frac{1}{3} + \frac{1}{5} - \frac{1}{7} + \frac{1}{9} - \frac{1}{11} \ldots)$.
Use your calculator and write out the values obtained by taking the
first term only, then the first two, the first three, until you have the
first twenty terms.
Describe how the series is progressing. Can you suggest to what the
series is converging?
The following infinite sum converges more quickly to π.

$$4\left[\left(\frac{1}{2} - \frac{\left(\frac{1}{2}\right)^3}{3} + \frac{\left(\frac{1}{2}\right)^5}{5} - \frac{\left(\frac{1}{2}\right)^7}{7} + \ldots\right) + \left(\frac{1}{3} - \frac{\left(\frac{1}{3}\right)^3}{3} + \frac{\left(\frac{1}{3}\right)^5}{5} - \frac{\left(\frac{1}{3}\right)^7}{7} + \ldots\right)\right]$$

Find the value that the terms shown produce.
See if you can find any other methods for finding π.

The irrational numbers of the form $\sqrt[n]{a}$, where a is not a perfect nth
power of a rational number, for example $\sqrt{3}, \sqrt[3]{5}, \sqrt[4]{\left(\frac{1}{2}\right)}$, are called **surds**.
Surds, like all other real numbers, obey the rules of algebra; of
particular use are the following:

$$\sqrt[n]{a} \times \sqrt[n]{b} = \sqrt[n]{(ab)} \qquad \sqrt[n]{\left(\frac{a}{b}\right)} = \frac{\sqrt[n]{a}}{\sqrt[n]{b}}$$

Example 13

(a) A surd such as $\sqrt{12}$ can be written $\sqrt{12} = \sqrt{(4 \times 3)} = \sqrt{4} \times \sqrt{3} = 2\sqrt{3}$
and so we have $\sqrt{3} + \sqrt{12} = \sqrt{3} + 2\sqrt{3} = 3\sqrt{3}$.

(b) In a similar way $\sqrt{45}$ can be written as $\sqrt{9} \times \sqrt{5} = 3\sqrt{5}$ and so we
have $\sqrt{5} \times \sqrt{45} = \sqrt{5} \times 3\sqrt{5} = 3 \times 5 = 15$.

(c) Brackets can be multiplied out:

$$(5\sqrt{3} - 2\sqrt{7})(4\sqrt{3} + 3\sqrt{7}) = (20 \times 3) - 8\sqrt{21} + 15\sqrt{21} - (6 \times 7)$$
$$= 18 + 7\sqrt{21}$$

EXERCISE 1.9

1 Given that $(\sqrt{5} - \sqrt{2})^2 = p - q\sqrt{10}$, find the values of the
integers p and q.

2 Without using a calculator, find the value of

(a) $(\sqrt{7})^2$ (b) $\sqrt{2} \times \sqrt{8}$ (c) $\frac{\sqrt{90}}{\sqrt{10}}$ (d) $\frac{\sqrt{27} + \sqrt{3}}{\sqrt{3}}$

(e) $\sqrt[3]{16} \times \sqrt[3]{4}$ (f) $(2\sqrt{5} - \sqrt{2})(2\sqrt{5} + \sqrt{2})$

3 Without using a calculator, show that $\sqrt{32} + \sqrt{128} = \sqrt{288}$.

4 Given that $\sqrt{2} = 1.41$, find the value of

    (a) $\sqrt{8}$ (b) $\sqrt{20000}$ (c) $\sqrt{0.02}$ (d) $\sqrt{2}(2 + \sqrt{2})$

5 Write, in the form $a + b\sqrt{c}$, where a, b and c are integers,

    (a) $(\sqrt{3} - \sqrt{2})^2$ (b) $(3 - 4\sqrt{2})(1 + \sqrt{2})$ (c) $\sqrt{5}(3\sqrt{5} + 4)$

6 Without using a calculator, find the largest number from

    (a) $\sqrt{125}$ (b) $6\sqrt{5}$ (c) $\sqrt{20} + \sqrt{45}$.

7 Simplify $2\sqrt{24} - \sqrt{54} + \sqrt{96} - 5\sqrt{6}$.

8 The number $\dfrac{3}{\sqrt{2}}$ can be written as $\dfrac{3\sqrt{2}}{2}$ by multiplying the numerator and denominator by $\sqrt{2}$.
Write each of the following numbers in the form $k\sqrt{a}$.

    (a) $\dfrac{1}{\sqrt{3}}$ (b) $\dfrac{5}{\sqrt{7}}$ (c) $\dfrac{1}{2\sqrt{5}}$ (d) $\sin 45°$ (e) $\tan 30°$

Investigation J

Using the the well-known 'difference of two squares' result,
$a^2 - b^2 = (a - b)(a + b)$, we see that if a and/or b is a square
root then the result is rational.
For example $(\sqrt{7} - \sqrt{2})(\sqrt{7} + \sqrt{2}) = (\sqrt{7})^2 - (\sqrt{2})^2 = 7 - 2 = 5$.
Use this fact to write the following numbers in the form $a + b\sqrt{c}$.

    (a) $\dfrac{1}{\sqrt{3} - 1}$ (b) $\dfrac{5}{4 + 3\sqrt{5}}$ (c) $\dfrac{\sqrt{2} + 3}{1 - \sqrt{2}}$ (d) $\dfrac{\sqrt{3}}{2 + 3\sqrt{3}}$

Check that your answer has the same calculator value as the given number.

Degrees of accuracy and approximations

As we have seen, irrational numbers can be expressed approximately
as decimal numbers to any degree of accuracy we please. Sometimes
it may be appropriate to take $\sqrt{5}$ as 2.24 and at other times as 2.236 07
depending on the accuracy of the other data being used at the time.

Note that both 2.24 and 2.236 07 are rational numbers and that both are approximations to √5, the first to 2 decimal places and the second to 5 decimal places. We could also say that 2.24 and 2.236 07 are approximations to √5, written to 3 significant figures and to 6 significant figures respectively.

Note: Approximations for π are often taken as 3.14 and $\frac{22}{7}$, but we must be aware that they are only approximations; they are not equivalent to π – an irrational number has no rational equal!

In all of our calculations involving measurements, such as length, time and mass, and quantities, such as speed, area and force, which depend on some of the measurements, we are dealing with approximations because no measurement can be absolute. If we use a ruler to measure the length of a line we can give our result to the nearest mm, or 0.1 cm.

Absolute errors

The absolute error is the greatest possible error in any measurement.

Example 14
We measure a line as 3.5 cm, say, and adopt the convention that this measure is correct to 2 significant figures. This is another way of saying that the true length lies between 3.45 cm and 3.55 cm and we say further that the **absolute error** is 0.05 cm; the length of the line is 3.5 ± 0.05 cm. This absolute error is then the greatest error possible in the measurement of the line as 3.5 cm.

Example 15
The length and breadth of a rectangle are each measured to the nearest cm as 8 cm and 6 cm. That is, the length lies between 7.5 cm and 8.5 cm and the breadth lies between 5.5 cm and 6.5 cm.

Largest possible perimeter: $2(8.5 + 6.5)$ cm $= 30$ cm.
Least possible perimeter: $2(7.5 + 5.5)$ cm $= 26$ cm.
Least possible area: 7.5×5.5 cm$^2 = 41.25$ cm^2.
Largest possible area: 8.5×6.5 cm$^2 = 55.25$ cm^2.

We conclude that the area lies somewhere between 41 cm^2 and 55 cm^2 (2 significant figures). This could be recorded, to 2 significant figures, as (48 ± 7) cm^2.

In cases such as this, we call the error, 7 cm, the **tolerance**. This term is widely used in industry.

EXERCISE 1.10

1 Express the following surds to (i) 2 decimal places, (ii) to 4 significant figures.

    (a) $\sqrt{11}$ (b) $\sqrt{(17^2 + 19^2)}$ (c) $(\sqrt{3} - \sqrt{2})^3$

2 For the following defined measures give an estimate in the form $x \pm y$ and then check with a published estimate.

    (a) The distance, in miles, from Bristol to London.

    (b) The population of India.

    (c) The height, in m, of the mountain K2.

3 A cube of volume V cm^3 has sides of length 2.4 cm, measured to the nearest cm. Find an inequality satisfied by V.

4 The number of matches, m, in a box of matches must be such that $110 \le m \le 130$.

    (a) How many boxes would you need to buy to be sure of having 2000 matches?

    (b) What is the least number of boxes that could be filled from 10^6 matches?

5 Given that the measurements in the following problems have been rounded, give a sensible range of values for the required values. Use your calculator value of π.

    (a) The circumference of a circle of radius 5.8 cm.

    (b) The radius of a circle of area 6.52 m^2.

    (c) The volume of a cuboid with dimensions 1 .2 cm by 3.4 cm by 5.6 cm.

6 The sides of a rectangle are measured as 2.5 cm and 3.3 cm.

    (a) Assuming the measurements are exact, calculate the area of the rectangle.

    (b) Assuming the measurements are correct to 2 significant figures, find the greatest and least possible values of the area.

7 Adrian was collecting data for his project on the heights of pupils in the school. The heights, measured to the nearest 0.5 cm, of the five pupils on his table were: 148.5, 150.0, 152.5, 146.5 and 149.0.

(*a*) Find the greatest possible average height of these pupils.

(*b*) What is the difference between the greatest and least possible average heights?

(*c*) He gave the average height of this group as $a \pm b$ cm. What should a and b be?

(*d*) Adrian intends to construct a histogram to display the data for the whole school. He collects the data in groups such as 145.5 – 149.5, 149.5 – 151.5,... Comment on this decision.

8 (*a*) A car, travelling at a constant speed of 40 m.p.h., measured to the nearest 1 m.p.h., covers a distance of 60 miles, measured to the nearest $\frac{1}{2}$ mile. Find the shortest possible time taken, to the nearest minute.

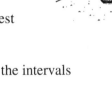

(*b*) Another car covers a distance of 1800 m, measured to the nearest 10 m, in a time of 2.5 minutes, to the nearest 10 seconds.
  (i) Find its greatest possible average speed, in m/s, to 3 significant figures.
  (ii) Find the difference between the greatest and least possible average speeds.

9 The two numbers x and y are known to lie in the intervals $0.5 \leq x \leq 1.5$ and $1.7 \leq y \leq 2.5$.
Find the greatest and least values of

(a) $x - y$ (b) $x + 3y$ (c) $\dfrac{2x}{5y}$ (d) $x^{-1} - y^{-1}$

10 Given that $x = \left(\dfrac{1}{a} - \dfrac{1}{b}\right) t$ and $a = 4.5$, $b = 7.4$ and $t = 1.9$, all correct to 1 decimal place, find the values of c and k, if $c \leq x \leq k$, where c and k are correct to 3 decimal places.

Relative and percentage errors

The absolute error is not very useful in practice. An error of 0.5 cm in the length of a 100-m running track is far less serious than an error of 0.5 cm in the diameter of a car axle of actual diameter 8 cm. We consider the error in relation to the true measurement itself by finding what is called the **relative error,** which is given by:

$$\text{Relative error} = \frac{\text{actual error}}{\text{measurement}}$$

We could also express the relative error as a percentage:

$$\text{Percentage error} = \frac{\text{error}}{\text{measurement}} \times 100$$

Example 16

For the running track, the relative error is $\dfrac{0.5}{100} = 0.005$, which is 0.5% as a percentage error.

For the car axle, the relative error is $\dfrac{0.5}{8} = 0.0625$, which is about 6% as a percentage error.

EXERCISE 1.11

1 Fergie thinks that $\sqrt{(a^2 + b^2)} = a + b$.
  Find her percentage error in the cases when

  (*a*) $a = 4, b = 3$ (*b*) $a = 4, b = -3$ (*c*) $a = 4, b = 0$

2 Sue uses $(1 + \frac{1}{2}x)$ to find $\sqrt{(1 + x)}$
  For example, to find $\sqrt{1.25}$ she uses $(1 + \frac{1}{2} \times 0.25) = 1.125$.

  (*a*) Use a calculator to find $\sqrt{1.25}$ to 4 significant figures and find Sue's percentage error in using her method.

  (*b*) Without using a calculator, find $\sqrt{1.44}$, and find the percentage error in the method in this case.

3 Correct to 1 decimal place, $\sqrt{2} = 1.4$ and $\sqrt{18} = 4.2$.

  (*a*) Write down the correct value of $\sqrt{2} \times \sqrt{18}$.

  (*b*) Calculate the percentage error in using the estimates of $\sqrt{2}$ and $\sqrt{18}$ for this value.

4 Correct to 1 decimal place, $\sqrt{3} = 1.7$ and $\sqrt{5} = 2.2$.

    (*a*) Find the percentage error obtained when these values
       (i) are squared to approximate to 3, 5, 15,
      (ii) are used to evaluate $(\sqrt{5} + \sqrt{3})(\sqrt{5} - \sqrt{3})$.

    (*b*) Find out by how much the percentage error is lessened if
       the approximations $\sqrt{3} = 1.73$ and $\sqrt{5} = 2.24$ are used.

5 Heidi measures three lines, each correct to the nearest mm, as
5.8 cm, 7.6 cm and 10.4 cm.

    (*a*) Why is it not possible to calculate the percentage errors
       she may have made in the measurements?

    (*b*) Calculate the maximum percentage error that she could
       have made in any one measurement.

6 The heights, measured to the nearest cm, of three students are
154 cm, 165 cm and 181 cm. Calculate, to 1 decimal place, the
maximum percentage error in calculating their average height.

7 Express π^2 as a decimal number written to (*a*) 4 significant
figures (*b*) 4 decimal places.
An engineer takes the value of π^2 as 10. Find the engineer's
percentage error to the nearest integer.

8 The diameter of a circular metal disc is measured, to the nearest
0.1 cm, as 7.8 cm. Find (*a*) the tolerance, (*b*) the greatest possible
percentage error in this measurement of the diameter.

9 An equilateral triangle is measured out on horizontal ground. Each
side of the triangle is measured as 14.2 m to the nearest 0.2 m.
Find the greatest possible percentage error in the area of the
equilateral triangle.

10 Nick found a formula in a book for estimating the value of
some cosines.
It said $\cos x° = 1 - \dfrac{\pi^2 x^2}{64800}$.

    (*a*) Calculate his value for $\cos 30°$, correct to 4 significant figures.

    (*b*) Find the percentage error in this value compared with the
       calculator value, corrected to the same degree of accuracy.

2. Arithmetical applications

Financial transactions in the family, and in business

Arithmetic processing is needed in many everyday situations ranging from simple transactions in shops and supermarkets to complicated dealings with shares on the Stock Exchange. We need to be able to control our own personal finances and to make decisions and judgements either on our own or in consultation with others.

The questions which you will face in examinations are about everyday situations, which you have met already in Books 3y and 4y. Very few formulae are needed and ones like the compound interest formula are given on the examination paper or in a separate data sheet. Try to keep your arithmetic skills sharp by regular practice. For example, if you do some food shopping, try to keep a rough tally of the total cost of the items in your trolley and then see how far out you are when the checker presents you with the bill. It is possible that an error has been made on either side if your estimate and the check-out total differ widely! Similarly when you are using your own calculator, keep in mind a rough estimate of what you expect the answer to be.

Example 1

After VAT has been added at 17.5%, the cost of a washing machine is £415.95.

This means that 117.5% of the cost of the washing machine is £415.95.

Without VAT the washing machine costs

$$\frac{100}{117.5} \times £415.95 = £354.$$

Example 2

On the day his son, Marcel, was born, M. Duval put 2000 francs into an investment account for him. The account earns compound interest at 6% per annum.

The compound interest formula is

$$A = P\left(1 + \frac{R}{100}\right)^N,$$

where A is the amount in the account, P is the amount invested, $R\%$ is the rate and N is the time.

On Marcel's eleventh birthday his investment is worth

$$2000\,(1.06)^{11}\text{f} = 3797\text{f (to the nearest franc)}.$$

Example 3

As an alternative investment policy, the bank recommended that M. Duval should invest 272f on each of Marcel's first ten birthdays, with the interest rate fixed at 6% per annum.

This method of investment would spread the payments of the total amount but make the total invested 2720f instead of 2000f. The formula needed in this case to evaluate the amount is

$$A = 272\left(1 + \frac{1}{r}\right)\left[(1 + r)^N - 1\right],$$

where A is the amount, r the rate and N the time.
We have then $r = 0.06$ and $N = 10$, which gives

$$A = 272\left(1 + \frac{1}{0.06}\right)(1.06^{10} - 1) = 3800\text{f}.$$

Note that the final amount is almost the same as that obtained in Example 2.

Many people use the investment method described in Example 3 for saving for the future. Others borrow to buy a house, which is then repaid by regular monthly payments over, say, 25 years.

EXERCISE 2.1

1 Without using a calculator, estimate to 1 significant figure, the value of (a) $7^2 + 77^2 + 777^2$, (b) $(7 + 77 + 777)^2$.
Obtain in each case an estimate to 2 significant figures, again without resorting to a calculator.

2 When the local weather centre gives the temperature in degrees Celsius Jan, a local sailor, converts to degrees Fahrenheit by using the rule 'double the degrees C and then add 30'. By using an accurate conversion, check and comment on the accuracy of Jan's method when applied to (a) an air temperature of 20°C, (b) a water temperature of 60°C, (c) a boiler temperature of 1500°C.

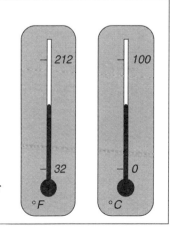

3 In a recent test, Mandy was asked to find the value of $\sqrt{2} + \sqrt{3} + \sqrt{5}$ but, by pressing incorrect buttons on her calculator, she evaluated $(\sqrt{2})(\sqrt{3})(\sqrt{5})$. Find her percentage error.

4 Winston bought ten items in a supermarket costing £1.45, £2.59, £0.75, £1.89, £3.54, £0.34, £0.67, £3.77, £2.67, £3.15. He decided to estimate the total spent by rounding each amount to the nearest £ and adding. What total did Winston get? What was the percentage error in his estimate?

5 This advertisement was shown in a local paper. Rahul bought a new door for which he paid £200. How much would the door have cost him without the reduction?

> **Replacement Doors and Windows**
> **20% OFF**
> *Special Reduced Prices*

6 How many glasses each containing $\frac{2}{9}$ of a pint can be filled from a full refrigerated tank holding 20 pints of fruit juice?
   The wholesaler charges £17.50 to clean and refill the tank. Find, to the nearest penny, the lowest price of a glass of fruit juice if a profit of at least 50% is to made when all the glasses that can be obtained from a full tank are sold?

7 At today's exchange rate I can get 8.325 french francs (f) for £1. I change £91 into francs and I receive 750f. Find the commission charged by the Bureau de Change for this transaction, giving your answer both as an amount in francs and as a percentage of the money exchanged.

8 In a local election only 71% of the electors actually voted. There were just two candidates and the ratio of the winner's votes to those of the loser was 8:7. The winner got 12 345 votes. How many failed to vote at all?

9 Study the following advertisement:

MOUNTAIN RACING BIKES	
CASH PRICE	FRIENDLY CREDIT TERMS
£224	Down payment: £25.20 followed by 101 weekly payments of £2.80.

Find the percentage of the cash price that is charged for the Credit Terms.

10 Three women, Andrea, Barbara and Cheryl lease premises and set up a hair salon. Their respective capital investments were:

Andrea	Barbara	Cheryl
£12 000	£13 000	£15 000

They agreed that the profits would be shared in the ratio of their investments. At the end of the first year profits of £5780 were made and all were withdrawn.

(a) Find the percentage profit made by Andrea on her investment.

Andrea withdrew her investment at this stage. Barbara and Cheryl each invested £6000 more in the salon to cover Andrea's withdrawal. At the end of the second year the profits were £4800.

(b) Find Barbara's percentage return for the second year.

(c) Find Cheryl's percentage return over the two years.

11 A sales executive is paid an annual salary in 12 equal monthly instalments. In addition, at the end of the year, the executive is paid a bonus amounting to 10% of the value of his total annual sales. In one year his total sales were £92 000 and his monthly salary was £1750.

(a) Find his total gross income for this year.

His income after deductions for income tax, national insurance and superannuation was £21 400.

(b) What percentage of his income was deducted?

In the following year, this executive made total sales of £101 000 and his gross annual income increased by 6% before any deductions were made.

(c) Find his gross monthly salary during this year.

12 Two million, seven hundred and thirty thousand, nine hundred and forty pounds was paid into a building society in a particular week.

(a) Write this amount in figures.

It is found that 0.2% of this amount was used by the society in administration costs including business rates.

(b) Find this amount and write it in words.

13 During the quarter October–December 1992, a family found that they had used 746 units of electricity. The first 100 units cost 21p per unit and the remainder cost 11p per unit. Calculate the cost of the electricity for this quarter. In the next quarter all charges were increased by 4%. The family received a bill for £107.20. Calculate the number of units of electricity used.

14 £2500 is invested at 7% each year compound interest. Find (*a*) the amount after 3 years, (*b*) the total interest after 5 years. After how many years does the investment double itself?

15 A man purchases a car by using his previous car as a deposit and borrowing £4000 at 1% compound interest per month over a year.

(*a*) Find the total cost of this loan.

(*b*) Find the annual rate of interest on this loan.

16 An accountant is checking the financial records of a firm when first-class letters cost 24p and second-class letters 18p.

(*a*) On one day he notices that a secretary posted the same number of first-class and second-class letters, and that the bill was recorded as £71.82. How many letters in all were posted on this day?

(*b*) Most Saturdays were blank in the records but on one occasion, a total of £3.60 was recorded. Investigate the number of letters that could have been dispatched on that day. Show that there is more than one possible solution. Find all the possible solutions.

17 A mixed tennis club rents covered, floodlit courts and meets once a week for 48 weeks of each year. The annual subscription for the club is £45 and each member pays an attendance fee of £3.50 on each weekly visit when they attend.

(*a*) Find the average weekly cost for a member who attends 40 of the possible 48 meetings.

(*b*) Find the number of times Peter attended if his average weekly outlay was £2.25.

18 A second-hand car dealer sells a van for for £2064. This makes a profit of 20% on the cost of the car to the dealer. Find the actual profit. During the first month after the sale, the van develops faults which cost the dealer £150 to rectify. Find the new percentage profit for the dealer on this sale.

19 Explain what is meant by (*a*) simple interest, (*b*) compound interest.

Derive the formula $I = \dfrac{PRT}{100}$ for simple interest, I,

where P is the principal, $R\%$ is the rate and T is the time. Selena found that she had a savings account amounting to £702 which had been gaining simple interest at 7% per annum for 5 years. What was the original investment?

20 Investigate which will give the better return for an investment of £1000 over 1 year:
Investment A: 1% compound interest per month
Investment B: 6% compound interest at the end of each 6 months
Investment C: 13% simple interest per annum

21 Using the formula given in Example 3, find the value of investing an annual increment of £250 for 20 years at a compound interest rate of (*a*) 4%, (*b*) 6% per annum.

Investigation A

A concentrated liquid fertiliser contains 10% water. How many litres of water should be added to 35 litres of the fertiliser so that the diluted solution contains 70% water?
Obtain a formula which could be applied to L litres of the 10%-concentrate fertiliser to dilute it to a solution containing $n\%$ water, where $n > 10$.

Investigation B

Two car dealers, Ron and Sid, have 35 old, 'banger' cars between them to dispose of. Ron sells all of his cars at the same price, £X, and Sid sells all of his cars at the same price, £Y, where X and Y are unequal integers.
If Ron had sold his cars at Sid's price, he would have received £5600.
If Sid had sold his cars at Ron's price, he would have received £3150.
How many cars could they each own?

Investigation C

Here are some popular shares which are quoted each day on the Stock Market.

Keep a daily record of three of these over a month and draw sketch graphs to show fluctuations in the price of each. Can you detect any trends? If so, were these in any way related to items of world or national news?

Mensuration: area, volume and speed

RETAILERS, FOOD				
ASDA 256	+1	5.8	9.2	1543
Appleby 420	+3	38.5	1.0	1336
Argyll 175	_1	19.5	2.2	4198
Brake Bros 465	+9	24.3	3.9	999
Budgens 312	+5	33.7	2.9	1073
Cullen's 213	+4	29.5	4.1	1222
Dairy Farm ...333	−5	41.1	2.7	1789
Farepak.........250	+3	46.3	4.0	4025
Fitzwilton 198	−1	35.8	3.3	2888
Fyffes 432	+2	11.8	1.9	3123
Gheest 276	+3	20.2	2.3	963
Greggs 256	+1	20.1	3.1	2000
Iceland 328	+3	10.8	1.7	4587
Kwik Save 197	−4	33.7	4.7	1954
Low (Wm)......550	+3	46.5	3.3	1313
M & W 389	−7	39.9	2.8	2482
Merchant 212	+2	21.7	5.0	987
Morrison (W) .315	+5	42.5	3.5	3497

A formula sheet is provided for the use of students in examinations giving information about the areas of some plane figures, and the surface areas and volumes of some solids. You should compare the one given here with the one issued by your examination board and note any differences carefully.

1 litre = 1000 cm^3

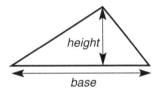

Area of triangle $= \dfrac{\text{base} \times \text{height}}{2}$

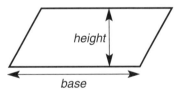

Area of parallelogram $=$ base $\times$ height

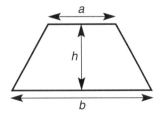

Area of trapezium $= \frac{1}{2}(a + b)h$

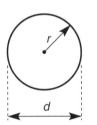

Circumference of circle $= \pi d$
$= 2\pi r$
Area of circle $= \pi r^2$

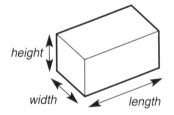

Volume of cuboid $=$ height $\times$ width $\times$ length

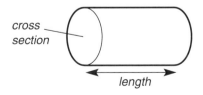

Volume of prism $=$ area of cross-section $\times$ length

Volume of cylinder $= \pi r^2 h$

Volume of sphere $= \frac{4}{3}\pi r^3$
Surface area of sphere $= 4\pi r^2$

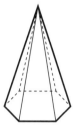

Volume of pyramid (including cone)
$= \frac{1}{3} \times$ area of base $\times$ height

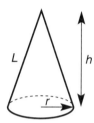

Volume of cone $= \frac{1}{3}\pi r^2 h$
Curved surface area $= \pi r L$

Example 4

A hollow sphere is made of metal which is 0.6 cm thick and has an outer radius of 9 cm.
The volume of a sphere of radius r is $\frac{4}{3}\pi r^3$.
The volume of metal in the hollow sphere is

$$\frac{4}{3}\pi(9^3 - 8.4^3) = 571 \text{ cm}^3.$$

If the density of the metal is 5.7 g/cm^3, then the mass of metal in the hollow sphere is

$$571 \times 5.7 \text{ g} = 3.25 \text{ kg (to 3 s.f.)}.$$

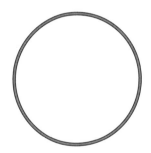

Example 5

A solid, metal rectangular block measuring 10 cm by 9 cm by 8 cm is melted down and re-formed without any waste into a solid cone of height 7 cm. Calculate the base radius of this cone and hence the curved surface area.
From the formula sheet:

Volume of cone $= \frac{1}{3}\pi \times r^2 \times h$, and
curved surface area of cone $= \pi \times r \times L$.

Volume of block $= 10 \times 9 \times 8 \text{ cm}^3 = 720 \text{ cm}^3$

We have then $\frac{1}{3} \times \pi \times r^2 \times 7 = 720$

So, $r = \sqrt{\left(\frac{720 \times 3}{7\pi}\right)} = 9.91$ cm

From Pythagoras, $L = \sqrt{(r^2 + 7^2)}$ cm $= 12.1$ cm

Curved surface area of cone $= \pi r L$
$$= 378 \text{ cm}^2.$$

Example 6

The scale of a map is 1:10 000.
This means that a line of length 1 cm on the map is equivalent to a
length of 10 000 cm $= 100$ m on the ground.
A region of area 8 cm^2 on the map is equivalent to a region of area
$8 \times (10\ 000)^2$ cm$^2 = 80\ 000$ m^2 on the ground.

Example 7

A journey from Bristol to Perth is undertaken in two stages. In the
first part, 247 miles are covered by motorway at an average speed of
65 m.p.h. and, in the second part, the remaining 200 miles are covered
at an average speed of 40 m.p.h.

The total travelling time $= \left(\frac{247}{65} + \frac{200}{40}\right)$ hours

$$= 8.8 \text{ hours}$$

Average overall speed $= \dfrac{\text{total distance}}{\text{total time}}$

$$= \frac{447}{8.8} \text{ m.p.h.}$$

$$\simeq 51 \text{ m.p.h.}$$

EXERCISE 2.2

1 Calculate the radius and the area of a circle in which a chord of
length 16 cm is at a distance of 15 cm from the centre of the
circle.

2 A drinking mug is in the form of a cylinder, open at one end
and made of thin glass. The radius is half the height and the
cylinder holds 0.5 litres.

Find the radius of the mug and its external surface area.

3

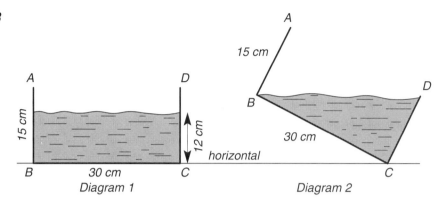

Diagram 1 *Diagram 2*

Diagram 1 represents a vertical cross-section of a fish tank.
standing on a flat table. The tank has a square base of side
30 cm and is 15 cm high. The depth of water in the tank is 12 cm.
Calculate the volume of water in the tank.
Diagram 2 shows the tank tilted so that BD is horizontal.
How much water has been spilled in order to achieve this?

4 A cone has radius R, height h and volume V. Giving each
answer in terms of V, find the volume of a cone which has

(*a*) radius $2R$ and height h

(*b*) radius R and height $2h$

(*c*) radius $3R$ and height $3h$.

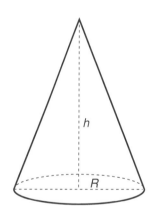

5 A train leaves Bath at 0831 and arrives at Plymouth at 1046.
The distance covered is 216 km. Find the average speed of the
train. The train then moved on to Penzance, 125 km away, at an
average speed of 80 km/h. Find the average speed of the
journey from Bath to Penzance.

6 A map has a scale of 1 : 25 000. Calculate, in cm^2, the area of a
region on the map which covers a region of area 8 km^2 on the
ground.

7 A map has a scale of 1: N. The area of a settlement on the map is
40 cm^2 and on the land it is 160 hectares. Find the value of N.

8 A circular lake has an area of 100 cm^2 on a plan whose scale is
1:120. Find the area and the circumference of the lake on the
ground.

9 Two maps of an island are drawn to different scales. The distance between two landmarks, A and B, is 8 cm on the first map and 12 cm on the second. The scale of the first map is 1:100 000.

(a) Find the scale of the second map.

A small-holding has an area of 8 cm^2 on the first map.

(b) Find the area of the small-holding on the second map and its actual area on the ground.

10 A solid glass paperweight has a diameter of 20 cm and weighs 1.6 kg. A similar solid paperweight of the same glass has a diameter of 10 cm. Calculate the weight of the smaller paperweight.

11 A pyramid of height 30 cm has a volume of 810 cm^3. Find

(a) the volume of a similar pyramid of height 10 cm

(b) the height of another similar pyramid whose volume is 51.84 cm^3.

12 A rectangular lawn is 9 m long and 5 m wide. A path of width x metres surrounds the lawn. The total area of the path and lawn is 61 m^2. Form a quadratic equation in x and solve it to determine the outside perimeter of the path, giving your answer to the nearest 0.1 m.

13

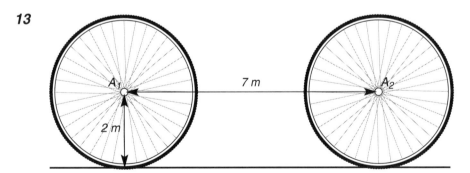

The diagram shows a wheel of radius 2 m which rolls, without slipping, on a smooth flat surface so that its centre, A, moves in a straight line. When A has moved through a distance of 7 m, as shown, find, to the nearest degree, the angle through which a spoke of the wheel has turned.

14 Kim walks at an average speed of 5 km/h to see his grandparents who live 18 km away in a village. He then cycles back to his starting point along the same route and takes one hour. Find his average speed for the whole 36 km journey.

15 A running track has an overall perimeter of 400 m. The two straights are each of length 80 m, are the opposite sides of a rectangle and are connected by two equal semicircles, as shown.
Calculate the radius of a semicircle and the total area enclosed by the track.
    On her morning training programme, Lucy covers eight circuits of the track in 12 minutes 43 seconds. Calculate her average speed in km/h.

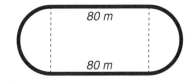

16 A solid cylinder and cone have the same radius, 12 cm, and are stuck together so that their bases are coincident. The cone has height 10 cm, and the combined volume of the cone and cylinder is 3000 cm^3.
Calculate the height of the cylinder and the external surface area of the combined body.

17 A cyclist covered a distance of 40 miles at an average speed of p miles per hour. She returned by the same route but her average speed was 2 miles per hour less. The difference in times between the two journeys was 1 hour. Form an equation in p and solve it.

18 The solid triangular prism shown has a horizontal rectangular base ABCD and a horizontal ridge XY parallel to AB and DC. The triangular faces XDA and YBC are vertical. AB = DC = XY = 8 cm, and BC = AD = XA = XD = YB = YC = 6 cm.
Calculate the total surface area and the volume of the prisim.

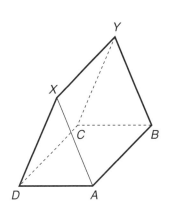

19 Solid cones are made to have height 8 cm and base radius 6 cm. How many cones of this specification can be made by melting down a solid metal sphere of radius 50 cm?

20 A flat rectangular plot of land is 7.8 m long and 6.4 m wide. Earth is excavated to a depth of 0.4 m all over this plot. The earth has mass of 960 kg/m^3. Find the mass of earth excavated.

21 Snow lies on a flat rectangular roof measuring 16 m by 13 m to a uniform depth of 10 cm. One cubic metre of this snow is estimated to have a mass of 654 kg. Find the total mass of the snow on the roof.

22 The diagram shows the cross-section of a tunnel in the form of a semicircle. The area of the cross-section is 12.4 m². Find the greatest height of the tunnel. A van is 2 m wide and is just able to drive through the tunnel. Find the height of the van.

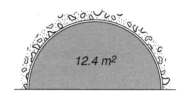

12.4 m²

23 Find the area of a regular octagon, with sides of length 5 cm. The octagon is the horizontal base of a pyramid whose vertex is 6 cm above the centre of the base. Calculate (*a*) the volume of the pyramid, (*b*) the total surface area of the sloping faces.

24 Calculate the volume of a sphere whose surface area is 47.3 cm³.

25 The cylinder of a sports-ground roller has diameter 0.78 m and width 1.2 m. Find, to the nearest m², the area covered by the roller when it moves along a straight path through 100 complete revolutions. without slipping.
   Given that the mass of the handle of the roller is negligible compared with that of the cylinder, find the density of the material in the cylinder which is of mass 445 kg.

26 A sphere S has radius *a*, a cylinder C has radius *a* and height 2*a*, and a cone D has base radius *a* and height 2*a*. Find, for S, C and D,

   (*a*) the ratio of their volumes,

   (*b*) the ratio of their total surface areas.

27 The curved surface of a hollow cone is made, without waste, from a semicircular sheet of metal of diameter 15 inches. Find the volume of the cone.

28 A station snack-bar sells drinks in cylindrical cups which are 9 cm high and hold 0.5 litres when filled to the brim. Calculate the radius of the base.

29 Anticorrosive spraying of the external curved surface of metal cylindrical pipes costs 14 pence for each square metre. Find the cost of the treatment for a gas main of length 2.5 km using pipes of diameter 27 cm.

30 A company purchases solid metal cylinders of length 1.5 m and diameter 15 cm for £93 each. The cylinder is melted down and refined before recasting into solid spheres of diameter 6 cm. In this overall process 10% of the original metal is lost and the manufacturing cost is £43. The spheres are sold so that a profit of 35% is made. Find the price at which a sphere is sold.

   Explain why a slightly higher profit than 35% will be made when a number of cylinders are melted down in this process.

31 When fully inflated a balloon forms a sphere of radius 5.4 m. Calculate the surface area and the volume of this balloon when it is fully inflated.

   When in flight, reduced air pressure causes the balloon to expand. Calculate the volume of the balloon when the surface area is increased by 10%.

Investigation D

In a recent 5000-m race, Ahmed finished 400 m in front of Bengi and Bengi finished 200 m in front of Chris. They all ran at constant speeds throughout the race. By how many metres did Ahmed finish in front of Chris?

Investigation E

A local council has just acquired a piece of flat ground for additional car parking. Explain, in detail, how you would investigate the marking out of parking spaces and roads on this site so that the maximum number of cars can be parked, but no car is blocked in.

   Write up your final report, with diagrams, in a form which could be presented to the Council's Engineering Department.

Investigation F

Jim is investigating possible sizes for a cylindrical water butt which he wants to use for storing rain water when it runs off the roof.

   The butt is going to stand with its circular base on horizontal ground and it has no top. As Jim has a big garden he wants the tank to have a capacity of 5000 litres. As little sheet metal as possible is to be used for the butt. By using the formula $V = \pi r^2 h$ and a formula for the area of sheet metal required, take some numerical values and investigate the problem. Write up your investigation; include the dimensions which you have found for the butt to give a capacity of 5000 litres but which contains the least sheet metal. (1 litre = 1000 cm^3)

3. Working with expressions and formulae

This chapter reviews and extends the work on formulae and algebraic expressions covered in Books 3y and 4y.

Substitution of numbers for letters

Reminders: 1. Evaluate means 'find the numerical answer'.
  2. $3a^2$ means 3 'lots of' a^2, *not* $(3a)^2$.

Example 1

Evaluate (*a*) $5x^2$ (*b*) $2xy - y^3$, when $x = 4$, $y = -2$.

(*a*) $5 \times (4)^2 = 5 \times 16 = 80$ [*not* $(20)^2 = 400$]

(*b*) $2 \times 4 \times (-2) - (-2)^3 = -16 - (-8) = -8$

Note: $-y^3 = -(y)^3$ just as $2y^3 = 2(y)^3$

EXERCISE 3.1

1 Evaluate the following expressions when $a = 2$, $b = -4$, $c = -1$ and $d = 5$:

(*a*) $2ab$ (*b*) $b^2 + d^2$ (*c*) $5 - b$ (*d*) $2d - a$ (*e*) $abc + d$

(*f*) $(a + b)(a - b)$ (*g*) $a^2 - b^2$ (*h*) $3ad - 7bd$ (*i*) $d(3a - 7b)$

(*j*) $d^2 - 3b^2$ (*k*) $c\,(d + 2b)^2$ (*l*) $bd - ac$ (*m*) $6 + b(a + d)$

2 For the given data evaluate the following expressions:

(*a*) $5xy$ when $x = 3$, $y = 7$ (*b*) $2x^2y^3$ when $x = 7$, $y = 2$

(*c*) $2x - 5y$ when $x = 4$, $y = -1$ (*d*) $x^2 + y^2$ when $x = -1$, $y = -2$

(*e*) $(2x - y)(4x^2 - y)$ when $x = \frac{1}{2}$, $y = -2$ (*f*) $\dfrac{3x + 6y}{x - 7y}$ when $x = -4$, $y = -2$

3 The table shows some values of y, where $y = 5x^2 - \frac{1}{2}x + 7$, for given values of x from -2 to $+3$.

x	-2	-1	0	1	2	3
y		12.5			26	

(a) Roger's value for $x = -2$ was -12. How do you know that his value cannot be correct, without making any calculations?

(b) Calculate the missing values.

EXERCISE 3.2

1 Use the formula $S = 180(n-2)$ to evaluate S when

(a) $n = 3$ (b) $n = 4$ (c) $n = 5$ (d) $n = 8$ (e) $n = 22$.

If n represents the number of sides of a polygon, what does S represent?

2 Use the formula $s = ut + \frac{1}{2}at^2$ to evaluate s when

(a) $u = 40$, $a = 0.6$, $t = 5$ (b) $u = -10$, $a = -2$, $t = 8$.

3 Use the formula $E = p(x - y)^2$ to evaluate E when

(a) $p = 0.3$, $x = -0.2$, $y = 0.4$ (b) $p = -3$, $x = 5$, $y = -2$.

You will see that the sign of E is the same as the sign of p.
Explain why this will always be the case, unless $x = y$.

4 Use the formula $N = \dfrac{2a - 4b}{2b - a}$ to evaluate N when

(a) $a = 7$, $b = 4$ (b) $a = -3$, $b = 2$ (c) $a = 5$, $b = -1$.

Explain why your answers are the same. Will all values of a and b give the same value of N?

5 The radius r of a sphere of surface area S is given by $r = \frac{1}{2}\sqrt{\left(\frac{S}{\pi}\right)}$.

Calculate the radius of the sphere, writing your answer in cm to 2 significant figures, when S is (a) 40 cm^2 (b) 0.8 m^2.

6 For the formula $A = \dfrac{a^2 - 2b^{\frac{1}{3}}}{3(a+b)}$:

    (*a*) (i) Write down an efficient calculator button sequence for evaluating A for given values of a and b.

        (ii) Evaluate A when $a = 4.17$, $b = 6.58$, giving your answer to 2 decimal places.

    (*b*) Without using a calculator, evaluate A when

        (i) $a = 3$, $b = 8$ (ii) $a = -3$, $b = -8$.

Investigation A

Check that the values of $2^{2^0} + 1$, $2^{2^1} + 1$ are 3 and 5 respectively.

Find the values of $2^{2^2} + 1$, $2^{2^3} + 1$.

The French mathematician, Fermat, once declared that numbers of the form $2^{2^n} + 1$ are always prime. Do your results support his statement?

Find the exact value of $2^{2^5} + 1$.

You should find that this number is divisible by 641.

What does that tell you about Fermat's statement?

(Even evaluating 2^{2^5} may well have taxed your ingenuity and patience but it emphasises the difficulty that mathematicians of earlier times had in testing theories. It took a super-computer, for example, ten days to show that $(2^{2^{20}} + 1)$ was not a prime!)

Working with brackets

It is important to use brackets when they are necessary. So often $3x + y$ is seen when 3 'lots of' $(x + y)$ is what is meant. Even if it is just carelessness in omitting the bracket, it is likely to lead to further errors.

    The expansions $x(y + z) = xy + xz$ and $a(b - c) = ab - ac$ are demonstrated below, the shaded areas being $x(y + z)$ and $a(b - c)$ respectively.

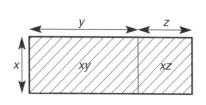
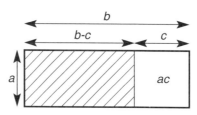

Example 2

(a) $3(x+y) = 3x + 3y$

(b) $10 - 6(1 + 2x) = 10 - 6 - 12x = 4 - 12x$

The result of multiplying two brackets can be found using the earlier
results for one bracket.

Example 3

(a) $(a+b)(y+z) = a(y+z) + b(y+z) = ay + az + by + bz$

(b) $(a-b)(y-z) = a(y-z) - b(y-z) = ay - az - by + bz$

Reminders:
$$(a+b)^2 = a^2 + 2ab + b^2$$
$$(a-b)^2 = a^2 - 2ab + b^2$$
$$(a+b)(a-b) = a^2 - b^2$$

EXERCISE 3.3

1 Expand and simplify where possible.

(a) $7(x-4)$ (b) $6(1-2x)$ (c) $2(x+4y)$

(d) $5(5x-2y)$ (e) $(2x+7) - (3x-8)$ (f) $5 - 2(1-2x)$

(g) $5(x+2y) - 4y$ (h) $2x - (1-2x)$ (i) $7(3-x) - 5(x+2)$

(j) $8(x+2y) + 3(4y-x)$ (k) $4(6-x) + 2(4x-3)$ (l) $1 - (6x-5) - 6(2-x)$

2 Expand and simplify.

(a) $(x+1)(x-2)$ (b) $(x+8)(x-4)$ (c) $(x+8)(x+2)$

(d) $(1-x)(2-x)$ (e) $(1+x)(x-3)$ (f) $(3x+5)(x-7)$

(g) $(2x+3)(3x-2)$ (h) $(2a+3b)(b-c)$ (i) $(5x-y)(x+7y)$

3 Expand and simplify.

(a) $(x+1)^2$ (b) $(x-5)^2$ (c) $(x-2y)^2$

(d) $(7-2x)^2$ (e) $(3x-2)^2$ (f) $(6x-4)^2$

(g) $(3x+4y)^2$ (h) $(x+7y)^2$ (i) $(x-1)(x+1)$

(j) $(x+5)(x-5)$ (k) $(x-5y)(x+5y)$ (l) $(4x-1)(4x+1)$

(m) $(2x-3)(2x+3)$ (n) $(3x+7y)(3x-7y)$

EXERCISE 3.4

1 Which of the following expressions are equivalent?

   (a) $(x-2)(x+4)$ (b) $x(x+2)-8$ (c) $(2-x)(4+x)$

   (d) $(x+1)^2-9$ (e) $(x-4)(x+2)$ (f) $(2x+1)(x+4)-(x+3)(x+4)$

2 The diagrams show a solid cube and cuboid. The cube has sides
x cm and the cuboid measures x cm by $(x+1)$ cm by $(x-1)$ cm.

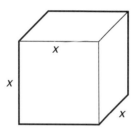 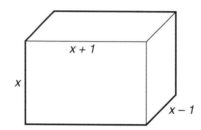

   Find which has the larger volume and by how much.

3 Expand $x^3 - y^2(y-1)$ and explain why it is always greater than
$x^3 - y^3$ for all non-zero values of x and y.

4 Tim said that $(x+y)^2$ is always greater than $x^2 + y^2$, whatever
the values of x and y, because $(x+y)^2 = x^2 + y^2 + 2xy$.
Is he correct? If not, how must x and y be related for it to be
untrue?

5 Expand and collect like terms where appropriate.

   (a) $(x^2 + y^2)^2$ (b) $(\sqrt{x} - \sqrt{y})(\sqrt{x} + \sqrt{y})$ (c) $(x^2 + 2)(3x - 5)$

6 (a) Show that $(a+b)^3 = a^3 + 3a^2b + 3ab^2 + b^3$.

   (b) Expand (i) $(x-1)^3$, (ii) $(2x+3)^3$.

   (c) A hollow cube, whose outer edges measure x cm, is made
of wood 0.5 cm thick. Find, in terms of x, the volume of
wood used.

7 (a) Find the value of c, if $4x^2 - 20x + c$ is a perfect square.

   (b) Find the value of k, if $2y^2 + 4y + 7 = a(y-1)(y+3) + k$.

8 The coordinates of a point on a particular curve are given as $x = 1 + t$, $y = 2t^2$. (Different values of t produce different points on the curve, for example: $t = 1 \Rightarrow (2, 2)$, $t = 2 \Rightarrow (3, 8)$.) Find a relationship between x and y, not involving t, and sketch the curve.

9 A group were asked to find the value of $x^2 + \dfrac{1}{x^2}$ given that $x + \dfrac{1}{x} = 5$.

(a) John said it was 25. Explain why this cannot be correct.

(b) Show that the correct value is 23.

10 (a) Simplify $(a^2 + b^2)^2 - (a^2 - b^2)^2$.

(b) Given that $a^2 + b^2 = 13$ and $ab = 6$, find the values of $a^2 - b^2$.

11 Given that $a + b = 6$ and $ab = 2$, write down the value of $a^2 b^2$ and (a) show that $a^2 + b^2 = 32$, (b) find the value of $a^4 + b^4$.

Factorisation

The reverse of multiplying out brackets is factorising; the aim is to write sums and differences of algebraic terms as products. An important application of this is seen in solving quadratic equations.

Reminder:
Two-termed expressions can only have a common factor, be a difference of two squares or be a combination of both.

Example 4

(a) $3x^3 - 9 = 3(x^3 - 3)$

(b) $x^3 y^2 + 2xy = xy(x^2 y + 2)$

(c) $4x^2 - 9y^2 = (2x)^2 - (3y)^2 = (2x + 3y)(2x - 3y)$

(d) $20x^2 - 45y^2 = 5(4x^2 - 9y^2) = 5(2x + 3y)(2x - 3y)$

EXERCISE 3.5

1 Factorise the following expressions.

(a) $5 + 35x$ 　　　　(b) $7x - 14x^2$ 　　(c) $108 - 24x$ 　　(d) $6x^2 + 15x^5$

(e) $abc + 4bc$ 　　　(f) $2a^3 - 8a^8$ 　　(g) $3x^4y^3 + 57x^2y^2$ 　　(h) $10a^5b^6 + 15a^7b^4$

(i) $x + y + (x + y)^2$ 　(j) $a(2a - c) - 5(2a - c)$ 　　　　(k) $x(y + z) - y - z$

2 Factorise, if possible, the following expressions.

(a) $x^2 - 25$ 　　(b) $1 - x^2$ 　　　　(c) $16 - x^2$ 　　(d) $b^2 - 81c^2$

(e) $2x^2 + 8xy$ 　(f) $y^2 + 16$ 　　　　(g) $9 - 4p^2$ 　　(h) $3p^2 - 147q^2$

(i) $36x^2 - 1$ 　(j) $(x + 2y)^2 - y^2$ 　(k) $(2x - 1)^2 - 1$ 　(l) $y^4 - 16$

(m) $x^2y^3 - 4y$ 　(n) $2xy^2z^3 + 10x^3y^2z$ 　(o) $3^x - 3^{2x}$ 　(p) $4^x - 1$

3 (a) Show that the shaded area in the diagram is $(x^2 - 4y^2)$ cm².

(b) Find the area when $x = 6.36$ and $y = 1.82$, showing your working clearly, without the aid of a calculator.

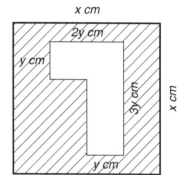

Investigation B

The difference between two integers is always a factor of the difference between the squares of the numbers, the cubes of the numbers and the fourth powers of the numbers. For example:

$$[(5 - 2) = 3] \text{ is a factor of } [(5^2 - 2^2) = 21], [(5^3 - 2^3) = 117] \text{ and } [(5^4 - 2^4) = 609].$$

Try a few more numerical examples and then try to prove that the statement is true for all integers.

Reminder:
Three-termed expressions of the form $ax^2 + bx + c$ only factorise if $(b^2 - 4ac)$ is a perfect square.

In the special case when $a = 1$, and $x^2 + bx + c$ factorises:

$$x^2 + bx + c = (x + p)(x + q), \text{ where } p + q = b \text{ and } pq = c.$$

Example 5

(a) $x^2 + 12x + 32$ factorises since $b^2 - 4ac = 144 - 128 = 16$.

As $(+8) + (+4) = +12$ and $(+8) \times (+4) = +32$,

$x^2 + 12x + 32 = (x + 8)(x + 4)$.

(b) It follows that: $x^2 + 12xy + 32y^2 = (x + 8y)(x + 4y)$

(c) $y^2 + 3y - 28$ factorises since $b^2 - 4ac = 121$.

As $(+7) + (-4) = +3$ and $(+7) \times (-4) = -28$,

$y^2 + 3y - 28 = (y + 7)(y - 4)$.

EXERCISE 3.6

1 Factorise the following expressions.

(a) $x^2 - 15x + 54$ (b) $y^2 + 5y - 66$ (c) $p^2 + 10p + 25$ (d) $c^2 - 9c - 10$

(e) $x^2 + 17x + 72$ (f) $x^2 + 5x - 14$ (g) $x^2 + 5xy - 14y^2$ (h) $x^2 - x - 56$

(i) $15 + 8x + x^2$ (j) $m^2 - 7mn + 12n^2$ (k) $x^2 - xy - 30y^2$ (l) $x^2 + 10xy + 16y^2$

2 By calculating the value of $b^2 - 4ac$ find which of the following expressions factorise and give their factors.

(a) $x^2 - 6x - 5$ (b) $x^2 - 6x + 5$ (c) $x^2 + 6x + 5$ (d) $x^2 - 5x - 6$

(e) $x^2 - 5x + 6$ (f) $x^2 + 5x - 6$ (g) $x^2 + 3x + 4$ (h) $x^2 + 4x + 3$

3 (a) Given that the expression $x^2 + kx - 12$ factorises, find the possible values of k.

(b) Explain how the problem changes if the expression is changed to $x^2 - 12x + k$.

4 Find the factor that is common to both $x^2 - x - 20$ and $(x + 4)(x - 7) + 18$.

5 Given that $(x + 3)$ is a factor of $x^2 + kx + 18$, find the value of k.

6 By first taking out the common factor, factorise completely the following expressions.

(a) $x^3 - 2x^2 - 3x$ (b) $2x^2 - 12x + 54$ (c) $5y^2 + 10y + 5$

7 (a) Factorise (i) $y^2 + 7y + 6$, and hence (ii) $(x - 1)^2 + 7(x - 1) + 6$.

(b) Factorise (i) $y^2 - y - 12$, and hence (ii) $x^4 - x^2 - 12$.

Reminder:
If $a \neq 1$ in $ax^2 + bx + c$, then the method of factorising is more involved but many expressions can be factorised by inspection with care.

Example 6

As $2x^2 + 3x - 5$ has prime numbers at each end we can write:
$(2x + p)(x + q)$ with $p = +5$ and $q = -1$ *or* $p = -5$ and $q = +1$.
A quick check to see which gives $+3x$ as the middle term determines that:

$$2x^2 + 3x - 5 = (2x + 5)(x - 1)$$

Note: Always multiply out your factors as a check.

An expression like $4x^2 - 4x - 15$ will have more options to consider in a solution by inspection but, if you find you have no difficulty, then the following example, outlining the method given in Book 4y, may be passed over.

Example 7

For $4x^2 - 4x - 15$ find two numbers that (*a*) multiply to give $4 \times -15 = -60$ and (*b*) add to give -4.
Having found the numbers, -10 and $+6$, rewrite the middle term, $-4x$, as $-10x + 6x$ and then factorise into two pairs:

$$
\begin{aligned}
4x^2 - 4x - 15 &= 4x^2 - 10x + 6x - 15 \\
&= 2x(2x - 5) + 3(2x - 5) \\
&= (2x - 5)(2x + 3) \qquad (2x - 5) \text{ is a common factor}
\end{aligned}
$$

EXERCISE 3.7

1 (*a*) Which of the following is the correct factorisation of $2x^2 - 13x + 15$?

(i) $(2x - 5)(x - 3)$ (ii) $(x - 5)(2x - 3)$ (iii) $(2x - 15)(x - 1)$

(*b*) Explain why both signs in the brackets have to be $-$.

2 For the following expressions of the form $ax^2 + bx + c$, either a or c or both are prime numbers. Complete the following statements.

(*a*) $3x^2 + 14x - 5 = (3x - \;)(x + \;)$ (*b*) $5x^2 + 7x + 2 = (5x...)(x...)$

(*c*) $7x^2 - 22x + 3 = (7x...)(x...)$ (*d*) $2x^2 + 7x - 15 = (2x - \;)(x + \;)$

(*e*) $8 + 10x + 3x^2 = (\; + 3x)(\; + x)$ (*f*) $6x^2 - 7x - 3 = (\; + 1)(\; - 3)$

3 Factorise the following expressions.

(a) $2x^2 - 9x - 11$ (b) $3x^2 + x - 14$ (c) $6x^2 - 19x - 7$

4 Consider the following products which were given by three students as the factorised equivalent of $4x^2 - 24x + 27$:

(i) $(2x + 9)(2x - 3)$ (ii) $(4x - 9)(x - 3)$ (iii) $(2x + 3)(2x + 9)$

(a) Why must the signs in (i) be incorrect?

(b) Why is (ii) incorrect?

(c) Why must the signs in (iii) be incorrect?

(d) Explain why the brackets cannot have $4x$ and x as their first terms.

(e) Give the correct factorisation.

5 Complete the following statements.

(a) $8x^2 - 2x - 15 = (4x + \ldots)(2x - \ldots)$

(b) $8x^2 - 19x - 15 = (8x \ldots)(x - \ldots)$

(c) $8x^2 - 23x + 15 = (\ldots)(\ldots - 3)$

6 Factorise the following expressions.

(a) $3x^2 - 11x + 10$ (b) $4x^2 - 21x - 18$ (c) $10x^2 - x - 21$

7 Find the value of k, if $2x^2 + kx - 12$ has a factor in common with $x^2 - 3x - 28$.

8 Show that $(2x - 3y)(2x + 5y) + 8y(3y + x)$ can be written as a perfect square.

Investigation C

As $x = 1$ and $x = 2$ both satisfy the equation $x^3 - 2x^2 - x + 2 = 0$, we know that $(x - 1)$ and $(x - 2)$ are both factors of $x^3 - 2x^2 - x + 2$. By writing $x^3 - 2x^2 - x + 2 = (x - 1)(x - 2)(x + k)$ we can see that $k = 1$ and we have factorised the cubic expression.

The following cubic equations have two small integer solutions. Find them by inspection and hence write down two factors of the expressions. Try to find their third factors.

(a) $x^3 - 13x + 12 = 0$ (b) $x^3 - 10x^2 + 23x - 14 = 0$

(This method of factorising uses the **factor theorem**. Look this up in an A Level textbook and write a few notes.)

Working with formulae

Deriving formulae

Questions such as: (*a*) 'What is the equivalent in °F of 20°C?',
(*b*) 'What is the sum of the interior angles of a 20-sided polygon?'
and (*c*) 'What is the speed of a car travelling with a constant
acceleration of 1 m/s^2 at the end of a 12-second period given that,
at the start of that period, its speed was 8 m/s?', require a specific
result from one or more pieces of given data.

A formula is more general; it gives an **algebraic** rule for
finding one quantity in terms of other quantities. When values are
substituted for the given quantities, the required result follows.

Some formulae we may have to be given as they are too difficult
to derive, for example $A = \pi r^2$ relating the area and radius of a circle;
but many can be derived using the mathematics we know.

Example 8

At 'Formula Two' they are giving interest-free credit if the car is
paid for within one year. The customer can pay a deposit of £*d* and
the balance by equal monthly instalments of £*i* over *m* months.
The salesman carries a formula for working out *i* in terms of *d*, *m*
and the cost of the car, £*c*. Find the formula.

The amount owed, in £, after paying the deposit is $c - d$.
This has to be divided by the number of months, *m*, to find

the monthly repayment and so $i = \dfrac{c - d}{m}$

Example 9

The gradient on a velocity/time graph represents acceleration;
constant acceleration, *a* m/s^2, therefore indicates a straight-line
graph with gradient *a*.

The diagram shows a starting speed, *u* m/s, and a final speed,
v m/s, at the end of a *t*-second interval.
As the gradient of the line is *a*, in triangle ABC,

$$a = \frac{y}{t} \Rightarrow y = at.$$

As $v = u + y$, $v = u + at$.

The answer to (*c*) above is, therefore, $v = 8 + 1 \times 12 = 20$ (m/s).

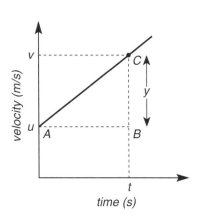

EXERCISE 3.8

1 Pete buys a television, on sale for £460, by paying £76 as a deposit and £12 per month, interest free.

(*a*) How much will he have paid in (i) 5 months (ii) *x* months?

(*b*) How much will he have left to pay after *y* months?

2 Leila's car averages 40 miles per gallon of petrol. Given that a gallon of petrol costs £2.20, write down a formula relating *C*, her petrol cost in £, and *x*, the number of miles travelled.

3 The diagram shows the conversion graph relating temperature in Centigrade and Fahrenheit.

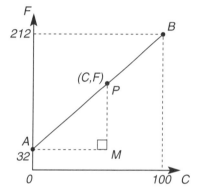

(*a*) What do the coordinates of the points A and B represent?

(*b*) Write down the gradient of the line joining A and B.

(*c*) Using triangle AMP and (*b*), derive the formula

$$F = \tfrac{9}{5}C + 32.$$

(*d*) Deduce the value of *F* when *C* is 20.

4 An inverted cone holds $V \, \text{m}^3$ of water, which is tipped into a rectangular tank that rests with its base on a horizontal table. Given that the dimensions of the base are *x* m by *y* m, find a formula relating *h*, the height of the water in the tank, and *x*, *y* and *V*.

5 If all the diagonals are drawn from one vertex of a polygon,

(*a*) write down the number of triangles that are formed when the polygon is (i) a triangle, (ii) a quadrilateral, (iii) a pentagon, (iv) a hexagon,

(*b*) suggest the number of triangles for a 30-sided polygon,

(*c*) derive the formula $S = 180\,(n - 2)$, for the sum of the interior angles of a polygon, *S*, in terms of the number of its sides (*n*).

Investigation D

In more advanced vector work than we have covered in the course, a multiplication of two vectors **a** and **b** is defined as:

$$\mathbf{a.b} = ab \cos x°,$$

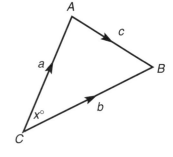

where $x°$ is the angle between the vectors.
Show that (i) $\mathbf{a.b} = \mathbf{b.a}$ (ii) $\mathbf{c.c} = c^2$.
Brackets can be multiplied as we do in algebra, for example:

$$(\mathbf{a} + \mathbf{b}).(\mathbf{c} + \mathbf{d}) = \mathbf{a.c} + \mathbf{a.d} + \mathbf{b.c} + \mathbf{b.d}$$

Show that (iii) $(\mathbf{b} - \mathbf{a}).(\mathbf{b} - \mathbf{a}) = b^2 + a^2 - 2\mathbf{a.b}$
Use these results to prove the cosine rule
for the triangle ABC shown, where $\mathbf{c} = \mathbf{b} - \mathbf{a}$.

Changing the subject of formulae

Often, particularly in the Science subjects, we know a formula but need to rewrite it with a different letter as the subject of the 'equation'. The following examples should remind you of the methods to adopt.

Example 10

Given that $w = \dfrac{m + 5n}{n}$, express n in terms of m and w.

Multiply both sides by n:	$nw = m + 5n$
Isolate all the terms that include n:	$nw - 5n = m$
Factorise:	$n(w - 5) = m$
Divide both sides by 'the bracket':	$n = \dfrac{m}{w - 5}$

Example 11

Make x the subject of 'the equation', $\dfrac{x - a}{a} + \dfrac{y}{b} = \dfrac{x}{c}$.

Multiply throughout by abc:	$bc(x - a) + acy = abx$
Multiply out brackets:	$bcx - bca + acy = abx$
Isolate terms in x:	$bcx - abx = abc - acy$
Factorise:	$bx(c - a) = ac(b - y)$
Divide both sides by $b(c - a)$:	$x = \dfrac{ac(b - y)}{b(c - a)}$

Example 12

Given that $T = k\sqrt{(a^2 + b)}$, express a in terms of b and T.

Square both sides:	$T^2 = k^2(a^2 + b)$
Multiply out:	$T^2 = k^2a^2 + k^2b$
Isolate term in a:	$k^2a^2 = T^2 - k^2b$
Divide by k^2:	$a^2 = \dfrac{T^2 - k^2b}{k^2}$
Take the square root of both sides:	$a = \pm\dfrac{1}{k}\sqrt{(T^2 - k^2b)}$

EXERCISE 3.9

1 Rewrite each of the following formulae with the starred letter as the subject.

(a) $V = \pi ab$, a^* (b) $V = \frac{4}{3}\pi r^3$, r^* (c) $P = 4a + 5b$, b^*

(d) $A = \pi r(r + l)$, l^* (e) $v = u + at$, a^* (f) $a = bc^2$, c^*

(g) $x = y\sqrt{z}$, z^* (h) $x^2 - y^2 = a^2$, y^*

2 Diane's attempt at solving the equation $\frac{x}{3} + \frac{x-1}{4} = 1 + \frac{x}{2}$ is given below.

$$4x + 3x - 1 = 1 + 6x$$
$$x = 2$$

(a) Why should she know her answer is wrong?

(b) What errors has she made?

3 Rewrite each of the following 'equations' to read $x = \ldots$.

(a) $a = \dfrac{7x - b}{3b}$ (b) $i = \dfrac{180x - 360}{x}$ (c) $S = \dfrac{n}{2}(x + a)$

(d) $y = \dfrac{2}{x + 2}$ (e) $p = xq^2 - qr$ (f) $2xy = ab + ax$

(g) $a = b\sqrt{(x - 1)}$ (h) $y = \dfrac{(x - a)c}{(b + x)}$ (i) $\dfrac{1}{\frac{1}{x} + \frac{1}{y}} = a$

4 Given that $d = \dfrac{ac}{a+b}$, express a in terms of b, c and d.

5 Given that $\dfrac{2}{R} = \dfrac{1}{R_1} + \dfrac{1}{R_2}$, express R_1 in terms of R and R_2.

6 Make R the subject of $V = d\,[R^2 - (R - c)^2]$.

7 For the circle with equation $(x - 1)^2 + (y + 2)^2 = 9$, express the equation in the form $y = \dots$.

8 Express x in terms of a and b given that $(x - a)(x + b) = x^2$.

9 Find b in terms of a, c and x if $x = \sqrt{(a^2 + b^2)} + c$.

10 Given that $s = t\,(2a + t)$,

   (*a*) express a in terms of s and t,

   (*b*) show that $s = (t + a)^2 - a^2$,

   (*c*) express t in terms of a and s.

EXERCISE 3.10

1 If $-1 < r < 1$, the 'answer', S, to the infinite sum

$$a + ar + ar^2 + ar^3 + \dots \text{ is } \frac{a}{1 - r}.$$

   (*a*) Find the sum of $12 + 4 + \frac{4}{3} + \frac{4}{9} + \dots$.

   (*b*) Given that $S = 2$, find r in terms of a.

   (*c*) For $S = 2$, find the possible range of values of a.

2 An operation $*$ is defined by $a*b = \dfrac{2b}{a + b}$, $b \neq -a$.

   (*a*) Find the value of (i) $3*4$ (ii) $2*{-}5$ (iii) $2*\frac{1}{2}$ (iv) $\frac{1}{3}*\frac{1}{4}$.

   (*b*) Given that $a*b = \dfrac{1}{a}$, $a \neq 0$, express b in terms of a.

   In this case is there a value of a for which b cannot be found?

3 The area, A cm^2, of a triangle with sides a cm, b cm and c cm can be found using the formula $A = \sqrt{\{s(s-a)(s-b)(s-c)\}}$, where

$s = \frac{1}{2}(a+b+c)$.

(*a*) For a triangle in which $a = b$ and $c = \frac{3}{4}s$, show that $2A = s(s-a)$.

(*b*) For this case express a in terms of s and A.

4 A teacher gave three tests but decided to weight them so that, if the marks scored in the three tests were a, b and c, the final mark, M, would be given by $M = \dfrac{3a + 2b + c}{6}$.

(*a*) Which test is the most important for the pupil?

(*b*) What happens if a pupil scores the same mark in each test?

(*c*) Find M when (i) $a = 50$, $b = 40$, $c = 10$, and (ii) $a = 30$, $b = 40$, $c = 70$.
When the M score is identical to the b score, what is the relationship between a, b and c ?

(*d*) Peter's final mark was 60 and his mark in the middle test was the average of his other two. Show that, for him, $c = 4b - 180$, and explain why he must have scored over 45 in the middle test. Given that $b = 70$, find his other two test scores.

5 The average age of g girls in a survey is x years and the average age of b boys iis y years. The average age of the whole group is a years.

(*a*) Show that $a = \dfrac{gx + by}{g + b}$.

(*b*) Express g in terms of a, b, x and y.

(*c*) If a is 3 more than y and 2 fewer than x, find the ratio of boys to girls in the survey.

6 (*a*) Write $x^2 - 2x + 3$ in the form $(x - a)^2 + b$.

(*b*) Hence show that $y = x^2 - 2x + 3$ may be rewritten in the form $x = 1 \pm \sqrt{(y - 2)}$.

(*c*) For what range of values of y does x have a solution?

(*d*) What does that tell you about the graph of y against x?

7 The equation of an ellipse is $\dfrac{x^2}{a^2} + \dfrac{y^2}{b^2} = 1$, where a and b are constants. Find, in terms of a and b, the x-coordinates of the points in which the curve crosses the line with equation $y = 4$.

8 In Example 9 we derived the formula $v = u + at$. Using this, together with the equation $s = \frac{1}{2}(u + v)t$, derive the equation $v^2 = u^2 + 2as$.

9 A game of 'Frogs' has the following rules:

The two sets of counters have one empty space between them. The counters are moved by either (i) sliding one square along into an empty space or (ii) jumping over one of the opponent's counters into an empty space; they can only be moved forwards. If there are x counters in one set and y counters in the other, the minimum number, m, of moves required to exchange positions of the sets is given by $m = xy + x + y$.

(a) Make x the subject of $m = xy + x + y$.

(b) Show that if the minimum number of moves is 11, there are two different possible games. Try out each one.

(c) Find possible values of x and y when m is (i) 8 (ii) 20 (iii) 28.

Sequences

A particular example of constructing formulae arises when we are looking for the nth term of a sequence. Here the formula only involves one variable, n, the number of the term. A common method is to consider the differences between the terms.

Example 13

Find a formula for the nth term of the sequence 3, 7, 11, 15… .
We can set this out in the following manner:

Number of term (n)	1		2		3		4 …	… n

Number of term (n)   1   2   3   4 …   … n

Value of term (T_n)   3   7   11   15 …   … ?

Differences   +4   +4   +4

Structure   3+4(1)   3+4(2)   3+4(3) $\Rightarrow$3+4(n−1)

The formula for the nth term is $T_n = \mathbf{4}n−1$

In general, if the differences are constant, the formula will be linear in n; if the points (1, 3), (2, 7), (3, 11), (4, 15) are plotted on graph paper they lie on a straight line of gradient **+4**. Sequences like this are called **arithmetic progressions**.

If the formula for the nth term of a sequence is *not* linear, more than one set of differences will be required before they are all the same; in some cases this will never occur.

Example 14

(*a*) The first few terms of the sequence whose nth term is $n^2 + 5n$ are:

6   14   24   36   50   66 …

First differences   8   10   12   14   16 …

Second differences   2   2   2   2 …

(*b*) The first few terms of the sequence whose nth term is n^3 are:

1   8   27   64   125   216 …

First differences   7   19   37   61   91 …

Second differences   12   18   24   30 …

Third differences   6   6   6 …

(*c*) The first few terms of the sequence whose nth term is 3^n are:

3   9   27   81   243   729 …

First differences   6   18   54   162   486 … [2×(3, 9, 27, 81…)]

Second differences   12   36   108   324 … [4×(3, 9, 27, 81…)]

Further differences also give multiples of the original sequence.

Investigation E

Investigate sequences for which the nature of the formula for the nth term is (*a*) quadratic, (*b*) cubic and (*c*) exponential, as in Example 14. Give a report of your findings to include how the final constant difference, where relevant, features in the appropriate formula.

EXERCISE 3.11

1 A single cube has five faces showing when it is placed on a table. When another equal cube is placed on top there are nine faces showing.

(*a*) Complete the table listing the number of faces, f, showing when there are n cubes in the vertical column.

n	1	2	3	4	5	6
f	5	9				

(*b*) Write down a formula for f in terms of n for this sequence.

(*c*) Deduce the number of faces showing when there are 120 cubes.

2 Examine the sequence 7, 13, 19, 25, 31, ...

(*a*) Write down the next seven terms.

(*b*) Find an expression for the nth term.

(*c*) How many of the first 12 terms are prime? Try to give a written explanation of why so many of the early terms in the sequence are prime.

3 The diagrams show the first three stages in building up a pattern when laying a floor with black and white tiles.

Stage 1   *Stage 2*   *Stage 3*

(*a*) Draw two more stages and then copy and complete the table.

Stage (*n*)	1	2	3	4	5
Black tiles	1	5			
White tiles	0	4		36	

(*b*) Write down a formula for the number of black tiles at the *n*th stage.

(*c*) Write down a sequence showing the total number of tiles at each stage and deduce the number of tiles in the *n*th stage.

(*d*) Deduce the formula for the number of white tiles in the *n*th stage.

4 The number of squares in the '3 by 3' square shown is 14.

9 squares (1 by 1)

4 squares (2 by 2)

1 square (3 by 3)

(*a*) Draw similar '4 by 4' and '5 by 5' squares and add the next two terms of the derived sequence 1, 5, 14, ...

(*b*) What do you think the next two terms are?

(*c*) For an '*n* by *n*' square, the formula for the total number, *N*, of squares is $\dfrac{n(n+1)(2n+1)}{6}$. Check that this does generate your sequence, and find the value of *N* in a '20 by 20' square. (*Note*: This sequence requires *three* sets of differences before they have the same value; the formula is a **cubic** in *n*.)

5 Noor was asked to find a formula for the *n*th term of the sequence 2, 6, 12, ..., given that the differences between consecutive terms continue to increase by 2.

(a) What are the next three terms of the sequence?
Noor noted that: the **first** term is **1** × 2,
the **second** term is **2** × 3,
the **third** term is **3** × 4.

(b) Continue her pattern for the next three terms and deduce the formula for the nth term of the sequence.

(c) Explain how this result shows that the formula for the nth triangle number is $\frac{1}{2}n(n+1)$.

(d) Deduce formulae, in a factorised form, for

(i) the nth term for the sequence 0, 2, 5, 9, 14, …,

(ii) the nth term of the sequence 1, $\frac{1}{3}$, $\frac{1}{6}$, $\frac{1}{10}$, $\frac{1}{15}$, …,

(iii) the sum of the first n natural numbers, that is

$1 + 2 + 3 + 4 + 5 + \ldots\ldots + n.$

6 The number of ways of choosing two discs from three differently coloured discs is 3.

We can record this without repeatedly drawing discs by listing:
AB, AC and BC.
The number of different combinations of choosing two discs from four discs is 6: AB, AC, AD, BC, BD and CD.

(a) Complete the table, where n is the number of discs to choose from, and C is the number of ways of choosing two different discs.

n	2	3	4	5	6	7
C	1	3	6			

(b) Suggest a formula for C in terms of n.

(c) Explain how this is related to the formula for the nth triangle number.

(d) Find the number of ways of choosing two discs from 30 different coloured discs.

7 The 'house of cards' shown has four storeys.

(*a*) Describe how the sequences
   (i) 2, 5, 8, 11, …
   (ii) 2, 7, 15, 26, …
relate to the house of cards.

(*b*) By adding two more layers to the 'house' give the next two terms of each sequence.

(*c*) Write down a formula for the *n*th term of sequence (i).

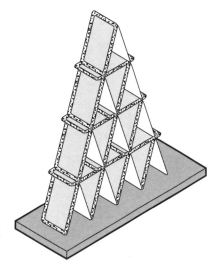

A class was given the task of finding a formula for the *n*th term of sequence (ii). Mischa spotted the following pattern:

$$n = 1 \Rightarrow 2 = \tfrac{1}{2} \times 1 \times 4$$
$$n = 2 \Rightarrow 7 = \tfrac{1}{2} \times 2 \times 7$$
$$n = 3 \Rightarrow 15 = \tfrac{1}{2} \times 3 \times 10$$
$$n = 4 \Rightarrow 26 = \tfrac{1}{2} \times 4 \times 13$$

and proceeded to find the correct formula.

(*d*) Find the *n*th term of the sequence 4, 7, 10, 13, … and hence deduce Mischa's formula for the *n*th term of sequence (ii).

8 There are an infinite number of sequences that have 1, 2, 4, 8, as their first four terms. One set of pupils was asked to provide a few. Angus produced 1, 2, 4, 8, 16, 32, 64, … and gave the formula for the *n*th term.

(*a*) Write down his formula.

(*b*) Write down observations about the sets of differences for this sequence and also how this formula differs from the others in this exercise.

Because Briony remembered an investigation in Book 4y into the number of regions formed when *n* points on the cirumference of a circle are joined to each other, she provided another two terms to give 1, 2, 4, 8, 16, 31, but could not remember how it continued.

(*c*) The diagrams show the first four results are correct. Check that the other two are correct.

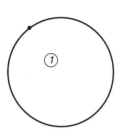 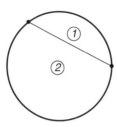 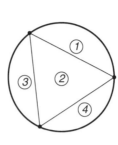 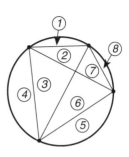

(d) The formula for the nth term of this sequence is $\dfrac{n^4 - 6n^3 + 23n^2 - 18n + 24}{24}$. Find the next two terms of this sequence.

After a lot of experimenting Calum found a formula, $\dfrac{n(n^2 - 3n + 8)}{6}$, which he thought generated the first four terms 1, 2, 4, 8.

(e) Check whether he was correct and find the next two terms generated using this formula.

Investigation F

The formula for the nth term of the triangle numbers is $\frac{1}{2}n(n + 1)$, as we saw in the last exercise, and that for the nth term of the square numbers is clearly n^2. In Book 3y we saw the sequence of pentagonal numbers, 1, 5, 12, 22, ..., which can be built up from the following diagrams.

 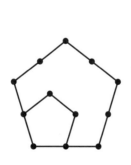 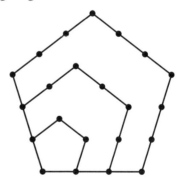

Write down the next few terms of the sequence and verify that the formula for the nth term is $\frac{1}{2}n(3n - 1)$.

From the following diagrams deduce the first four hexagonal numbers and then extend the sequence to seven terms.

You should find that the formula $n(2n - 1)$ will generate your sequence.

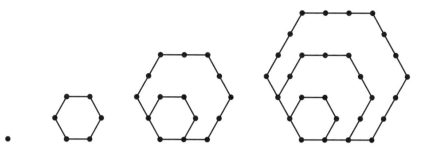

The four formulae (given above) themselves follow a clear pattern if you write them all in the form $\frac{1}{2}n(an + b)$. Investigate this and try to predict the sequence for the heptagonal numbers. Check with diagrams.

Investigation G

We have seen that $1 + 2 + 3 + 4 + 5 + \ldots + n$, the sum of the first n natural numbers, gives the nth triangle number, for example:

$1 + \underline{2} = 3$ (2nd triangle number), $1 + 2 + \underline{3} = 6$ (3rd),

and so a formula for this sum is $\frac{1}{2}n(n + 1)$.

Jason's teacher posed the following problem. By observing the answers to 1^3, $1^3 + 2^3$, $1^3 + 2^3 + 3^3$, $1^3 + 2^3 + 3^3 + 4^3$, could anyone suggest a formula for the sum of the cubes of the first n natural numbers?

Jason saw the connection with the triangle numbers and proposed a formula which happily agreed with his calculator results for the cases when $n = 5$ and $n = 10$. See if you can be as successful. This clearly does not constitute a proof but does lead into a method of proof called **proof by induction**. Try to find this in an A Level book and write some notes, including examples, on the method.

Investigation H

In trying to find the nth term for sequence (ii) in question 7 in Exercise 3.11, Dorian decided to look at the differences between the terms. She noted that the first set of differences, 5, 8, 11, 14, 17, ..., were not constant, but that the differences between these, 3, 3, 3, 3, ..., were. As it was the second set of differences that were constant she thought the required formula might be a quadratic in n and decided to let $T_n = an^2 + bn + c$.

As $T_1 = 2$, when $n = 1$, she found that $a + b + c = 2$.

Write down two other equations in a, b and c and try to solve the three equations. You should find that this agrees with Mischa's result.

Now form other sequences in which it requires two sets of differences before the values are constant and try to find their formulae in the same way. Write up any interesting observations.

Further simplification of algebraic expressions

Using factorisation

Evaluation of two arithmetic expressions such as $\dfrac{7+6}{3}$ or $\dfrac{5^2 + 2 \times 5}{5^2 - 3 \times 5}$ should cause little trouble – even without the aid of a calculator! It is not likely that you would dream of simplifying in the following way:

$$\frac{7+6}{3} = 7 + 2 = 9 \quad \text{or} \quad \frac{5^2 + 2 \times 5}{5^2 - 3 \times 5} = \frac{1+2}{1-3} = -1\tfrac{1}{2}!!$$

However, similar algebraic expressions such as $\dfrac{7+3x}{3}$ and $\dfrac{x^2 + 2x}{x^2 - 3x}$ seem to tempt 'cancelling' a little too easily.

The same rules apply in algebra as they do in arithmetic; cancelling is not allowed between terms separated by $+$ or $-$ signs, only $\times$ or $\div$. However, factorisation will often considerably simplify algebraic fractions and in further mathematics this is often necessary.

Example 15

$$\frac{x^2 + 2x}{x^2 - 3x} = \frac{x(x+2)}{x(x-3)} = \frac{x+2}{x-3}$$

There is no further simplification. It is useful to substitute a value for x in the given and the final expressions to test equivalence.

Example 16

$$\frac{x^2 + 7x + 10}{x^2 + 5x} = \frac{(x+2)(x+5)}{x(x+5)} = \frac{x+2}{x}$$

In this case the answer may be written in the form $1 + \dfrac{2}{x}$.

Note: If there is *only* one term in the denominator then the numerator can be split up as in the last example, but if there is more than one term then no further simplification should be attempted. (Terms are separated by $+$ and $-$ signs, for example $x^2 + 7x + 10$ has three terms, but $7x$ is a single term.)

Example 17

$\dfrac{x+y}{xy} = \dfrac{x}{xy} + \dfrac{y}{xy} = \dfrac{1}{y} + \dfrac{1}{x}$ just as $\dfrac{2+3}{6} = \dfrac{2}{6} + \dfrac{3}{6}$, but

$\dfrac{xy}{x+y}$ is *not* equal to $\dfrac{xy}{x} + \dfrac{xy}{y} \;(= y + x)$ just as $\dfrac{6}{2+3} \neq 3 + 2!$

Reminders: (*a*) $\dfrac{a+b}{b+a} = 1$ (*b*) $\dfrac{a-b}{b-a} = -1$

EXERCISE 3.12

1 Which, if any, of the following expressions is equivalent to $\dfrac{3x+6y}{6}$?

   (*a*) $3x + y$ (*b*) $\frac{1}{2}x + y$ (*c*) $\frac{1}{2}x + 6y$ (*d*) $x + 3y$

2 Which, if any, of the following expressions is equivalent to $\dfrac{x}{x+2}$?

   (*a*) $1 + \frac{x}{2}$ (*b*) $\frac{1}{2}$ (*c*) $\frac{1}{3}$ (*d*) $1 + \frac{2}{x}$

3 Emily found the correct answer for $\dfrac{10.8^2 - 1.7^2}{10.8 + 1.7}$ by incorrectly cancelling as follows:

$\dfrac{10.8^2}{10.8} = 10.8$, and $\dfrac{1.7^2}{1.7} = 1.7$, and $\dfrac{-}{+} = -$, giving $10.8 - 1.7 = 9.1$.

Explain why this wrong method happens to give the correct answer.

4 Simplify the following expressions.

   (*a*) $\dfrac{2x+3y}{3y+2x}$ (*b*) $\dfrac{1-5x}{5x-1}$ (*c*) $\dfrac{x^2-9x}{x}$ (*d*) $\dfrac{x^2-y^2}{x-y}$

   (*e*) $\dfrac{5x-3y}{15x-9y}$ (*f*) $\dfrac{9x}{3x+6x^2}$ (*g*) $\dfrac{x^3+7x}{7+x^2}$ (*h*) $\dfrac{(x-2)^2}{x^2-x-2}$

   (*i*) $\dfrac{x^2+3x-4}{x^2-2x+1}$ (*j*) $\dfrac{2x+3y}{9y^2+6xy}$ (*k*) $\dfrac{x^4-16y^4}{(x-2y)(x+2y)}$ (*l*) $\dfrac{6x^2+x-2}{2x^2+7x-4}$

   (*m*) $\dfrac{2x^2+9x+10}{3x^2-12}$ (*n*) $\dfrac{2x+4}{3x^2+x-10}$ (*o*) $\dfrac{x^3-9x}{2x^2+6x}$ (*p*) $\dfrac{x^2-xy-12y^2}{x^2+2xy-3y^2}$

When algebraic fractions are multiplied or divided it is even more beneficial to simplify.

Example 18

$$\frac{x^2 - 3x}{x^2 + 2x + 1} \div \frac{x^2 - x - 6}{x^2 + 3x + 2} = \frac{x\cancel{(x-3)}}{(x+1)\cancel{(x+1)}} \times \frac{\cancel{(x+2)}\cancel{(x+1)}}{\cancel{(x-3)}\cancel{(x+2)}} = \frac{x}{x+1}$$

EXERCISE 3.13

1 Simplify the following products of algebraic fractions.

(a) $\dfrac{2}{x+1}$ and $\dfrac{3x^2 - 12x - 15}{6}$ (b) $\dfrac{x+1}{x}$ and $\dfrac{x^3 - x}{x^2 + 2x + 1}$

(c) $\dfrac{2x^2 + xy}{4}$ and $\dfrac{8x^2 - 2y^2}{4x^2 + 4xy + y^2}$ (d) $\dfrac{x^2 + 3x + 2}{3x^2 - 2x - 5}$ and $\dfrac{6x + 3}{2x^2 + 5x + 2}$

2 Simplify the following.

(a) $\dfrac{x}{x+6} \div \dfrac{x^2}{xy + 6y}$ (b) $\dfrac{6}{5x + 10} \div \dfrac{2}{x^2 - 3x - 10}$

(c) $\dfrac{2x - 8}{x^2 - 4y^2} \div \dfrac{x^2 + 3x - 28}{x^2 + 2xy}$ (d) $\dfrac{x - 5}{2x + 4} \div \dfrac{x^2 - 4x - 5}{x + 2}$

Addition and subtraction of algebraic fractions

Think through the process of adding $\frac{1}{2}$ and $\frac{2}{3}$, without using a calculator. Each fraction is written as an equivalent fraction with the same (lowest) denominator, $\frac{3}{6}$ and $\frac{4}{6}$, and then the answer is clearly $\frac{7}{6}$. The same process should be used for algebraic fractions.

Example 19

$$\frac{x}{2} + \frac{5x - 3}{3} = \frac{3x}{6} + \frac{2(5x - 3)}{6} = \frac{3x + 10x - 6}{6} = \frac{13x - 6}{6}$$

Notice the addition of the bracket when $5x - 3$ is multiplied by 2. A bracket is always needed when one expression is multiplied by another.

Example 20

$$\frac{5}{x+2} - \frac{2}{x+3} = \frac{5(x+3) - 2(x+2)}{(x+2)(x+3)}$$

$$= \frac{5x + 15 - 2x - 4}{(x+2)(x+3)}$$

$$= \frac{3x + 11}{(x+2)(x+3)}$$

Here the LCM of $x + 2$ and $x + 3$ is $(x + 2)(x + 3)$ as they have no common factor, just as the LCM of 4 and 3 is 12. However, if there is a factor in common the LCM will not be the product of the factors, just as the LCM of 4 and 6 is not 24 but 12. One way of finding the LCM is to multiply all the prime factors together, having first discarded the common factor(s) from the second number.

Example 21

(*a*) Written as a product of prime factors, $4 = 2 \times 2$ and $6 = 2 \times 3$. The LCM $= 2 \times 2 \times 3 = 12$.

(*b*) As $18 = 2 \times 3 \times 3$ and $30 = 2 \times 3 \times 5$, the LCM of 18 and 30 is $2 \times 3 \times 3 \times 5 = 90$.

Although with numbers the LCM can easily be found using a calculator, the process should ensure that you find the correct LCM for algebraic expressions.

Example 22

(*a*) As $x^2 = (x) \times (x)$ and $x^2 + x = x(x + 1)$, their LCM is $x^2(x + 1)$.

(*b*) The LCM of $(x + 1)(x + 2)$ and $(x + 2)(x + 3)$ is $(x + 1)(x + 2)(x + 3)$.

Example 23

$$\frac{3}{x^2} + \frac{4}{x(x + 1)} = \frac{3(x + 1) + 4x}{x^2(x + 1)} = \frac{7x + 3}{x^2(x + 1)}$$

Notice that the numerator is not $3x(x + 1) + 4x^2$. Why would that be wrong?
Always check that your answer is in its lowest terms.

Example 24

$$\frac{x}{(x+1)\,(x+2)} - \frac{2}{(x+2)(x+3)} = \frac{x(x+3) - 2(x+1)}{(x+1)(x+2)(x+3)}$$

$$= \frac{x^2 + x - 2}{(x+1)(x+2)(x+3)}$$

$$= \frac{(x+2)(x-1)}{(x+1)(x+2)(x+3)}$$

$$= \frac{(x-1)}{(x+1)(x+3)}$$

EXERCISE 3.14

Express each of the following as a single fraction in its lowest terms.

1 $\dfrac{x}{4} + \dfrac{x}{7}$
    2 $\dfrac{x}{4} - \dfrac{x}{5}$
    3 $\dfrac{2x}{3} + \dfrac{5x}{6}$
    4 $\dfrac{4x}{9} - \dfrac{x}{4}$

5 $\dfrac{5x}{7} + 1$
    6 $\dfrac{x+2}{5} + \dfrac{x}{2}$
    7 $\dfrac{x-1}{2} - \dfrac{x-5}{3}$
    8 $\dfrac{1}{4} + \dfrac{x}{5} - 2x$

9 $\dfrac{2x+5}{12} + \dfrac{3x}{8}$
    10 $\dfrac{3x+4}{6} - \dfrac{1-x}{7}$
    11 $\dfrac{x}{2} + \dfrac{x+6}{6} - \dfrac{3x}{4}$
    12 $\dfrac{2x-1}{10} + \dfrac{4x+3}{12}$

EXERCISE 3.15

1 (*a*) Which one, or more, of the following is equivalent to $\dfrac{1}{x} + \dfrac{1}{y}$?

    (i) $\dfrac{2}{x+y}$
  (ii) $\dfrac{2}{xy}$
  (iii) $\dfrac{x+y}{xy}$
  (iv) $\dfrac{y+x}{x+y}$
  (v) $\dfrac{y+x}{xy}$

(*b*) One of the expressions above can be simplified further.
Identify it and give its simplified version.

(*c*) Prove, showing your working clearly, that $\dfrac{1}{\dfrac{1}{x} + \dfrac{1}{y}} = \dfrac{xy}{x+y}$

(*Note:* The answer to this is not $x + y$!)

(*d*) Write down, without using a calculator, the answers to:

(i) $\dfrac{1}{\frac{1}{2}+\frac{1}{3}}$ (ii) $\dfrac{1}{\frac{1}{5}+\frac{1}{7}}$ (iii) $\dfrac{1}{\frac{1}{2}-\frac{1}{5}}$ (iv) $(\frac{1}{3}+\frac{1}{4})^{-1}$

2 Namayola travels to a point 12 km away to fetch water for her family. She walks at x km/h on the way there and at y km/h on the return journey.

(*a*) Express T, the total time taken in hours, in terms of x and y, giving your answer as a single fraction.

(*b*) Evaluate T when $x = 5$ and $y = 3$, without using a calculator.

3 Express each of the following as a single fraction in its lowest terms.

(*a*) $\dfrac{4}{x}+\dfrac{5}{2x}$ (*b*) $\dfrac{7}{2x}-\dfrac{5}{3x}$ (*c*) $\dfrac{1}{4x}+\dfrac{5}{6x}$ (*d*) $\dfrac{1}{x}+\dfrac{1}{x^2}$

(*e*) $\dfrac{1}{x+4}+\dfrac{1}{x-3}$ (*f*) $\dfrac{2}{x+1}-\dfrac{7}{x}$ (*g*) $\dfrac{4}{x}+\dfrac{5}{x-2}$

(*h*) $\dfrac{3}{2x+3}-\dfrac{4}{3x-5}$ (*i*) $\dfrac{5}{2(x+2)}+\dfrac{4}{3(x-2)}$ (*j*) $\dfrac{x^2+7}{2x}-\dfrac{x}{2}$

(*k*) $\dfrac{1}{x^2+x}+\dfrac{1}{x}$ (*l*) $\dfrac{2}{1-x^2}-\dfrac{3}{1+x}$ (*m*) $\dfrac{x}{(x+1)(x+2)}-\dfrac{3}{x+2}$

(*n*) $1-\dfrac{12}{x}+\dfrac{15}{x+1}$ (*o*) $\dfrac{3}{x^2-3x}-\dfrac{4}{x^2-2x-3}$

4 Show that $\dfrac{1}{(x-2)(x+1)}+\dfrac{2}{3(x+3)(x+1)}=\dfrac{5}{3(x-2)(x+3)}.$

5 (*a*) Show that $x+\dfrac{a}{x}=\dfrac{x^2+a}{x}.$

(*b*) Write each of the following as a simplified single fraction.

(i) $\sqrt{x}+\dfrac{1}{\sqrt{x}}$ (ii) $\sqrt{(x+3)}-\dfrac{3}{\sqrt{(x+3)}}$ (iii) $\sqrt{(5-2x)}+\dfrac{2x}{\sqrt{(5-2x)}}$

Investigation I

In Example 20 we saw that $\dfrac{3x+11}{(x+2)(x+3)} = \dfrac{5}{x+2} - \dfrac{2}{x+3}$.

To split up an expression like this into its **partial fractions** on the right-hand side, is a little more difficult than forming this expression from the separate fractions. Look at the answers for question 3 (a), (b) and (c), and try to see how to break them down into the given expressions. If you think you have succeeded try the following:

(a) $\dfrac{12x-1}{(x+2)(x+7)}$ (b) $\dfrac{9x-38}{(x-7)(x-2)}$ (c) $\dfrac{17x+16}{(2x-1)(3x+2)}$

4. Solving equations

This chapter revises and relates the various methods used during the course to solve algebraic equations.

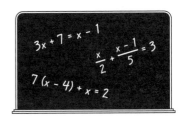

Linear equations in one unknown

Whatever the form in which the equation is given it will be possible to rearrange into the form $ax = b$, and so there will always be one solution (or root) $x = \dfrac{b}{a}$.

All linear equations can be solved algebraically, that is by using the operations $+$, $-$, $\times$ and $\div$, in just the same way that x is made the subject of an equation involving several letters.

Example 1

Solve $7(x - 2) = 5 + 4x$.

Multiply out:	$7x - 14 = 5 + 4x$
Collect terms in x on one side:	$7x - 4x = 5 + 14$
Simplify:	$3x = 19$
Divide by coefficient of x:	$x = \dfrac{19}{3} = 6\dfrac{1}{3}$

Example 2

Solve $\dfrac{x - 1}{3} = 1 - \dfrac{1 + 2x}{5}$.

Multiply through by 15:	$5(x - 1) = 15 - 3(1 + 2x)$
Multiply out:	$5x - 5 = 12 - 6x$
Collect terms in x:	$5x + 6x = 12 + 5$
Simplify:	$11x = 17$
	$x = \dfrac{17}{11} = 1\dfrac{6}{11}$

The final step, where you need to divide by the coefficient of x, is often the weakest in examinations. If $11x = 17$, then x is clearly greater than 1 and so there is no excuse for giving the answer $\dfrac{11}{17}$!
The intermediate step in the answer line, $\dfrac{17}{11}$, should also prevent errors like $1\dfrac{6}{17}$.

EXERCISE 4.1

Solve for x, giving your answer in fractional form where necessary.

1 $5x = 32$ **2** $-6x = -5$ **3** $-6x = 2$ **4** $0.6x = 5.4$

5 $0.4x = 2$ **6** $1.25x = 0.75$ **7** $4x - 15 = 0$ **8** $1 + 2x = 0$

9 $4 - 0.2x = 0.6x$ **10** $3x - 14 = 5 - x$ **11** $4 - 9x = 2x$ **12** $6(x + 5) = 2 - x$

13 $3(5 - 4x) = -9$ **14** $3 - (5 - x) = 7$ **15** $x - 3(4 - 2x) = 5x$

16 $2(x + 7) = 7(2x - 3)$ **17** $2(3x - 0.5) = 0.6(3 + 2x)$ **18** $\frac{3x}{5} = 12$

19 $1 + \frac{3}{x} = 5$ **20** $\frac{2x}{3} = \frac{5}{4}$ **21** $\frac{x}{2} - \frac{1}{3} = \frac{x}{5}$

22 $\frac{x + 7}{6} = 2(3 - x)$ **23** $\frac{2}{1 - x} + \frac{x}{1 + x} = 1$ **24** $\frac{4x - 3}{2x - 5} = \frac{3}{4}$

EXERCISE 4.2

1 Find the point in which the line $3y + 2x = 5$ intersects (*a*) the
x-axis, (*b*) the y-axis.

2 Jacques bought x bottles of *panachée* at 1.40 francs each and
$(\frac{1}{2}x + 5)$ bottles of Orangina at 4.6 francs each. The total cost
was 67.4 francs. Find the value of x.

3 For each of the first x articles that Mr Cash sells he receives £5
commission; he receives £6 commission on each article sold
above this number. In one month he sold 115 articles and
received £650 commission. Form an equation in x and solve it.

4 The cost of tickets for Elsa's school play was £1.50 for adults
and 50p for children. On a night when there were 220 tickets
sold, x of which were for adults, the takings amounted to £210.
Find the value of x.

5 A path of width 0.5 m surrounds a lawn with dimensions x m
by 2 m. Given that the area of the path is 14.7 m^2, find the
value of x.

6 Last year in Michelle's year group there were eight more boys than girls. This year there are two new boys and one of the girls has left; the ratio of boys to girls is 6 : 5. Let the number of boys last year be x and form an equation in x. Solve the equation and deduce the number of pupils in Michelle's year group this year.

7 In each of the following solutions there is one line which has an error. Correct the error and complete the solutions.

(a) $6(2 + x) = 15$
$12 + x = 15$
$x = 3$

(b) $4x + 1 = 7x - 4$
$5 = 3x$
$x = 1\frac{2}{5}$

(c) $5x - (1 - x) = 2$
$5x - 1 + x = 2$
$6x = 1$
$x = \frac{1}{6}$

(d) $\frac{x}{3} + 2(x + 1) = 13$
$x + 6x + 6 = 13$
$7x = 7$
$x = 1$

(e) $5 - 3(4 + x) = 14$
$2(4 + x) = 14$
$8 + 2x = 14$
$2x = 6$
$x = 3$

8 After he had marked the exam papers Mr Fudge decided to scale the marks using the formula $m = \frac{4}{3}r + 20$, where r is the raw mark and m is the mark the pupil is given, m being corrected to the nearest integer.

(a) What is the lowest mark any pupil could be given by Mr Fudge?

(b) Jennie's raw mark was 47. What mark was she given?

(c) Lucy came top in the exam with 96. What was her raw mark?

9 For what value of x is $\dfrac{1 + x}{2 - x}$ equal to $\dfrac{2 - x}{1 + x}$?

10 (a) For the pentagon shown find the value of x.

(b) Azif read angle A as $(80 - x)°$. Why is this unfortunate for him?

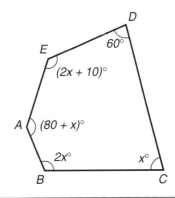

11 In the grid we see an H centred on 55. The shape may be
translated in the grid but no part of the shape must be outside
the grid.

1	2	3	4	5	6	7	8
9	10	11	12	13	14	15	16
17	18	19	20	21	22	23	24
25	26	27	28	29	30	31	32
33	34	35	36	37	38	39	40
41	42	43	44	45	46	47	48
49	50	51	52	53	54	55	56
57	58	59	60	61	62	63	64

(a) Write down the sum of the seven numbers of the H
centred on (i) 55 (ii) 11.

(b) If the H is centred on x, write down in terms of x the sum
of the seven numbers.

(c) The sum of the seven numbers centred on y is 203. Find
the value of y.

(d) Explain why the total of the seven numbers of an H
cannot be (i) 142 (ii) 280.

12 To help Susie with her maths revision her father sets her
100 questions and gives her 5p for each one she gets right
but deducts 2p for each one she gets wrong.

(a) How many questions would she need to get right in order
not to have to pay her father?

(b) If she was given £3.11, how many did she get right?

13 On a journey of 180 miles from Bristol to Cambridge a driver
stops for refreshments when he has reached x miles from
Bristol. Before the stop he averaged 50 m.p.h. and after the
stop he was able to average 60 m.p.h. Given that his total
driving time was 3 hours 16 minutes, find the value of x.

14 The perimeter of the isosceles trapezium is 20 cm.

(a) Find, in terms of x, an expression for DE.

(b) Given that the distance between the parallel sides is 3 cm, form an equation in x and solve it.

15 A hollow hemispherical container holds a quantity of liquid. The diameter of the circular surface of the liquid is 4 m and the maximum depth of the liquid is 1 m. Calculate the radius of the hemisphere. (Volume of a sphere of radius r is $\frac{4}{3}\pi r^3$.)

Linear equations in two unknowns

An equation such as $3x + 4y = 11$ is a linear equation in two unknowns; the graph of y against x is a straight line of gradient $-\frac{3}{4}$. In general, therefore, there are an infinite number of pairs of values of x and y that satisfy the equation, represented by each point on the line. If we have another equation relating x and y, this too can be represented by a line and so we know that, providing the lines are not parallel, there will be *one pair of values of x and y,* the coordinates of the point of intersection of the lines, that satisfy the two equations simultaneously.

In general two equations in two unknowns, x and y, have a unique solution pair that can be found graphically or algebraically.

EXERCISE 4.3

This exercise should be worked through *without* using algebraic methods. Questions 1–7 can be solved by 'testing values' and question 8 requires a graphical solution.

1 It is known that $x = c$ and $y = d$ are positive integers that satisfy the equation $3x + 4y = 11$.

(a) Find the values of c and d.

(b) Which of the following equations are also satisfied by $x = c$ and $y = d$?

(i) $x + y = 3$ (ii) $7x - 4y = -1$

(iii) $4x + 3y = 11$ (iv) $4x + 3y = 10$

(c) Solve the equations $3x + 4y = 11$ and $4x + 3y = 10$ simultaneously.

2 It is known that p is a positive integer and that q is a positive number such that $3p + 2q = 10$.

(a) Write down the solution pairs.

(b) State the values of p and q that satisfy both $3p + 2q = 10$ and $5p + 2q = 16$.

3 Which of the following equations have no solutions in common with $2x - 3y = 2$?

(a) $2x + 3y = 2$ (b) $4x - 6y = 4$ (c) $6x - 9y = 1$ (d) $3y = 2x + 1$.

4 On one particular day a firm hired out x coaches at £80 each and y at £120 each. Given that the total income received was £1480 and that the total number of coaches hired out was 15,

(a) show that $2x + 3y = 37$,

(b) form another equation in x and y,

(c) deduce the values of x and y.

Why can this problem be solved without using a graph or an algebraic method?

5 The three 2-digit numbers xy, yx and $x2$ add up to 100.

(a) Explain how you know that $x + y = 8$ and $2x + y = 9$.

(b) Write down the values of x and y that satisfy both equations.

6 For all values of x the expression $a(x + 2) + b(3 - x)$, where a and b are positive integers, always has the same value as $3x + 11$.

(a) By putting $x = 1$, show that $3a + 2b = 14$.

(b) Write down pairs of values of a and b that satisfy this equation.

(c) By choosing a different value of x form another equation in a and b.

(d) Deduce the values of a and b.

7 Hamish has £1.70 made up of x five-pence pieces and y twenty-pence pieces.

(a) Show that $x + 4y = 34$, and list possible pairs of values of x and y.

If there had been y five-pence pieces and x twenty-pence pieces the total would be £1.55.

(b) Write down and simplify another equation in x and y, and deduce the values of x and y.

8 For each of the following pairs of equations draw the corresponding straight-line graphs and hence find the solution common to both equations.

(a) $x - y = 1$, $4x + 2y = 16$ (b) $3x + y = 5$, $2x - 3y = 7$

(c) $x + 4y = 30$, $4y = 5(x + 3)$ (d) $2x + 3y = 7$, $x - y = 2$

Algebraic methods

Even when solutions are integers we are often not aware of the fact when trying to solve the equations simultaneously and so trying values would not be worthwhile. Solving graphically is time consuming and will often not be accurate enough, and so the algebraic approach is more usual. The methods used are substitution and elimination; the latter is possibly more common here but the method of substitution is most useful when the equations are not both linear.

Example 3 (Substitution)

This method is usually used when the coefficient of x or y is ± 1 in one of the equations.

Solve simultaneously $6x - y = 12$ and $4x - 2y = 6$.

Rewrite the first equation as $y = 6x - 12$ and replace the 'y' in the second equation by this expression to give an equation in x only.

$$4x - 2(6x - 12) = 6 \Rightarrow 4x - 12x + 24 = 6 \Rightarrow 8x = 18 \Rightarrow x = 2\frac{1}{4}$$

Use either equation with $x = 2\frac{1}{4}$ to find $y = 1\frac{1}{2}$. The solution should be checked in the other equation.

Example 4 (Elimination)

Find the values of x and y common to (a) $4x + 3y = 5$ and (b) $3x + 2y = 3$.

Scale the equations so that the coefficients of either x or y are equal and of opposite sign.

Multiply (a) by 2 and (b) by -3: $8x + 6y = 10$
$$-9x - 6y = -9$$

Add the equations: $-x = 1 \Rightarrow x = -1$

We can find y as before. Check that $y = 3$.

EXERCISE 4.4

1 Solve the following equations simultaneously, using an algebraic method.

(a) $2x - 5y = 3$ (b) $5x + 2y = 0$ (c) $4x + 3y = 6$ (d) $11x + 2y = 12$
   $3x + y = -4$ $x - y = 12$ $6x + y = 9$ $3x + 2y = 4$

(e) $2x - 6y = 1$ (f) $4x - 2y = 2$ (g) $2x - 6y = 14 = -x - 4y$
   $5x + 12y = 25$ $8x + 8y = -5$

2 Find the point of intersection of the straight lines with these equations.

(a) $y = 5x + 2, y = 3$ (b) $y = 2x - 3, y = 0$ (c) $y = x, y = 4 - x$

(d) $3x - y = 1, y = 2x$ (e) $x + y = 5, 7x - 2y = -1$ (f) $y = 3(x - 1), \frac{x}{2} + \frac{y}{3} = 4$

3 Jack bought 40 first-class and 25 second-class postage stamps for £14.10; Jill bought 30 of each type for £12.60. Let the price of a first-class stamp be x pence and the price of a second-class stamp be y pence.

(a) Show that $8x + 5y = 282$ and $x + y = 42$.

(b) Find the values of x and y.

(c) An equal number of each type of stamp are bought for £31.08. Calculate the total number of stamps bought.

4 The curve with equation $y = \dfrac{ax + 2}{x - b}$ passes through the points (1, 1) and (3, 4). Flnd the values of a and b and verify that the point (25, −29) also lies on the curve.

5 Moira has two brothers whose average age is the same as the difference between their ages; three years ago the elder was four times as old as the younger. If the younger brother is x years old now and the elder is y years old now, (a) show that $y = 3x$ and $y = 4x - 9$, (b) deduce the values of x and y.

6 The marked price of a TV and a midi-system are £400 and £450 respectively. In a sale they are reduced by $x\%$ and $y\%$ respectively. In the sale one person who bought a TV and a midi-system made a saving of £105.

(a) Show that $8x + 9y = 210$.

Another person who bought 2 TVs and 4 midi-systems made a saving of £300.

(b) Form another equation in x and y and use the two equations to solve for x and y.

7 Twenty litres of petrol and $\frac{1}{2}$ litre of oil cost a driver £12.20; another driver bought 25 litres of petrol and 1 litre of oil from the same garage for £16.15.

(a) Without working out the cost per litre of petrol and oil find the cost of 10 litres of petrol and 1 litre of oil.

(b) Let the cost per litre of petrol and oil be x pence and y pence respectively, and form two equations in x and y.

(c) Solve the equations for x and y and check your result for (a).

8 A teacher organised a trip to an international hockey match. The cost of the tickets was £7 for adults and £4 for children; the total cost of all the tickets being £460. For the coach journey he charged £5 for adults and £2 for children which exactly covered the hire cost of £260.

(a) Let the number of adults and children on the trip be x and y respectively and form two equations in x and y.

(b) Without calculating x and y find the total number of people in the party.

(c) Solve the two equations simultaneously and check your result for (b)

9 A train covers the first x miles of a journey at an average speed of 30 m.p.h. and the remaining y miles at an average speed of 75 m.p.h.; the total time for the journey being 26 minutes.

(*a*) Show that $5x + 2y = 65$.

If the average speeds for the two parts of the journey are 40 m.p.h. and 50 m.p.h., the time taken is 27 minutes.

(*b*) Show that x and y also satisfy $5x + 4y = 90$.

(*c*) Find x and y and hence deduce that the average speed of the train for the complete journey is approximately 47.3 m.p.h.

10 (*a*) Factorise $x^2 - y^2$.

(*b*) Given that $x^2 - y^2 = 16$ and that $x + y = 2$, state the value of $x - y$.

(*c*) Deduce the values of x and y that satisfy the two equations.

11 Using a similar method to that in question 10 find values of x and y that satisfy the following pairs of equations.

(*a*) $x^2 - 4y^2 = 20$, $x - 2y = 2$ (*b*) $x^2 - 25y^2 = 1$, $x + 5y = 1$

(*c*) $9x^2 - 16y^2 = 4$, $3x - 4y = 1$ (*d*) $2x^2 - 8y^2 = 10$, $x + 2y = 2$

Investigation A

Design a computer program to solve the simultaneous equations $Ax + By = E$ and $Cx + Dy = F$, where A, B, C, D, E and F are known constants. Test your program on the equations in Exercise 4.4, question 1.

Quadratic equations

Algebraic, graphical and numerical methods have been used to solve equations of the form $ax^2 + bx + c = 0$.

(1) Using factorisation

If $b^2 - 4ac$ is a perfect square then the equation can be solved by using factorisation. (The methods can be revised using Chapter 3.)

Example 5

Solve $6x^2 + 7x - 3 = 0$.

As $b^2 - 4ac = 49 - 4(6)(-3) = 121$, a perfect square, factorisation can be used.

$$6x^2 + 7x - 3 = 0 \Rightarrow (3x - 1)(2x + 3) = 0$$
$$\Rightarrow x = \tfrac{1}{3} \text{ or } x = -1\tfrac{1}{2}$$

(2) Completing the square and 'the formula'

These methods can be used in all cases.

Completing the square enables the equation to be rewritten in the form $(x + p)^2 = q$, which can then easily be solved.

Example 6

Solve $2x^2 + 8x - 1 = 0$.

Divide through by 2: $\qquad\qquad\qquad\qquad x^2 + 4x - \tfrac{1}{2} = 0$

Rewrite: $\qquad\qquad\qquad\qquad\qquad\quad x^2 + 4x = \tfrac{1}{2}$

Complete the square by adding 4 to both sides: $\quad x^2 + 4x + 4 = 4.5$

$$(x + 2)^2 = 4.5$$

Take the square root of both sides: $\qquad\qquad x + 2 = \pm\sqrt{4.5}$

The solutions are: $\qquad\qquad\qquad\qquad\qquad x = -2 \pm \sqrt{4.5}.$

As the solutions are irrational, decimal answers should be given to an appropriate degree of accuracy, for example $-4.12, 0.121$ (to 3 significant figures).

'The formula' is the result of completing the square on the general equation $ax^2 + bx + c = 0$.

$$ax^2 + bx + c = 0 \Rightarrow x^2 + \frac{b}{a}x = -\frac{c}{a}$$

Complete the square:
$$x^2 + \frac{b}{a}x + \frac{b^2}{4a^2} = -\frac{c}{a} + \frac{b^2}{4a^2}$$

$$\Rightarrow (x + \frac{b}{2a})^2 = \frac{b^2 - 4ac}{4a^2}$$

Square root:
$$\Rightarrow \quad x + \frac{b}{2a} = \frac{\pm\sqrt{(b^2 - 4ac)}}{2a}$$

The solutions are:
$$x = \frac{-b \pm \sqrt{(b^2 - 4ac)}}{2a}$$

Example 7

Solve $2x^2 - x - 5 = 0$, giving answers correct to 3 significant figures.

As $a = 2$, $b = -1$, $c = -5$, the solutions, using the formula, are

$$x = \frac{+1 \pm \sqrt{41}}{4} = -1.35 \text{ or } 1.85$$

(3) Graphical

If the graph, a parabola, of $y = ax^2 + bx + c$ is drawn, its intersections with the x-axis are the solutions of $ax^2 + bx + c = 0$. This method will often lack the accuracy of algebraic and numerical methods but can also be used for equations of higher power and for finding a starting value to use in the methods of trial and improvement, and of iteration.

All of the above methods find both solutions in one operation; the numerical methods need a separate operation for each solution.

(4) Trial and improvement

This method homes in on a solution until the required degree of accuracy is reached.

Example 8

Find, to 3 signficant figures, the solutions of $x^2 - x - 5 = 0$.

Let $y = x^2 - x - 5$. The graph shows one solution to be about 2.8.

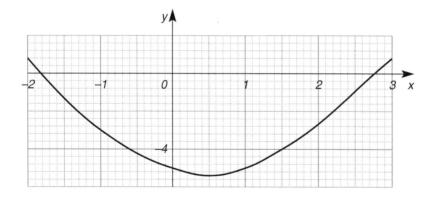

When $x = 2.8$,　　$y = 0.04$
　　　　$x = 2.75$,　　$y = -0.1875$　$\Rightarrow x$ lies between 2.75 and 2.8 ($x = 2.8$, to 2 s.f.)
　　　　$x = 2.79$,　　$y = -0.0059$　$\Rightarrow x$ lies between 2.79 and 2.8
　　　　$x = 2.795$, $y = +0.017$　$\Rightarrow x$ lies between 2.79 and 2.795

One solution, to the required degree of accuracy, is 2.79.

The graph shows the other solution to be approximately -1.8. Use this method to show that, to 3 significant figures, it is -1.79.

(5) Iteration

As we saw in Book 4y an iteration formula may produce, for some starting values, sequences which converge but, for other starting values, sequences that diverge. If a sequence defined by the iteration formula $x_{n+1} = \dfrac{5}{x_n - 1}$ converges then this **limiting value** will be a solution of the equation $x = \dfrac{5}{x - 1}$ or $x^2 - x - 5 = 0$.

An equation can be solved by rearranging it to form an iterative formula which produces, for some starting value, a limit; this value is a solution of the equation. To find the other solution another formula must be found.

Example 9

Let us consider the equation in Example 8.

The graph has given us good starting values, -1.8 and 2.8. (Athough we can try various starting values, one near a solution is an advantage.)

We now need to devise an iteration formula from the equation $x^2 - x - 5 = 0$. One possibility is given above, that is,

$x^2 - x - 5 = 0$ can be rearranged in the form $x(x - 1) = 5$ or $x = \dfrac{5}{x - 1}$,

which provides the iteration formula:

$$x_{n+1} = \frac{5}{x_n - 1}$$

For this formula, the starting value -1.8 quickly converges to give -1.79. (The starting value 2.8 converges a little more slowly.)

Another formula is needed to provide the other solution; a suitable one being:

$$x_{n+1} = \sqrt{(x_n + 5)} \quad \text{(from } x^2 = x + 5)$$

Both of the starting values produce the other solution, 2.79 (3 s.f.), very quickly.

EXERCISE 4.5

1 Solve the following quadratic equations without using a calculator.

(a) $x(2x - 3) = 0$

(b) $x^2 - 2x - 15 = 0$

(c) $x^2 - 7x + 10 = 0$

(d) $3x^2 + 15x - 42 = 0$

(e) $x^2 + 60 = 19x$

(f) $x(x - 1) = 2$

(g) $(x - 3)(x + 3) = 7$

(h) $(x + 8)^2 = 25$

(i) $3(2x + 1)(5x - 2) = 0$

(j) $(x - 4)(3 - x) = 2(x - 4)$

(k) $12x = 3x^2$

(l) $2x^2 + 5x - 3 = 0$

(m) $3x^2 + 14x - 5 = 0$

(n) $2x(x - 2) = 3 + x$

(o) $\frac{4x}{5} = \frac{45}{x}$

(p) $\frac{3x + 5}{x + 7} = x$

(q) $\frac{x - 2}{9} = \frac{1}{x - 2}$

(r) $5 + \frac{11}{x} = \frac{x + 1}{2}$

2 (a) Solve the equation $x^2 - 6x + 8 = 0$.

The diagram shows the sketch of $y = x^2 - 6x + 8$.

(b) Write down the coordinates of A, B and C.

(c) Deduce the solution set of $x^2 - 6x + 8 < 0$.

(d) State the equation of the line of symmetry.

(e) Deduce the coordinates of D.

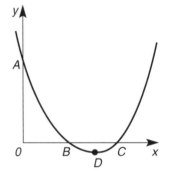

3 Write down the solutions of the following equations, leaving square roots in your answers.

(a) $2x^2 = 34$

(b) $\frac{x}{8} = \frac{3}{x}$

(c) $(2x + 1)^2 = 6$

(d) $x^4 = 25$

4 Solve the following equations. If the solutions are irrational, give answers to 3 significant figure accuracy.

(a) $x^2 - 3x - 5 = 0$

(b) $8x^2 = 2x$

(c) $(x - 1)^2 = 9$

(d) $16x^2 = 25$

(e) $3x^2 + x - 3 = 0$

(f) $2x^2 = (2 + x)^2$

(g) $2x^2 + 13x - 7 = 0$

(h) $x^2 + 3x + 1 = 0$

(i) $\frac{2x - 1}{4} = \frac{1}{x}$

5 (a) $x^2 + 8x + k$ is a perfect square. State the value of k.

(b) Solve the equation $x^2 + 8x + 14 = 0$, giving your answer to 2 decimal places.

6 (*a*) Find the values of p and q such that $x^2 + 4x - 6 = (x + p)^2 + q$.

(*b*) Deduce the solutions of $x^2 + 4x - 6 = 0$, correct to 3 significant figures.

7 (*a*) Without calculating the solutions show that a solution of $x^2 + 2x - 5 = 0$ lies between 1 and 2.

(*b*) Use your calculator and the method of trial and improvement to find this solution correct to 2 decimal places.

8 The graph shows $y = x^2 + 2x - 1$ from $x = -4$ to $x = +2$.

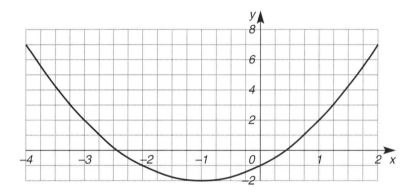

(*a*) To solve the following equations, draw the suggested lines and read off the x values where the line crosses the curve drawn.

(i) $x^2 + 2x - 1 = 0$; line: $y = 0$

(ii) $x^2 + 2x = 2$; line: $y = 1$

(iii) $x^2 = -2x$; line: $y = -1$

(iv) $x^2 + 3x - 1 = 0$; line: $y = -x$

(v) $x^2 + x - 4 = 0$; line: $y = x + 3$

(vi) $2x^2 + 4x - 9 = 0$; line: $y = 3\frac{1}{2}$

(*b*) Check your answers by solving the equations algebraically; that is by factorising, where appropriate, or by using 'the formula', or by completing the square.

9 Draw the graph of $y = x^2 - x - 3$ for values of x in the interval $-3 \leq x \leq 4$, using scales of 2 cm to represent 1 unit on the x-axis and 1 cm to represent 1 unit on the y-axis. By adding appropriate lines to your graph, estimate as accurately as you can the solutions of (a) $x^2 - x - 7 = 0$, (b) $x^2 - 2x - 3 = 0$, (c) $x^2 - 2 = 0$. How can you tell from the graph that $x^2 - x + 1 = 0$ has no solutions?

10 (a) Use the graph of $y = 2x^2 - 10x + 8$ to solve (i) $x^2 - 5x + 4 = 0$, (ii) $2x^2 - 13x + 18 = 0$.

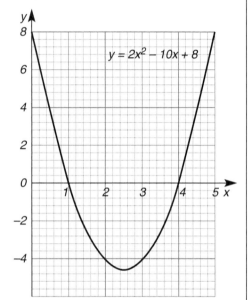

(b) Add the line $y = 3$ and estimate, to 1 decimal place, the solutions of $2x^2 - 10x + 5 = 0$.

(c) Use the iteration formula $x_{n+1} = \dfrac{2x_n^2 + 5}{10}$, with a starting value of 1, to estimate the smaller solution to the equation in (b), to the nearest 0.001.

(d) Use the iteration formula $x_{n+1} = \sqrt{\{\frac{1}{2}(10x_n - 5)\}}$ to find the other solution to the same degree of accuracy.

(e) Check your solutions by solving the equation using an alternative method.

11 The graph shows the speed, v, in m.p.h., for a train over a forty-minute period, where t is the time in minutes after 1240. The curved part of the graph has equation $v = \dfrac{800}{t} - \dfrac{1}{2}t$.

(a) Write down the speed of the train at 1254.

(b) Estimate the value of t when the train is travelling at 10 m.p.h.

(c) Use this estimate with the iteration formula
$$t_{n+1} = \dfrac{1600}{t_n + 20}$$
to calculate this time to the nearest second.

(d) Explain clearly how this iteration formula is derived.

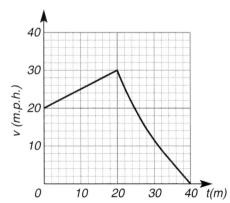

Investigation B

(a) Explain how the following statements can be deduced from 'the formula' used to solve $ax^2 + bx + c = 0$.

(i) If $b^2 - 4ac$ is a perfect square, factorisation can be used to solve the equation.

(ii) If $b^2 > 4ac$, there are two distinct solutions whose sum is always $-\dfrac{b}{a}$;

if $b^2 = 4ac$, the two solutions are equal;

if $b^2 < 4ac$, there are no (real) solutions.

(b) Make up an equation of the form $ax^2 + bx + c = 0$ for each of the cases in (a)(ii) and, for each, sketch the corresponding graph of $y = ax^2 + bx + c$. How does the graph indicate the number of solutions possessed by the corresponding equation?

EXERCISE 4.6

1 Given that $x = -2$ is a solution of $2x^2 - 3x + k = 0$,

(a) find the value of k,

(b) deduce the other solution.

2 Show that the equation $\dfrac{4}{x-1} - \dfrac{3}{x} = 1$ reduces to $x^2 - 2x - 3 = 0$

and hence find its solutions.

3 Given that $a = \dfrac{1}{x}$ and $b = \dfrac{x+3}{x^2}$ find the values of x for

which $a + b = 1$.

4 Form the equations, in their simplest form, whose solutions are

(a) $x = 3$ or $x = 4$ (b) $x = -1$ or $x = -6$ (c) $x = 2\frac{1}{2}$ or $x = -1$

(d) $y = 0$ or $y = 5$ (e) $t = 0.5$ or $t = 0.4$ (f) $p = \pm 7$

5 The sum of the first n terms in the series $1 + 4 + 7 + 10 + \ldots$ is $\frac{1}{2}n(3n - 1)$. For example the sum of the first five terms is $2\frac{1}{2} \times 14 = 35$.

(a) Write down in terms of n the value of the nth term.

(b) Find the number of terms in the series whose sum is 1335 and deduce the last term of the series.

6 The height, s metres, above the ground, after t seconds, reached by a particle projected vertically upwards with a speed of 40 m/s is given by the formula $s = 40t - 5t^2$. Calculate

(a) how long the particle takes to return to the ground,

(b) for how long the particle is above 60 m,

(c) the greatest height reached by finding the value of s for which the equation has only one solution for t. Why does this value give the greatest height?

7 The shaded area in the diagram is 114 cm².

(a) Show that $2x^2 + 9x - 110 = 0$.

(b) Solve the equation and find the length of AB.

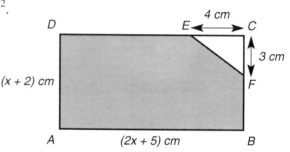

8 The sum of the squares of two consecutive odd numbers is 1570. Find the two numbers by forming and solving a quadratic equation.

9 Last year Carole worked for a certain number of hours in her holiday and earned £240. This year the hourly rate has increased by 20p and she noted that she earned as much as last year in five fewer hours. Find the number of hours she worked last year and deduce her hourly rate this year.

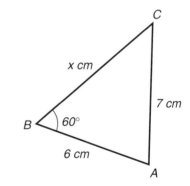

10 Use the cosine rule on triangle ABC to form a quadratic equation in x and hence find the length of BC, correct to 3 significant figures.

11 The surface area of the solid figure shown is 768π cm². Form and solve a quadratic equation in r and hence find the volume of the solid.

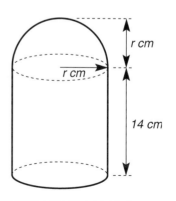

12 For the first 3 km of a journey a motorist travels at x km/h; for the next 5 km he travels 6 km faster. Given that his average speed for the 8 km is 43 km/h, form an equation in x and hence find the times for each part of the journey.

13 (a) By squaring both sides of the equation $\sqrt{(x+15)} = x+3$ form and solve a quadratic equation in x. By substituting your answers in the given equation you will find that only one solution satisfies it; why is the other solution produced?

(b) Solve $1 - \sqrt{x} = 2x$.

14 (a) Write down the solutions of the equation $4(x-2)(x-3) = 0$, and rewrite the equation in the form $ax^2 + bx + c = 0$.

(b) Repeat the exercise for the equation $a(x-p)(x-q) = 0$.

(c) Deduce that, for the equation $ax^2 + bx + c = 0$, with solutions p and q,
 (i) the sum of its solutions, $p+q$, is equal to $-\dfrac{b}{a}$,
 (ii) the product of its solutions, pq, is equal to $\dfrac{c}{a}$.

(d) The line $y = 3x + 1$ cuts the parabola $y = x^2$ in the points A and B. Given that the x-coordinates of A and B are x_1 and x_2 respectively, show that $x_1 + x_2 = 3$ and deduce the coordinates of the mid-point of the chord AB.

Higher degree equations

Although some equations of higher degree can be solved using factorisation, the general methods are: (a) trial and improvement, (b) graphical and (c) iterative.

In Book 3y we saw that simple equations of the form $ax^n = b$ can be solved using the $x^{\frac{1}{n}}$ button on your calculator and that the method of trial and improvement can be used for more complex equations.

Example 10
Solve $3x^5 = 16$.

$$x^5 = \frac{16}{3} \Rightarrow x = (\frac{16}{3})^{\frac{1}{5}}, \text{ the fifth root of } \frac{16}{3},$$
$$= 1.40 \text{ (correct to 3 significant figures)}.$$

Calculator sequence: $\boxed{1}\ \boxed{6}\ \boxed{\div}\ \boxed{3}\ \boxed{=}\ \boxed{x^{\frac{1}{y}}}\ \boxed{5}\ \boxed{=}$

Graphs can be used in their own right to find solutions of equations, as we saw in Books 3y and 4y, but often the accuracy is not good enough; this can be improved by using numerical methods.

Example 11

(a) Show that $x^3 - 7x^2 + x + 3 = 0$ has a solution between 0 and 1 and use your calculator to find a solution correct to 2 decimal places.

(b) Show that the equation can be rewritten as $x = \sqrt{\left\{ \dfrac{10}{(7-x)} - 1 \right\}}$.

(c) Use the iteration formula $x_{n+1} = \sqrt{\left\{ \dfrac{10}{(7-x_n)} - 1 \right\}}$ with $x_1 = 1$,

to find the solution correct to 4 decimal places.

(a) A graph will show a solution but is unlikely to produce the degree of accuracy required.
Let $y = x^3 - 7x^2 + x + 3$

When $x = 0$, $y = +3$
$\quad\quad x = 1$, $y = -2$ $\quad\quad\quad \Rightarrow$ there is a solution between $x = 0$ and $x = 1$
$\quad\quad x = 0.5$, $y = +1.875$ $\quad\Rightarrow x$ lies between 0.5 and 1
$\quad\quad x = 0.75$, $y = +0.234$ $\Rightarrow x$ lies between 0.75 and 1
$\quad\quad x = 0.8$, $y = -0.168$ $\quad\Rightarrow x$ lies between 0.75 and 0.8
$\quad\quad x = 0.775$, $y = +0.036 \Rightarrow x$ lies between 0.775 and 0.8
$\quad\quad x = 0.78$, $y = -0.0042 \Rightarrow x$ lies between 0.775 and 0.78

Correct to 2 decimal places, the solution is 0.78.

(b) $x^2(7 - x) = x + 3 = 10 - (7 - x) \Rightarrow x^2 = \dfrac{10}{7 - x} - 1 \Rightarrow x = \sqrt{\left(\dfrac{10}{7-x} - 1 \right)}$

(c) A calculator with the sequence

$$\boxed{x_n}\;\boxed{+/-}\;\boxed{+}\;\boxed{7}\;\boxed{=}\;\boxed{\tfrac{1}{x}}\;\boxed{\times}\;\boxed{1}\;\boxed{0}\;\boxed{=}\;\boxed{-}\;\boxed{1}\;\boxed{=}\;\boxed{\surd}$$

produces the results shown; the required answer of 0.7795 is found quite quickly. A computer with a spreadsheet is very useful for iteration problems.

One problem with equations of higher degree is knowing how many (real) solutions it has. Again this is where a graph can be useful.

0.8164965
0.7856247
0.7804948
0.7796441
0.779503
0.7794797
0.7794758
0.7794751
0.779475
0.779475

EXERCISE 4.7

1 For each of the following equations

(a) give a 2-figure guesstimate of the solution(s),

(b) use your calculator to find the solution(s) correct to 3 significant figures.

(i) $x^5 = 40$ (ii) $x^3 = -1205$ (iii) $x^4 = 100$ (iv) $x^7 = 160$

2 Use the method of trial and improvement to find the two solutions, correct to 3 significant figures, for the following equations.

(a) $x^2 - 2x - 7 = 0$ (b) $x^2 + 3x - 5 = 0$ (c) $x^2 - 4x = 2$

3 The equation $x^3 - 6x^2 + 14 = 0$ has a solution between 1 and 2. Find it, correct to 3 significant figures.

4 For the equation $x^5 - 3x + 2 = 0$,

(a) show that $x = 1$ is a solution,

(b) show that there is another solution between $x = -2$ and $x = -1$,

(c) find this solution, correct to 3 significant figures.

5 (a) Show that $x^3 + 6x - 5 = 0$ has a solution between 0 and 1.

(b) Use your calculator to find this solution, correct to 2 significant figures, by trial and improvement.

(c) Explain how you could show that this is the only solution of this equation.

6 (a) Verify that $x = +\frac{1}{2}$ is a solution of $2x^3 - 3x^2 - x + 1 = 0$.

(b) Draw the graph of $y = 2x^3 - 3x^2 - x + 1$ for values of x in the interval $-1 \le x \le 2$, using scales of 4 cm for 1 unit on the x-axis and 1 cm for 1 unit on the y-axis.

(c) Check that your curve crosses the x-axis between 1.6 and 1.7, and use your calculator to give this solution correct to 2 decimal places.

(d) Use your graph and calculator in a similar way to find the third solution to the same degree of accuracy.

7 (a) Draw the graphs of $y = \frac{1}{4}x^3$ and $y = (x^2 + x - 2)$ in the interval $-2 \le x \le 5$, using scales of 2 cm for 1 unit on the x-axis and 1 cm for 1 unit on the y-axis.

(b) Use your graph to write down approximate solutions of $x^3 = 4(x^2 + x - 2)$.

(c) Show that this equation can be rewritten as $x = \frac{1}{2}[\sqrt{(x^3 + 9)} - 1]$.

(d) Using the derived iteration formula with $x_1 = 1.1$, find the smallest positive solution to 5 significant figures.

8 (a) Draw, on the same axes, the graphs of $y = x^2 - 1$ and $y = \sqrt{x}$, using scales that are as large as possible.

(b) Deduce that there is only one solution of $x^2 - 1 = \sqrt{x}$ and write down the solution, correct to 2 significant figures.

(c) Show that the equation can be rewritten as $x = \sqrt{(1 + \sqrt{x})}$ and, using the iteration formula $x_{n+1} = \sqrt{(1 + \sqrt{x_n})}$, find the solution of the equation, correct to 4 significant figures.

9 (a) Using the graph of $y = x^2 - \frac{6}{x}$ write down (correct to the nearest integer) the solutions of $x^2 - \frac{6}{x} = 8$.

(b) Show that the equation can be rewritten as $x = \sqrt{\left\{\frac{2(4x + 3)}{x}\right\}}$ and using the derived iteration formula find a solution correct to 5 significant figures.

(c) By using the iteration formula $x_{n+1} = -\sqrt{\left\{\frac{2(4x_n + 3)}{x_n}\right\}}$, with $x_1 = -1$, find a second solution to the same degree of accuracy.

(d) Derive another iteration formula to find the third solution and show that this is -0.81859 to 5 significant figures.

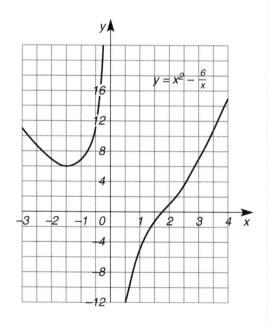

Extension work

Two equations in two unknowns; one equation non-linear

To calculate the coordinates in which a line meets a curve requires solving simultaneously the equation of the line and the non-linear equation of the curve. Although a few special methods were seen in Exercise 4.5, the method of substitution is generally used.

Example 12

Find the points in which the line $y = 3x - 2$ meets the circle $2x^2 + 2y^2 = 17$.

Substituting for y:

$$2x^2 + 2(3x - 2)^2 = 17 \Rightarrow 2x^2 + 2(9x^2 - 12x + 4) = 17$$
$$\Rightarrow 20x^2 - 24x - 9 = 0$$
$$\Rightarrow (2x - 3)(10x + 3) = 0$$
$$\Rightarrow x = 1.5 \text{ or } x = -0.3$$

Using the linear equation the points are $(-0.3, -2.9)$ and $(1.5, 2.5)$.

In many cases fractional equations result from the substitution.

Example 13

Find the values of x and y that satisfy
$x^2 - 4y^2 = 9$ and $3x + 4y = 7$ simultaneously.

Substitute $x = \dfrac{7 - 4y}{3}$ in the first equation $\Rightarrow \dfrac{(49 - 56y + 16y^2)}{9} - 4y^2 = 9$

$$\Rightarrow 49 - 56y + 16y^2 - 36y^2 = 81$$
$$\Rightarrow \quad 20y^2 + 56y + 32 = 0$$
$$\Rightarrow \quad 5y^2 + 14y + 8 = 0$$
$$\Rightarrow \quad (5y + 4)(y + 2) = 0$$
$$\Rightarrow \quad y = -\tfrac{4}{5} \text{ or } y = -2$$

The solutions are $(3\tfrac{2}{5}, -\tfrac{4}{5})$ and $(5, -2)$.

Note: A common error is to 'square' the second equation to get
$9x^2 + 16y^2 = 49$! Where is the error?

EXERCISE 4.8

1 Solve the following pairs of simultaneous equations, giving
answers to 3 significant figures where necessary.

(a) $x^2 + y^2 = 4$
$\quad y = x + 2$

(b) $y = 4x - 14$
$\quad xy = 8$

(c) $\quad 2x + 3y = 1$
$\quad 3x^2 + 4xy - y^2 = 6$

(d) $x^2 + y^2 = 8$
$\quad y = 1 - 3x$

(e) $\quad\quad y - 2x = 1$
$\quad 5x^2 - x^2 - x - y + 12 = 0$

(f) $\quad 2x - y = 7$
$\quad y^2 - x(x + y) = 11$

2 Find where the straight line $y = 3x + 1$ meets the parabola $y^2 = 12x$.
Draw a sketch graph to illustrate your answer.

3 Find the points of intersection of the line $x + 2y = 4$ and the
ellipse $x^2 + 4y^2 = 16$. Draw a sketch to illustrate your answer.

4 For the values of x and y, that satisfy both $x + y = 5$ and
$x^2 - 2xy + y^2 = 1$,

(a) without finding x and y, show that $xy = 6$ and $x^2 + y^2 = 13$,

(b) use two of these equations and the method of substitution
to find x and y.

(c) Factorise $x^2 - 2xy + y^2$ and hence solve the problem by
using linear equations only.

5 A class was asked to work out the dimensions of a
rectangle given that its area was 60 cm^2 and that it
must just fit in a circle of radius 6.5 cm; they were
told to let the sides be x cm and y cm.

(a) Show that $x^2 + y^2 = 169$ and $xy = 60$.

(b) Dave solved the equations simultaneously.
Write out a solution.

(c) Sushie found the values of $(x + y)^2$ and $(x - y)^2$,
which gave her a neat way of finding x and y.
Write out her solution.

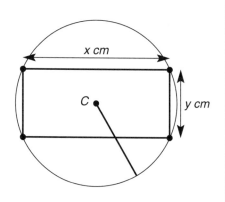

Linear equations in three unknowns

If there are three unknowns then three equations are needed to find
the solutions. For the case when the equations are linear, such as
$2x + 3y - 4z = 2$, the three equations may be solved by eliminating
one of the unknowns from each of two pairs of equations and then
solving the resulting equations in two unknowns simultaneously.

Example 14

Find the values of x, y, z which satisfy simultaneously the equations
(1) $2x + 3y - 2z = 3$, (2) $3x - y + z = 9$ and (3) $x - 4y + 2z = -2$.

Suppose we choose to eliminate z from each of two pairs of equations.
Add (1) and (3), $3x - y = 1$
Multiply (2) by 2 and add to (1), $8x + y = 21$
The two resulting equations can be solved to give $x = 2$, $y = 5$.
Substitution of these values into (1), (2) or (3) will give z.
Using (2), $6 - 5 + z = 9 \Rightarrow z = 8$.
The solution is $x = 2$, $y = 5$, $z = 8$, which can be checked in (1) or (3).

In general, and certainly in the following exercise, there is a unique
solution to three linear equations in three unknowns.

EXERCISE 4.9

1 Find the values of x, y and z that satisfy the following sets of
equations.

(a) $2x - 5y + 8z = 5$
    $x + 2y + 3z = 6$
    $4x - 2y + 3z = 5$

(b) $x + y + z = 4$
    $3x - 2y + 2z = 13$
    $2y + z = 2$

(c) $2x - 3y + 2z = 5$
    $2x + y + z = 1$
    $2x - 3y = 5$

(d) $x - 2y + z = 1$
    $2x + 4y - z = 9$
    $-x + 8y + z = 0$

(e) $2x + 3y - 2z = 0$
    $5x + y + 8z = 26$
    $-x - y + z = 1$

(f) $2x + 4z = 15$
    $x + 2y = 4$
    $y + z = 3$

2 The curve with equation $y = ax^2 + bx + c$ passes through the
points $(-1, 18)$, $(1, -4)$ and $(6, 11)$. Form three equations in
a, b and c, and solve them. Deduce the points in which the
curve crosses the axes.

3 In the diagram $AB = 7.7$ cm, $BC = 9.3$ cm and $CA = 8$ cm and
these are all tangents to the circle.

(a) Explain why $x + y = 7.7$, $y + z = 9.3$ and $z + x = 8$.

(b) Find the values of x, y and z.

4 Gavin has £11 in his charity jar, which contains 60 coins made
up of x 5p pieces, y 10p pieces and z 50p pieces. The total
number of 10p and 50p pieces is double the number of 5p
pieces. Find the values of x, y and z.

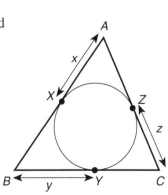

5. Applying trigonometry

Solving problems in 2-dimensions and 3-dimensions

In Books 3y and 4y we calculated lengths, angles and areas for right-angled triangles and later for general triangles using the sine and cosine rules. The following summary covers what is needed in your examinations. The work in this chapter provides you with an opportunity to improve, enhance and extend your knowledge and processing skills .

In the examinations you will be provided with a list of formulae similar to the one shown below. It is vitally important that you have a copy of the one provided by your Examination Group so that you are completely at ease with using it well before the examination.

Trigonometry

Right-angled triangle

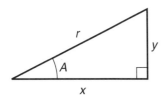

$r^2 = x^2 + y^2$, (result of Pythagoras')
$x = r \cos A$, $y = r \sin A$, $y = x \tan A$

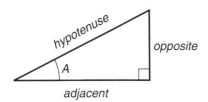

$$\sin A = \frac{\text{opposite}}{\text{hypotenuse}}, \quad \cos A = \frac{\text{adjacent}}{\text{hypotenuse}},$$

$$\tan A = \frac{\text{opposite}}{\text{adjacent}}$$

Any triangle

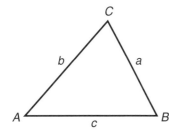

In any triangle ABC: $\dfrac{a}{\sin A} = \dfrac{b}{\sin B} = \dfrac{c}{\sin C}$

$$a^2 = b^2 + c^2 - 2bc \cos A$$

$$\cos A = \frac{b^2 + c^2 - a^2}{2bc}$$

Area of triangle ABC $= \frac{1}{2}ab \sin C$

Strategy for solving practical problems

Read the question carefully once and then build up a sketch of the
data given as you read the question again. Make sure that you have
included all the given facts in your sketch. Choose which formulae
you need for your calculations and *do not* leave any steps out as you
write up the solution.

Example 1

Calculate the length of the shadow cast by a vertical television mast,
of height 15 m, when the sun has an elevation of 33°. Find also the
elevation of the sun when the shadow has length 13 m.

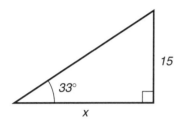
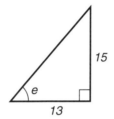

Using the first sketch we have,

$$\tan 33° = \frac{15}{x} \quad \Rightarrow x = \frac{15}{\tan 33°} = 23.1 \text{ m}$$

Using the second sketch we have,

$$\tan e = \frac{15}{13} \quad \Rightarrow e = 49°$$

Example 2

On a survey using a helicopter, the following
information was recorded about three landmarks A, B and C:
The distance AB = 40 km and B is due east of A.
C is the same distance from A and B.
The bearing of C from A is 035°.
Calculate the bearing of B from C and the
distance, to the nearest km, between B and C.

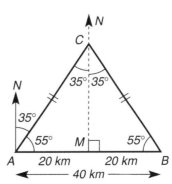

The sketch diagram shows the information given.
The broken line from C to the mid-point of AB is an axis of symmetry for triangle ABC since CA = CB.
The angle giving the bearing of B from C is the angle at C between north and CB, that is $180° − 35° = 145°$.
In triangle CMB, we have angle M = 90°, MB = 20 km and angle B = 55°.

$$\cos 55° = \frac{20}{BC} \Rightarrow BC = \frac{20}{\cos 55°} = 34.9 \text{ km}$$

The bearing of B from C is 145° and BC = 35 km, to the nearest km.

The angle between a line and a plane

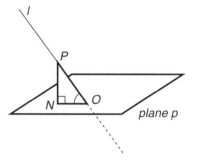

The line, l, meets the plane, p, at a point O. From any point, P, on l, draw the line perpendicular to p to meet p at N. The angle PON is defined to be the angle between l and p.

The angle between two planes

Any two non-parallel planes meet in a line.
The planes, p_1 and p_2, meet in the line AB. Take any point, P, on the line AB. Draw from P a line PQ in the plane p_1 and another line PR in the plane p_2 such that PQ and PR are both perpendicular to AB. The angle QPR is defined to be the angle between the planes p_1 and p_2.

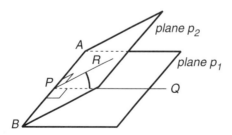

Problems in three dimensions are solved using the same formulae as those already used for two dimensions. Always draw sufficient sketches to support your solutions and to explain where each statement comes from.

Example 3

A rectangular metal sheet ABCD has AB = 12 cm and BC = 9 cm.
It is suspended 18 cm below a point O by four equal strings
OA, OB, OC and OD, as shown.

Calculate:

(a) the length of a string,

(b) the angle between a string and the horizontal,

(c) the angle triangle OAB makes with the horizontal.

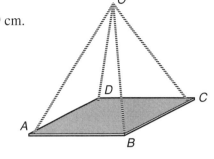

(a) $AC^2 = AB^2 + BC^2$
$ = 144 + 81$
$ = 225$
$AC = 15$ cm, AM = 7.5 cm

$OA^2 = AM^2 + OM^2$
$ = 56.25 + 324$
$ = 380.25$
$OA = 19.5$ cm

The length of a string is 19.5 cm.

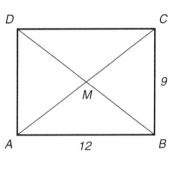

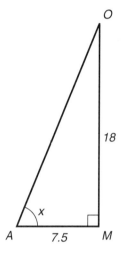

(b) The angle marked x in the second diagram is
the angle made by a string and the horizontal.

$$\tan x = \frac{18}{7.5} \Rightarrow x = 67.4°$$

(c) N is the mid-point of AB.

$$MN = \tfrac{1}{2}BC = 4.5$$

The angle between triangle OAB
and the horizontal is marked as y

$$\tan y = \frac{18}{4.5}$$

$$\Rightarrow y = 76°$$

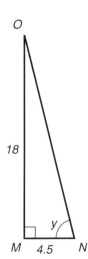

EXERCISE 5.1

Numbers 1–10 below provide routine practice questions. If you
have difficulty with these, consult your teacher and obtain help.
Then ask for some more questions of this type from Book 4y.

In questions 1–4, work out the lengths of the sides and the angles
indicated by letters.

1

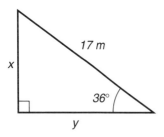

2

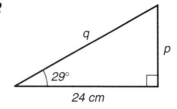

3

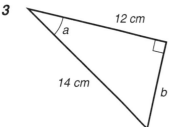

4

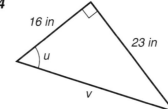

5 Angle ADC $= 90°$ and triangle BCD is equilateral. Calculate z.

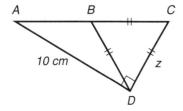

6 O is the centre of the circle, radius R and AC $= 0.8$ R.
Calculate angles ABC and AOC.

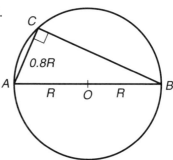

7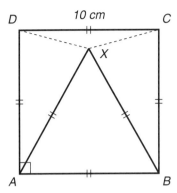

ABCD is a square and AXB is an equilateral triangle. Calculate the length of CX.

8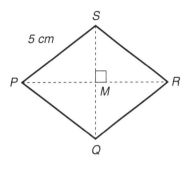

PQRS is a rhombus with PS = 5 cm, QS = 6 cm. Calculate the length of PR and the angle SPQ.

9 In triangle ABC, AB = AC, angle C = 72° and the bisector of angle B meets AC at the point X. AB = 10 cm. By calculation, find AX and CX.

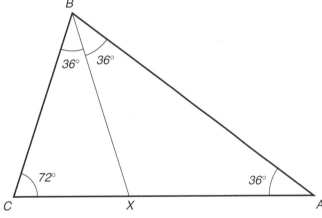

Verify that $AX^2 = AC.XC$.

By considering the similar triangles ABC and BCX, prove that $AX^2 = AC.XC$.

The point X is said to divide line AC in 'The Golden Ratio'.

10 The triangle XYZ has a right angle at X; YZ = 20 cm. Neither XY or XZ is less than 8 cm long. Calculate:

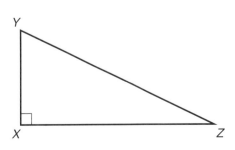

(*a*) The greatest and least values of angle Y which are possible.

(*b*) The greatest and least possible areas of triangle XYZ.

11 A radio mast is vertical and of height 32 m. Calculate the length of the shadow of the mast when the sun has an elevation of (*a*) 62°, (*b*) 37°.

12 A supply ship moves from port A on a course of 109° for 80 miles to a lighthouse L. From L, the ship moves for a further 120 miles on a course of 148° to a weather station W. Find how far A is (*a*) north of W, (*b*) west of W. Find the bearing of W from A.

13 A motor launch leaves harbour P and moves due north for 13 km to harbour Q. From Q the launch moves on the bearing 322° for a further 13 km and reaches a small island R. Calculate the distance that R is (*a*) north of P, (*b*) west of P. Find the bearing of P from R.

14 A tree grows on the far bank of a river. At the point A on the near bank and directly opposite the base B of the tree, Winston measures the angle of elevation of the top T of the tree as 43°. He walks directly away from A along BA produced for 50 m to the point C. From C, he measures the angle of elevation of T as 27°. Using Winston's measurements find the width of the river and the height of the tree.

15 The angles of elevation of the top of a pylon from two points due west of it, and 50 m apart, are 40° and 28°. Find the height of the pylon.

16 A flag pole stands on the roof of an embassy building. Tina measures a distance of 44 m from the building and, from there, finds that the top and bottom of the flag pole have angles of elevation of 48° and 35° respectively. Find the heights of the building and the flag pole.

17 A hot-air balloon is rising vertically at a constant speed and is observed to have an angle of elevation of 30°. After one minute it has an angle of elevation of 36°. Find its angle of elevation after a further minute.

18 A tower stands to the north of a straight road running West–East. The point on the road nearest to the base B of the tower is A. The distance AB = 125 m, AB is horizontal and the angle of elevation of the top T of the tower from A is 16°. Calculate the height of the tower.

  A guard post is situated at C on the road 120 m east of A and AC is horizontal. Calculate the angle of elevation of T from C.

19 An aircraft is flying at constant height and speed in the direction due south. Two observers on level ground are at A and B where AB = 1000 m and A is due north of B. The aircraft is north of both observers at the instant when A and B record the angle of elevation of the aircraft as 28° and 21°. Calculate the height of the aircraft.

  The aircraft is moving with speed 240 km/h and flies directly over the observers. Find the angle of elevation of the aircraft from the observer at (*a*) A, (*b*) B one minute after the first observation.

20 The angles of elevation of the top of a château from two points P and Q are 20° and 27° respectively. P and Q are on ground level with the base B of the château where P is due south of B and Q is due west of B. Given that PQ = 250 m, find the height of the château.

21 A rectangular trapdoor XYZW is hinged along XY and is open upwards so that plane XYZW is at an angle of 34° to the horizontal. Given that XY = 4 m and YZ = 3 m, calculate the angle that ZX makes with the horizontal.

  Calculate also the angle that the plane XYZW makes with the horizontal when it is in the position where the line ZX makes an angle of 6° with the horizontal.

22 The rectangular brick ABCDEFGH has rectangle ABCD horizontal and uppermost, and has vertical edges AE, BF, CG and DH each of length 6 cm; AB = 24 cm and BC = 8 cm. Calculate

  (*a*) the angle between plane ABGH and the horizontal,

  (*b*) the angle between the line AG and the horizontal.

23 A vertical mast AT stands at the corner A of a horizontal square ABCD of side 60 m. The angle of elevation of T from B is 18°. Calculate

(a) the height of the mast AT,

(b) the angle of elevation of T from C,

(c) the angle BTD.

24 A pyramid has a horizontal square base ABCD and its vertex V is vertically above M, the centre of the base. Given that VA = 10 cm and AB = 8 cm, calculate the angle between (a) VA and the horizontal, (b) plane VAB and the horizontal, (c) planes VAB and VDC.

25 A girl stands on level ground at A, 450 m due south of a vertical radio mast TB. She measures the angle of elevation of T, the top of the mast, as 36°. She now walks in the direction 040° until she reaches C which is due east of the mast. Calculate (a) the distance she walks, (b) the height of the mast, (c) the angle of elevation of the mast from C.

26 Sketch a triangle ABC in which angle B = 90° and the side AC is r. Write down the lengths of the sides AB and BC in terms of r and angle C.
Deduce that $(\cos C)^2 = (\sin C)^2 - 1$.
This identity is more often written as

$$\cos^2 x + \sin^2 x = 1$$

and it is true for all values of x. (Try a few if you need convincing.)

27 Given that $\cos x = \frac{4}{5}$, find the possible values of $\sin x$. Why do two possible values arise?

28 Given that $\sin x = \frac{12}{13}$ and $90° < x < 180°$, find the exact value of $\cos x$.

29 Find two different angles for which $\sin x = \cos x$, where x is an angle between 0° and 360°.

30 Given that $\tan x = \frac{20}{21}$, and $180° < x < 270°$, find the exact value of (a) $\sin x$, (b) $\cos x$.

Practical work using the sine and cosine rules

The sine rule

The sine rule, $\dfrac{a}{\sin A} = \dfrac{b}{\sin B} = \dfrac{c}{\sin C}$,

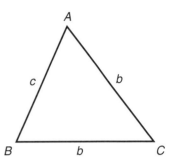

is used in the general triangle ABC, shown,
when (1) two angles and the length of a side are given,
　　　(2) the lengths of two sides and a non-included angle are given.

Example 4

In a flat desert region the distance between two fortified villages G
and H is 35 km and H is due east of G. A water hole W is on a
bearing of 047° from G and on a bearing of 302° from H. Find the
distance of each village from W.

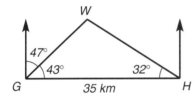

The diagram shows the information given.
The angle GWH $= 105°$.

$$\frac{GW}{\sin 32°} = \frac{35}{\sin 105°} \Rightarrow GW = \frac{35 \sin 32°}{\sin 105°} \Rightarrow GW = 19.2 \text{ km}$$

$$\frac{HW}{\sin 43°} = \frac{35}{\sin 105°} \Rightarrow HW = \frac{35 \sin 43°}{\sin 105°} \Rightarrow HW = 24.7 \text{ km}$$

Example 5

Consider the triangle ABC, in which $b = 6$ cm, $c = 8$ cm and
angle B $= 45°$.

Using the sine rule we have $\dfrac{\sin C}{8} = \dfrac{\sin 45°}{6}$.

This gives $\sin C = \dfrac{8 \sin 45°}{6} = 0.9428$, so

angle C $= 70.5°$ or $109.5°$.

The diagram below shows why two answers arise in this case.

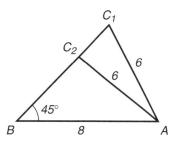

The cosine rule

For the triangle ABC, the cosine rule is written as

either $b^2 = c^2 + a^2 - 2ca \cos B$

or $\cos B = \dfrac{c^2 + a^2 - b^2}{2ca}$

The first form is used when two sides (a and c) and the included angle
(B) are given and the third side (b) is required.
The second form is used when the three sides (a, b and c)
are given and the angle B is required.

Example 6

A surveyor records the following information about a horizontal field
ABCD: AB = 57 m, AD = 48 m, BC = 62 m, CD = 87 m and
angle DAB = 117°. Calculate the length BD and the size
of angle BCD.

All the given information is put into a sketch:

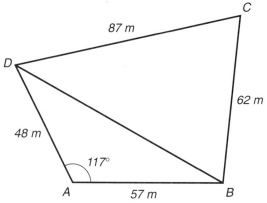

In triangle ADB we have two sides and the
included angle given. To find BD we apply
the cosine rule in its first form:

$$BD^2 = 48^2 + 57^2 - 2 \times 48 \times 57 \cos 117°$$
$$= 2304 + 3249 - (-2484)$$
$$= 8037$$
$$BD = 90 \text{ m (nearest m)}$$

To find angle BCD we apply the cosine rule in triangle BCD
where the three sides are known, using the second form:

$$\cos C = \frac{87^2 + 62^2 - 8037}{2 \times 87 \times 62} = \frac{3376}{10\,788}$$

angle C = 72° (nearest degree)

EXERCISE 5.2

Questions 1–10 provide routine practice questions in which you need to apply the sine and cosine rules. If you experience difficulty with these questions, consult your teachers and ask for some more routine questions from a book such as 4y.

In questions 1–6, find the sides and angles denoted by the letters x, y, z, w, p, q_1 and q_2.

1
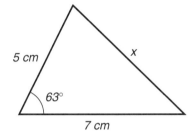

2
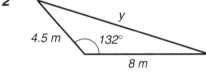

3
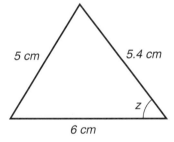

4
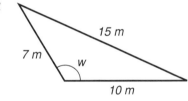

5
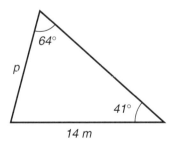

6
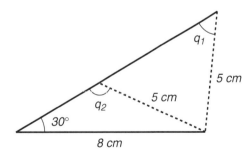

In questions 7–10 find the sides and angles marked
as *x*, *y*, *p*, *q*, *a*, *b*, *m* and *n*.

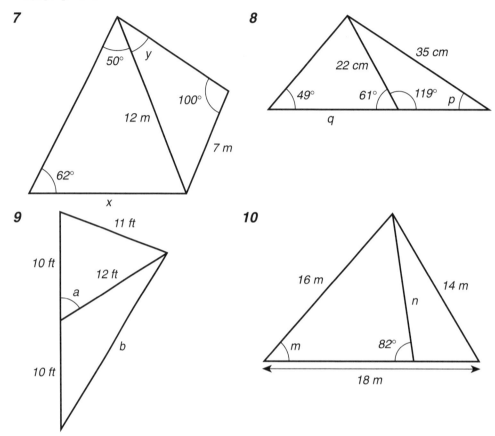

7

50° *y*
100°
12 m
7 m
62°
x

8

22 cm
35 cm
49° 61° 119° *p*
q

9

11 ft
10 ft
12 ft
a
b
10 ft

10

16 m
14 m
n
m 82°
18 m

11 Southampton is 120 km from London on a bearing of 224°.
Northampton is 105 km from London on a bearing of 319°.
Calculate:

(*a*) the distance of Southampton from Northampton,

(*b*) the bearing of Southampton from Northampton.

12 A vertical mast TB stands with its base B on horizontal
ground. The points A and C are on the ground, where A is
due South of the mast and AB = 75 m; C is on a bearing of
120° from the mast and BC = 100 m. The angle of elevation
of T from A is 12°. Calculate

(*a*) the distance AC,

(*b*) the height of the mast,

(*c*) the angle of elevation of T from C,

(*d*) the angle between the plane TAC and the horizontal.

13 Two ships A and B leave Plymouth at noon and move in the directions 132° and 217°, with speeds of 15 km/h and 18 km/h respectively. Calculate their distance apart and the bearing of B from A at 1400.

14 In the usual notation for a triangle ABC, $b = 36$ cm, $c = 48$ cm and angle C $= 45°$. Calculate the angle at B and the length a.

15 In a triangle ABC, $b = 36$ cm, $c = 48$ cm and angle B $= 45°$. Find the two possible values of angle C and the length a in each case.

16 In the triangle ABC, AB $= 24$ cm, BC $= 19$ cm and angle B $= 110°$. Calculate the length of AC .
      The triangle ABC is horizontal and the point D is 13 cm vertically below B. Calculate angle ADC.

17 A tetrahedron VABC has a horizontal equilateral triangle ABC as base, where AB $= 6$ cm. The vertex V is above the level of ABC and VA $=$ VB $=$ VC $= 7$ cm. Calculate the height of V above the plane ABC and the angle between planes ABC and VAB .

18 A tanker is moving due north at constant speed 5 km/h. The helmsman observes a look-out at the top of a vertical cliff to be on a bearing of 315° and at an elevation of 2°. Half an hour later the tanker is due west of the look-out. Calculate the height of the cliff.

19 All the faces of the tetrahedron OABC are equilateral triangles and AB $= 6$ cm. Calculate the angle between the planes ABC and OAB.

20 The points A(2, 3, 4), B(4, 5, 9) and C(1, 7, 7) are fixed in space relative to an origin O. Calculate

(a) the lengths of AB, BC and CA,

(b) the largest angle of triangle ABC.

Further practical examples

In many practical questions vectors such as forces and velocities are involved. In Book 4y answers were obtained in most cases by scale drawing but the sine and cosine rules can be used when greater accuracy is needed.

Example 7

An aircraft has a speed through still air of 650 km/h and this is called the **airspeed**. The aircraft is headed in the direction 049°, called the **course,** in a wind blowing at 91 km/h from 298°.
    Calculate the velocity of the aircraft over the ground, giving the **groundspeed** to the nearest km/h and the **track** (direction as a bearing) to the nearest degree.

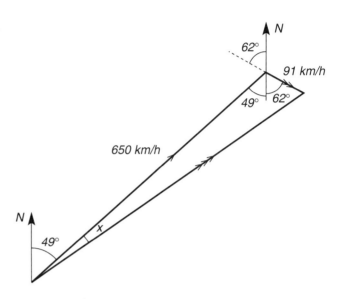

Using the notation in the diagram, where v km/h is the groundspeed and x is the angle between the course and the track, sometimes called the **drift.**

From the data, we see that we need the third side of a triangle for which two sides are known and the included angle is $49° + 62° = 111°$.
Using the cosine rule, we have

$$v^2 = 650^2 + 91^2 - 2 \times 91 \times 650 \cos 111°$$
$$= 422\,500 + 8281 + 42\,395 = 473\,176$$
$$v = 688 \text{ (nearest whole number)}$$

Groundspeed is 688 km/h.

Using the sine rule, we have

$$\frac{\sin x}{91} = \frac{\sin 111°}{688} \Rightarrow \sin x = \frac{91 \sin 111°}{688}$$

$$x = 7° \text{ (nearest degree)}$$

Track is $(49° + 7°) = 056°$.

Example 8

Two tugs are attempting to pull a stranded boat from a sand bank S. The first tug pulls with a force of 278 kN and the second tug pulls with a force of 223 kN. The angle between these two forces is 34°.

Calculate the size and the direction of a single force (called the resultant force) which would be equivalent to the combined forces from the two tugs.

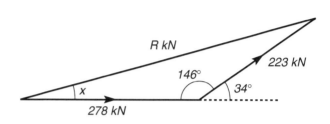

The first diagram shows the situation with the tugs pulling at an angle of 34°. The second diagram shows how the forces are combined using the vector law of addition, where the resultant has magnitude R kN and x is the angle between R and the pull of 278 kN.

Using the cosine rule, we have

$$R^2 = 278^2 + 223^2 - 2 \times 278 \times 223 \cos 146°$$
$$= 77\ 284 + 49\ 729 + 102\ 791 = 229\ 804$$
$$R = 479.4$$

The resultant is 479 kN (nearest kN).

Applying the sine rule, we have

$$\frac{\sin x}{223} = \frac{\sin 146°}{479.4} \Rightarrow \sin x = \frac{223 \sin 146°}{479.4} \Rightarrow x = 15.1°$$

The angle between the resultant and the pull of 278 kN is 15°.

EXERCISE 5.3

1 An aircraft, capable of flying at 250 km/h in still air, is headed due east in a wind blowing steadily from the north-east at 50 km/h. It flies from A to B taking 2.5 hours. Calculate

  (*a*) the bearing of B from A,

  (*b*) the distance between A and B.

2 An aircraft is tracking due south in a wind blowing at 55 km/h from the direction 063°. The airspeed is 290 km/h. Calculate the course and the groundspeed.

3 A boat is headed straight across a river flowing at 4 m/s between parallel banks which are 120 m apart. The boat can move at 6 m/s in still water. Find the resultant velocity of the boat through the water.

   The boat leaves point A which is directly opposite point B on the other bank. Calculate the distance from B to point C at which the boat lands.

   On another journey the boat leaves A and lands at B. Find the course set and the time taken to cross the river in this case, giving your answer to the nearest second.

4 For each of the following situations calculate the missing values. (All speeds are in km/h.)

	Airspeed	Course	Wind speed	Wind from	Groundspeed	Track
(a)	440	000°	80	240°		
(b)	400	310°	68	327°		
(c)	597	099°			530	090°
(d)	759	166°			636	180°
(e)	450		90	270°		102°
(f)	600		78	228°		029°

5 Two forces of magnitudes 40 N and 30 N act at a point at right angles to each other.
Show that the resultant force is of magnitude 50 N and that it acts in a direction making an angle p with the 40-N force, where $\tan p = \frac{3}{4}$.

6 Two forces of magnitude P newtons and Q newtons act at a point O and the angle between them is $c°$. Find the resultant of P and Q to 2 significant figures, and the angle between the resultant and P, to the nearest degree, in each of the cases, shown in the table.

	P	Q	c
(a)	47	47	50
(b)	48	28	66
(c)	39	39	132
(d)	82	69	141

7 Three forces of magnitude U, V and W act at a point as shown. The forces are measured in newtons. The angles between the forces are $a°$ and $b°$.
Calculate the resultant of U, V and W when:

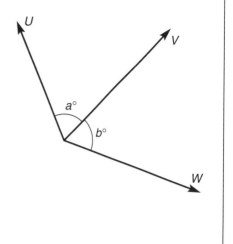

	U	V	W	a	b
(a)	40	50	60	90	90
(b)	40	50	60	120	60
(c)	40	40	40	120	120
(d)	40	50	40	50	50

8 Three forces of magnitude T, U, V newtons act at a point and are such that each has the same magnitude as the resultant of the other two forces. Explain a situation where this occurs.

Generating the graphs of trigonometric functions

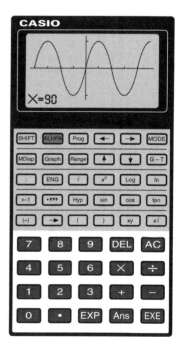

In this section you will find it useful to use a calculator which can produce a graphical display of curves. One such calculator is the Casio fx–7000GA. Most of these calculators have a number of functions, such as $\sin x$, $\cos x$, $\tan x$, 10^x, x^2, built in and the graphs of these functions can be produced directly as a visual display. The Casio booklet calls these 'built-in function' graphs. You will need to read the manual which accompanies your graphic calculator.

The sine curve, $y = \sin x$, is shown below for $-360° \leq x \leq 360°$

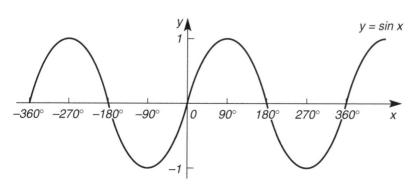

We now show the effects of a few simple transformations on this sine curve. In each case we first produce the graph of $y = \sin x$ (shown as a broken line) and then we superimpose the curve obtained by the simple transformation. It cannot be emphasised enough that you need to try these for yourself and, even without a curve-producing calculator or computer, you will soon be able to sketch transformed curves very quickly from the original curve. A summary about the effect of each transformation is given with further comments in some cases.

(1) $y = -\sin x$

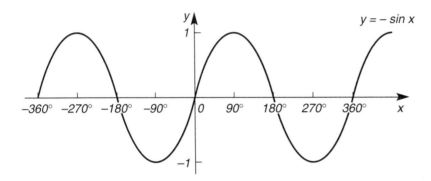

The curve $y = \sin x$ is reflected in the x-axis to give the curve $y = -\sin x$.

(2) $y = \sin (x + 130°)$

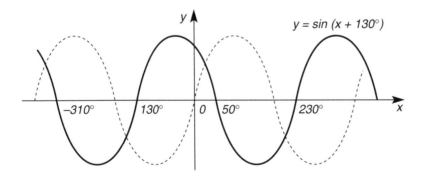

The curve $y = \sin x$ is translated 130° in the negative x-direction to give the curve $y = \sin (x + 130°)$.

(3) y = 2 sin x

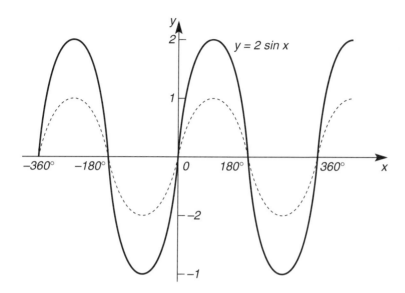

Every y value of the curve $y = \sin x$ is doubled to give the curve $y = 2 \sin x$.

(4) y = 4 + sin x

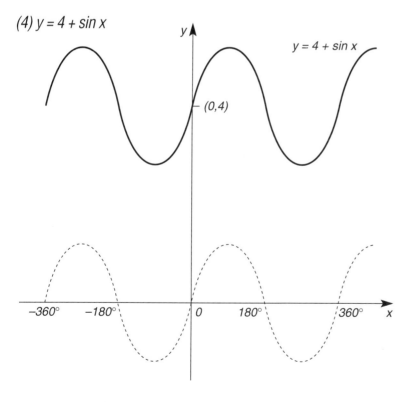

Every y value of the curve $y = \sin x$ has 4 added to it to give the curve $y = 4 + \sin x$.

(5) y = sin 2x

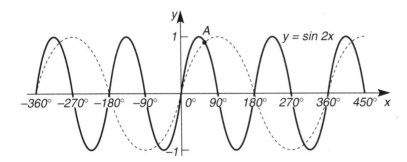

A complete cycle (or wave) of the curve $y = \sin x$ takes place over 360°. A complete cycle of the curve $y = \sin 2x$ takes place over 180°. That is, the original curve is compressed (or doubled up) as shown.

The curves meet at the point A ($0 \le x \le 90°$). Your calculator has a cursor which can 'home in' on this point A so you can see that $x = 60°$ at this point.

The equation $\sin 2x = \sin x$ has a solution 60°.

Further intersections give solutions ($-360° \le x \le 360°$) at $-360°$, $-300°$, $-180°$, $-60°$, 0°, 180°, 300°, 360°. Your calculator can locate any of these once the two graphs are displayed by using the cursor.

EXERCISE 5.4

(A calculator with a curve-sketching facility can be used when answering the questions in this exercise.)

1 (a) Obtain a sketch of the curve $y = \cos x$ for values of x from $-360°$ to 360°.

(b) Starting with a sketch of the curve $y = \cos x$ in each case, show, on separate diagrams, the curves (i) $y = 3 + \cos x$, (ii) $y = \cos 3x$, (iii) $y = -3 \cos x$.

2 In the same diagram sketch, for $0 < x < 90°$, the curves (a) $y = \tan x$, (b) $y = 4 \tan \left(\frac{x}{2}\right)$.

Using a curve-sketching calculator or otherwise, estimate, in degrees to 1 decimal place, a value of x for which

$$\tan x = 4 \tan \left(\frac{x}{2}\right)$$

3 In the same diagram sketch, for $0 < x < 360°$, the curves
(a) $y = \sin x$, (b) $y = 2 \sin 2x$.
Using a curve-sketching calculator, or otherwise, estimate in
degrees, to 1 decimal place where necessary, the values of x
for which $2 \sin 2x = \sin x$ for $0 < x < 360°$.

4 Sketch the curve $y = 3 \cos (x - 20°) + 4$ for $0 < x < 360°$.

(a) Find the coordinates of the point on the curve at which
    (i) y is greatest, (ii) y is least.

(b) Find two values of x for which $3 \cos (x - 20°) = 1.5$.

5 For $0 \le x \le 90$, sketch the curve $y = \cos x° + \sin x°$.
Find the coordinates of the point on the curve at which the
tangent to the curve is parallel to the x-axis.

Solve the equations in the interval $0 \le x \le 90$:

(a) $\sin x° + \cos x° = 1$ (b) $45(\sin x° + \cos x°) = x$

6 For $0 \le x \le 180$ draw a graph of the curve

   $y = 2 \cos 2x° + 1$

Add a straight line to your graph which would enable you to
solve the equation $20 \cos 2x° = x - 10$.
Write down a value of x which satisfies the equation.

7 Using a curve sketching calculator, or otherwise, sketch, on
the same diagram, the curves

   $y = 2 \sin 3x°$ and $y = 3 \sin 2x°$, for $0 \le x \le 120$.

Find a value of x which satisfies $2 \sin 3x° = 3 \sin 2x°$.

8 By using a graphical method, estimate, in degrees to 1
decimal place, a value of x between 0 and $90°$ for which

(a) $\cos^2 x = \sin x$, (b) $\cos^3 x = \sin x$.

9 Taking values of x from 0 to 90 sketch the curves $y = \tan 3x°$
and $y = 10 \sin 2x°$ on the same diagram. Find all the values
of x in the interval $0 \le x < 90$ for which $\tan 3x° = 10 \sin 2x°$.

10 Using a graphical calculator, or otherwise, sketch the curves
$y = \cos x°$ and $y = \sin (x° + 90°)$.
Deduce that $\sin (x° + 90°) = \cos x°$ for *all* values of x.

11 Using a similar approach to that used in question 10, sketch
the curves:

(*a*) $y = \cos (x° + 180°)$

(*b*) $y = \sin (x° + 270°)$

(*c*) $y = \tan (x° + 180°)$

Write each of these curves with a simpler equation.

12 The curve with equation $y = \sin x$ 'repeats' itself every 360°;
we say that $\sin x$ has a period of 360°.
State the period of (i) $\cos x$, (ii) $\tan x$.
   Giving a sketch curve to support your answer in each case,
find the period of (*a*) $\sin 2x$, (*b*) $\sin 3x$, (*c*) $\cos \frac{x}{2}$, (*d*) $\sin^2 x$,
(*e*) $\tan \frac{x}{3}$.

13 The curve with equation $y = \sin x°$ takes all values of y
between -1 and $+1$ inclusive; we say that the range of y
is $-1 \leq y \leq 1$.
   Similarly $y = 3 \sin x°$ has a range of $-3 \leq y \leq 3$ and we
say that $y = \tan x°$ has a range which includes all real
numbers or we say y can take all real values.
Find the range of the curves

(*a*) $y = 2 \cos x°$

(*b*) $y = \cos 2x°$

(*c*) $y = 4 \cos (2x° - 90°)$

(*d*) $y = \tan 2x°$

(*e*) $y = 3 \tan 2x°$

14 Using the same axes, plot the graphs of the curve $y = 2 \sin (90x°)$
and the line $y = 2 - x$ for values of x in the interval $0 \leq x \leq 1$.
Use your graphs to find a value of x for which

$$2 \sin (90x°) + x = 2.$$

6. Linear inequalities and linear programming

Linear inequalities

We know that any equation of the form $ax + by + c = 0$ represents a straight line. Two lines will always meet in a point unless they are parallel, and we find their point of intersection by solving the equations of the lines simultaneously.

Example 1

Consider the lines given by the equations:

$$7x + 2y - 14 = 0$$
$$5x + 2y - 10 = 0$$

By subtracting the second from the first, we see that

$$7x - 5x - 14 + 10 = 0$$
$$2x = 4 \text{ and } x = 2$$

Putting $x = 2$ in the first equation gives:

$$14 + 2y - 14 = 0 \text{ and } y = 0$$

The lines and their common point (2 , 0) are shown below.

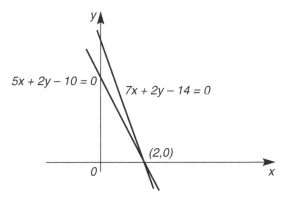

The line $ax + by + c = 0$ cuts the plane containing the coordinate axes into two regions. For one region we have $ax + by + c < 0$ and for the other $ax + by + c > 0$.

Example 2

For the line with equation $7x + 2y - 14 = 0$ the region which contains the origin O, has every point (x, y) satisfying the linear inequality $7x + 2y - 14 < 0$. It is conventional to show this region by shading out the other region which is *not* satisfied by the inequality.

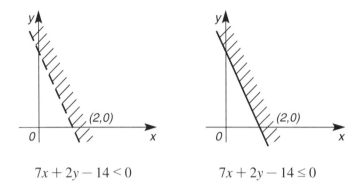

$$7x + 2y - 14 < 0 \qquad\qquad 7x + 2y - 14 \leq 0$$

Note: A broken line indicates that the points on the line are not included in the **solution region** but a continuous line indicates that all points on the line are included.

Example 3

The region satisfied simultaneously by both the linear inequalities $7x + 2y - 14 < 0$ and $5x + 2y - 10 > 0$ is shown as the region *not* shaded out in the diagram.

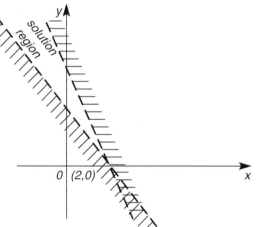

Example 4

The region satisfied simultaneously by the three inequalities $x - 2 \geq 0, y + 3 \geq 0, \quad 3x + 4y - 12 \leq 0$ is shown in the diagram as the region *not* shaded out. This solution region is sometimes called the solution set.

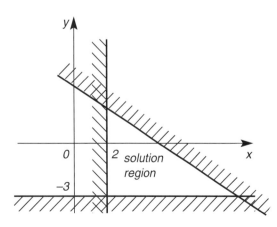

It is important to note at this stage that inequalities *do not* have all the same properties as equations.

If $A = B$ and $C = D$, we know that $A - C = B - D$.

If $A < B$ and $C < D$, it does not always follow that $A - C < B - D$.

One counter-example is suffcient to show this:

Example 5

It is true that $15 > 13$ and that $20 > 9$. It is clearly untrue to say that $15 - 20 > 13 - 9$ because -5 is less than 4.

Even more care is needed when we are discussing linear inequalities which are represented by regions in the plane of the coordinate axes.

Example 6

Returning to the simultaneous equations $7x + 2y - 14 = 0$ and $5x + 2y - 10 = 0$, you will remember that we subtracted to obtain $x = 2$. No such approach should be used when we consider the inequalities $7x + 2y - 14 < 0$ and $5x + 2y - 10 < 0$.

We could assert that $2x - 4 < 0$ by subtracting the second inequality from the first but we could assert also that $-2x + 4 < 0$ by subtracting the first inequality from the second. The first statement contradicts the second statement. Linear inequalities are best approached by considering the corresponding regions formed by sketching all the lines on a graph.

EXERCISE 6.1

1 In each part, a region is defined by the inequalities given. Show this region in a sketch by shading out all the regions *not* required. Use a broken line to indicate that points on the line are excluded.

(a) $x \geq 0$, $y < 4$, $y > 2x - 4$

(b) $2x + 3y > 6$, $y < 2$, $x \leq 4$

(c) $y \geq x$, $y \leq 2$, $x + y \geq 2$

(d) $x \geq 0$, $y \geq 0$, $y \geq 3x - 2$, $y \leq 2x + 1$

In each part write, on your sketch, the coordinates of the vertices of the solution region.

2 In each part, write down an appropriate set of inequalities to describe the region shown.

(*a*)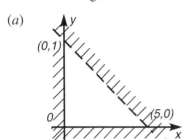

(*b*)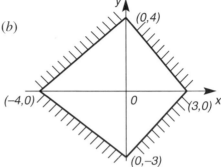

(*c*)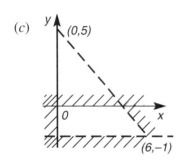

(*d*)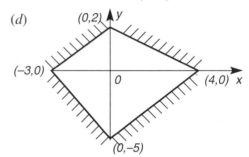

3 Given that *x* and *y* are integers, find, by drawing graphs, possible solutions of the inequalities when they are considered simultaneously.

(*a*) $x > 2$, $3x - 5y \leq 10$, $3x + 5y < 10$

(*b*) $3x - 3y > -4$, $2x + 2 < y$, $5x + 2y > -9$

4 Show, in a sketch, the region A defined by the inequalities

   $y \leq x$, $x \leq 4$, $y + x \geq 2$.

The origin is O and P is any point in A. Find the greatest possible distance between P and O.

5 The points A(3, −1), B(7, 3), C(10, 0) are three vertices of the parallelogram ABCD. Find the coordinates of D. Find four linear inequalities which, when taken together, for a point P(*x*, *y*) would ensure that P lies inside the parallelogram.

6 The equations of the sides PQ and PR of a triangle PQR are $3x + y - 1 = 0$ and $5x - y - 7 = 0$ respectively. The point R is at (3, 8) and Q lies on the *y*-axis.
Find the coordinates of P and Q.
Find three linear inequalities which would ensure that any point Z(*x*, *y*) lies inside the triangle PQR.

Practical illustrations of linear programming

Example 7

Two sizes of minibus, X and Y, are to be used to transport 70 students from their hall to the college each day. The following information is known:

Minibus	Number available	Maximum passengers
X	4	15
Y	5	10

The college can provide up to seven drivers but no driver can repeat the journey.
We take x and y as the numbers of X- and Y-minibuses used and form the following inequalities from the data:
$x \leq 4, y \leq 5$
From the drivers available, we have $x + y \leq 7$.
$15x$ students travel in the X-minibuses and $10y$ travel in the Y-minibuses so we have $15x + 10y \geq 70$, which ensures that all 70 students are included. This inequality reduces to $3x + 2y \geq 14$.
We draw the four lines for the equations:

$x = 4, y = 5, x + y = 7$ and $3x + 2y = 14$

We shade out to leave the region simultaneously satisfied by $x \leq 4, y \leq 5, x + y \leq 7$ and $3x + 2y \geq 14$ as shown.

As x and y must be integers we can list the solutions as (x, y). There are seven possible solutions and these are $(2, 5), (2, 4), (3, 3), (3, 4), (4, 1), (4, 2), (4, 3)$.

The cost of using an X-minibus is £23 and the cost of using a Y-minibus is £15.
By considering each possible solution in turn, the college finds that using 2 X- and 4 Y-minibuses gives them a minimum daily cost of £106 for transporting the 70 students.

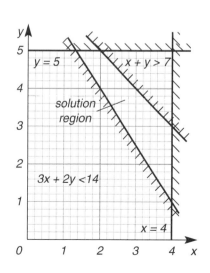

Example 8

A primary school decides to celebrate its centenary by hiring a train for a day for the parents, teachers and children. It was decided that

(*a*) the total number travelling should not exceed 200,

(*b*) there must be either one parent or one teacher with every four children, or fewer,

(*c*) the fare for an adult is £16 and for a child £10,

(*d*) sufficient people must travel in order to at least cover the cost, £1600, of the train.

If *x* children and *y* adults took part, we then have:

  x and *y* both need to be positive integers,

  $x + y \le 200$, because 200 is the maximum number,

  $y \ge \frac{x}{4}$, because there must be one adult with every four children or fewer,

  $10x + 16y \ge 1600$, because £1600 is needed to cover cost.

The graphs can now be drawn and the solution space identified as the region *not* shaded out.

The organisers would probably wish to know the minimum number of adults required to make the expedition viable. We can read this off at the point marked V on the diagram. This gives the number of adults as 29 and the greatest number of children would then be 115.

Solutions to practical problems using linear graphs as shown in Examples 6 and 7 are often called linear programming.

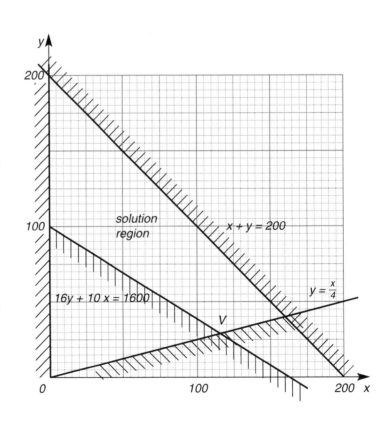

EXERCISE 6.2

1 A Veterinary Practice provides facilities for boarding
dogs and cats. There are kennels for 25 dogs and
cages for 20 cats. The staff need a total of at least
16 dogs and cats in residence at any time to make the
boarding pay. Daily each dog requires 20 minutes and
each cat 15 minutes of the staff's time and only a total
of 8 hours is allowed for the boarding side of the
Veterinary Practice.

Taking x as the number of dogs and y as the number
of cats in residence, form four inequalities for the data
given. Show the possible numbers of dogs and cats
which can be boarded as a solution space by drawing
graphs and labelling each clearly.

2 A coach, capable of carrying up to 50 passengers, is hired for a
day trip at a cost of £200. An adult pays £10 and a child pays
£6. Each adult must be responsible for at least one child and
not more than three children. The trip is cancelled if
insufficient people book and the hire change is not met. Taking
x as the number of children and y as the number of adults who
take part, find, by using a graphical method:

(*a*) the greatest and least possible numbers of adults,

(*b*) the greatest and least possible numbers of children,

(*c*) the greatest and least possible profit,

(*d*) the number of adults when the profit is least.

3 A rectangle of length x cm and breadth y cm is drawn
according to the four conditions:

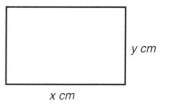

(i) the length is greater than the breadth,

(ii) the breadth is greater than one-third of the length,

(iii) the perimeter is greater than 400 cm,

(iv) the perimeter is less than 560 cm.

y cm

x cm

Write down four inequalities which together cover all the facts
given in the data.

Show by drawing linear graphs the possible solution region.
Investigate whether there are any integer values, in cm, of x
and y for which the area of the rectangle is 10 000 cm^2.

4 A shop stocks two types of calculator, A and B, which cost the owner £8 and £24 respectively from the manufacturer.

 The owner decides to buy 80 calculators of which there are more of A than of B, and he has up to £960 available for purchasing the calculators from the manufacturer. The owner sells type A and type B at £12 and £32 respectively.

 Investigate graphically how many of each type the owner should buy to maximise the profit, assuming that all are sold.

5 In an examination two papers, P and Q, are sat by all candidates and each carry a total of 100 marks. In order to pass the examination a student needs to score more than

 (i) 30 marks on paper P,

 (ii) 40 marks on paper Q,

 (iii) 150 marks for the sum of his mark on P and *twice* his mark on Q.

A student scored x marks and y marks on P and Q respectively. Using a graphical method, find the least value of $(x + y)$ for which this student could pass and state the value of x and of y in this case.

6 A country craft shop makes two types of rustic table, round R and square S. The following data is known:

	Raw materials cost (£)	Man-hours needed
Table R	20	10
Table S	12	15

The profit made on a table of either type is £15. The shop has capital of up to £500 available for materials and up to 330 man-hours for making tables.

 By forming appropriate linear inequalities for this data and drawing relevant graphs, find the greatest profit that is possible and the number of each type of table that are made in this case.

7. Networks

Network diagrams

Network diagrams provide a clear and easy way to display data in many practical situations. Some important practical problems can be identified, discussed and solved by considering networks. In this section we look at some simple cases of these and you can apply the techniques shown here in solving problems with data of your own.

Consider this road network which connects 11 major towns and cities in England. The distances between some of them are shown in miles.

Example 1

Shortest routes can be found by trial and improvement.
A route from Preston to Cardiff via Liverpool is of length (29 + 200) miles = 229 miles. The route from Preston to Cardiff via Manchester and Birmingham is of length (32 + 88 + 107) miles = 227 miles, which is the shortest route on the network between Preston and Cardiff.

Example 2

A large firm has offices in each of the 11 centres shown on the network. The head office is at Cardiff. Regular mailshots using couriers are sent out in the following way.

One courier drives from Cardiff to Birmingham with some of the mail. A second courier takes the remaining mail to Exeter. At Birmingham, further couriers take the mail to the next centres, where more couriers continue the despatch until all centres receive their mail.

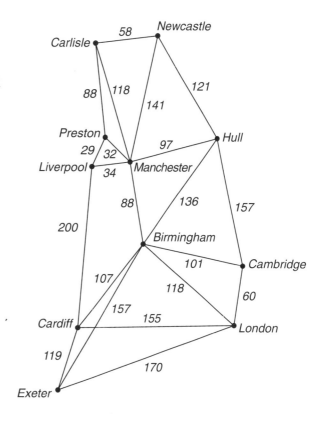

The accountants have worked out the shortest possible paths through the network so that each centre receives the mailshot but the couriers travel the shortest distance. Their solution is shown in the diagram. You should check carefully that these paths make the minimum distance connection between the centres.

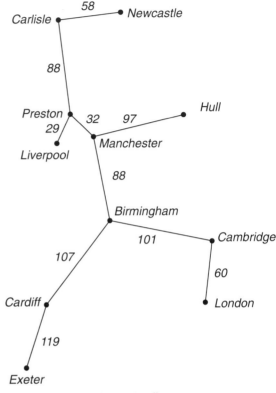

Minimum connection 779 miles

Example 3

The network shows the main building M and the four dormitory blocks A, B, C and D at a Youth Centre. The distances between buildings are shown in metres.

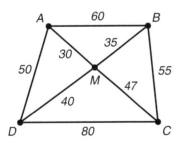

For security, the officer on duty each evening has to start and finish at M and visit each of the blocks A, B, C and D. On Monday evening, the officer took the path

$$M \rightarrow D \rightarrow A \rightarrow B \rightarrow C \rightarrow M,$$

a total distance of $(40 + 50 + 60 + 55 + 47)$ m $= 252$ m.

On Tuesday evening a second officer took the path

$$M \to A \to B \to C \to D \to M,$$

a total distance of $(30 + 60 + 55 + 80 + 40)\ m = 265\ m$.

They compared their paths with the officer on duty on the Wednesday evening, who told them that he only walked 250 m on his path, which he claimed was the shortest possible. Then he told them how he had investigated and solved the problem.

First, he recorded all the eight distances, smallest first, as 30, 35, 40, 47, 50, 55, 60, 80 with a total of 397 m.

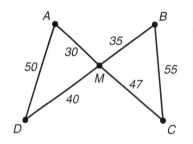

In order to cover M → (A, B, C, D in any order) → M he reasoned that five or six of the sections had to be walked. The shortest path using six sections should omit CD (80) and AB (60), the two greatest; see the diagram opposite.

The path $M \to A \to D \to M \to B \to C \to M$ is 257 m, which is rejected as this path is longer than the 252-m path found by Monday's officer.

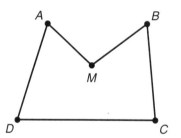

A network, starting and finishing at M, and passing through A, B, C and D with only five sections must be similar to the diagram opposite. This contains 2 'inside' and 3 'outside' sections. There are four possibilities, which are shown below.

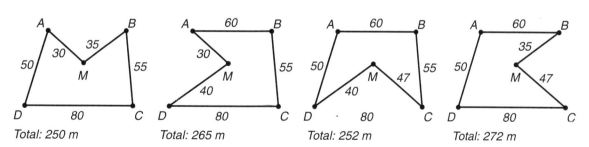

We see that the path

$$M \to A \to D \to C \to B \to M$$

produced the minimum distance of 250 m.

Investigation A

Some networks can be moved around completely, starting and finishing at the same vertex, and without repeating any route:

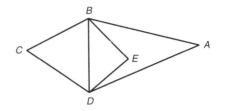

Other networks can be traversed without repeating a route, but the starting vertex and the finishing vertex are different:

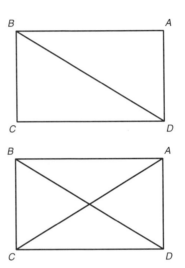

There are also many networks which cannot be traversed in this way:

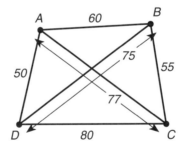

Investigate and find simple rules for these different cases.

Example 4

The warden at the Youth Centre asked his groundsman to check that all of the six paths, shown in the network diagram, were in good order.

The groundsman had to walk all the paths at least once. He started at a vertex and he covered the minimum distance possible in his route. Investigate how he achieved this. We appreciate from our work in Investigation A that this network cannot be traversed unless he walks one path twice.

For the whole route to be a minimum, we choose AD, the shortest of the six paths, to be repeated.

The shortest route is then

$$B \rightarrow C \rightarrow D \rightarrow A \rightarrow B \rightarrow D \rightarrow A \rightarrow C$$

Minimum distance is 447 m.

Investigation B

A famous network question arose in the eighteenth century known as the Königsberg Bridges Problem.

The city of Königsberg in central Europe had seven bridges over the River Pregel, as shown. Is it possible to start at any point A, cross every bridge just once, and then return to A? Investigate.

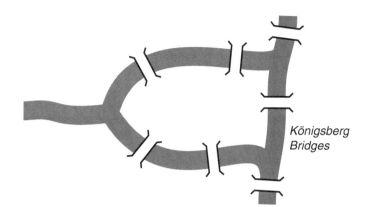

Königsberg Bridges

Investigation C

Working in pairs, make up networks of your own region and test your partner's ability to find the shortest route or the minimum connection between specific places on the network.

Investigation D

Sort out routes by Underground from Heathrow to all the London main-line railway stations.

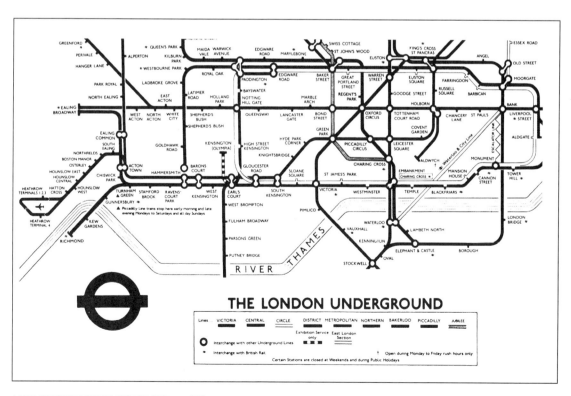

EXERCISE 7.1

1 By drawing an appropriate diagram find the minimum
connection between all the towns and cities in each of the three
networks shown. Distances are in miles.

(a)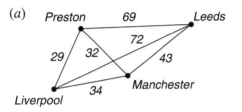

(b)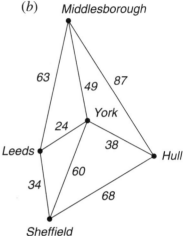

(c)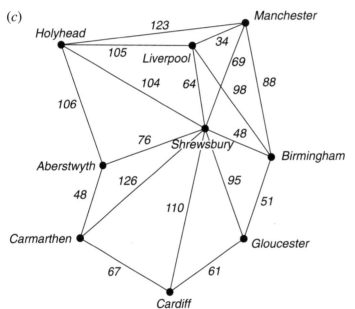

2 An executive wishes to buy a house in
the area which will minimise his
travelling each week. Every week he has
to visit Bristol, Oxford, Taunton,
Salisbury and Guildford (one city each
day of the week). The network shows the
distances between these places. Giving
reasons, recommend which city of the
five he should choose to live in so that
his weekly travelling distance is the least.

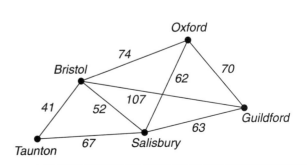

3 A television company wishes to connect the towns of Barnstaple, Taunton, Dorchester and Plymouth with a cable line for satellite transmissions. The distances in miles between the towns are :

	Taunton	Dorchester	Plymouth
Barnstaple	49	93	66
Taunton		41	73
Dorchester			94

Find the minimum length of cable which will be required to connect these towns and draw a sketch to illustrate your solution.

4 Repeat the investigation in question 3 for the six towns shown in the network, where distances are in miles.

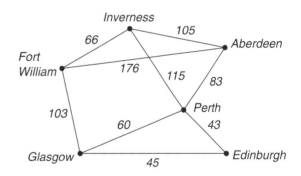

5 The network shows the distances of a London-based company from its nine regional offices. Calculate the minimum distance so that each office is linked either directly or via other offices to London, and show your minimum connection in a sketch graph.

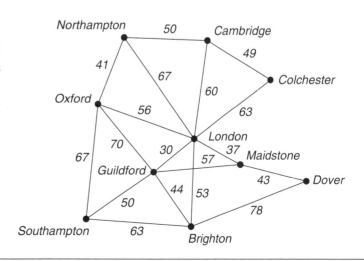

Critical path analysis

Several different activities are often required when we are undertaking a project. By careful planning we are often able to minimise the time required to complete all the activities.

Example 5

The JJ Country Garden Service is run by Jack and Jill in a locality and they do garden jobs ranging from mowing grass to building greenhouses for their customers. One daily project consisted of the following tasks, some of which had to be done before others could be started. The time required to complete each task is given in hours.

Task	Description	Time (hours)	Preceded by
A	Mow the lawns	3	
B	Cut hedges	4	A
C	Pick raspberries	2	
D	Weed borders	6	C
E	Bag-up rubbish and take to local tip	1	A, B, C, D

Any of the tasks A, B, C and D can be done by either Jack or Jill but task E requires both of them for 1 hour.

The project is analysed by drawing an activity network, in which we have given Jack tasks A and B, and Jill tasks C and D before they do E together.

The earliest possible starting time for an activity is written in the corresponding circle, as shown.

    Although the activities A and B take only 7 hours, the activities C and D take 8 hours. Therefore the earliest starting time for activity E is 8 hours after the start. As activity E takes 1 hour, the whole project would take 9 hours to complete as a minium.

    The route through the network which completes the project in the least time is called the **critical path**.

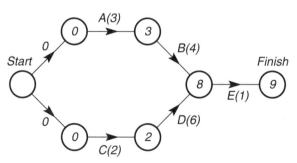

Activity network and earliest starting times

$$\text{Start} \rightarrow C \rightarrow D \rightarrow E \rightarrow \text{Finish}$$

is the critical path in this case.

Example 6

The secretary of the Sailing College Former Students Association has to arrange the annual dinner of the SCFSA. The secretary and his helpers (who can number as many as required) have the following tasks to do:

Task	Description	Time (days)	Preceded by
A	Send out tickets, finalise numbers	5	
B	Choose menu and order food	4	A
C	Apply for licence for bar	2	A
D	Buy drinks and set up bar	3	A, C
E	Organise speakers	2	A
F	Make final preparations	2	A, B, C, D, E

First we draw the activity network, as shown in the first diagram

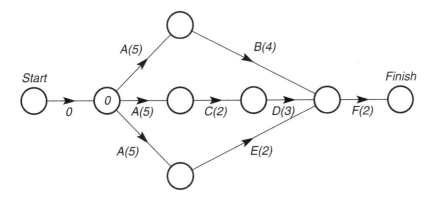

We now add the earliest finishing times, as shown in the second diagram.

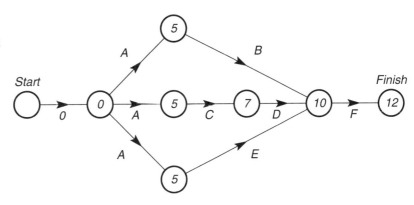

The critical path is

Start → A → C → D → F → Finish

The least time needed for the project is 12 days.

A general strategy

First draw the activity network.

In more complicated networks, we move forwards through the network, writing in the earliest starting time for each activity. Then we move backwards through the network noting the latest starting time for each activity.

Activities with equal earliest and latest starting times are on the critical path, which can then be identified.

EXERCISE 7.2

1 The friends of a bridegroom have the following tasks:

1.	Help the groom prepare	20 min
2.	Collect buttonholes	15 min
3.	Drive the groom to church	10 min
4.	Collect service sheets from vicarage	5 min
5.	Hide the groom's car	7 min
6.	Greet and direct the early arrivals at the church	30 min

Note that tasks 1 and 2 must be done before task 3 which must be done before tasks 4 and 5. Task 6 is independent. At what time should the friends start if the wedding is at 2 p.m. and all the six tasks must be completed by 1.45 p.m.?

2 A charity collection requires the following:

		Time (days)
1.	Arrange collection of tins and envelopes	2
2.	Print leaflets	3
3.	Find volunteers for collection.	5
	The envelopes and tins then need to be distributed and collected, and the money counted.	
4.	In area A, distribution	2
5.	collection	2
6.	In area B, distribution	3
7.	collection	3
8.	Counting money (in either area)	1
9.	Preparing final accounts	2

Note that 1, 2 and 3 must precede 4, 5, 6 and 7, which in turn must precede 8; all tasks, 1–8, must be complete before 9 can start.

The accounts are due on 30 June. On what date should work begin?

3 The following activities are used in the manufacture of frozen Yorkshire Puddings.

	Activity	Preceded by	Time (min)
A	Defrost freezers and sterilise	–	45
B	Sterilise mixers	–	20
C	Add milk, flour, eggs and seasoning to mixers	B	10
D	Beat ingredients	C	10
E	Pour mixture in trays	D	15
F	Preheat oven	–	20
G	Bake	E, F	25
H	Fast-freeze puddings	A, G	30
I	Pack frozen puddings	H	20

Draw a network to illustrate this information. Identify the critical path in your network and hence find the shortest time required to complete the whole operation.

4 A group of friends decide to help Pat decorate her room at home. Here is a list of activities they need to do.

Draw an activity network to illustrate all of this information. Draw in the critical path and hence find the shortest time required to complete the redecorating of Pat's room.

	Activity	Preceded by	Time (hours)
A	Prepare surfaces for painting and papering	–	6
B	Identify and fetch the materials required	–	3
C	Paint doors, skirting-board and window	A, B	4
D	Hang wallpaper	C	5
E	Hang curtains	D	1
F	Re-lay carpet tiles	D	2

Investigation E

Plan and write up the set of tasks you would need to do in order to decorate your bedroom at home, including an order of precedence.

Investigation F

Ken wants to build a garage on a rough piece of sloping ground at the side of his house. Write up a set of tasks which could be undertaken to complete this project, noting any tasks which should take precedence over others.

Winning strategies

In each of the following you are required to find a winning strategy.

EXERCISE 7.3

1 The diagram shows a strip of five squares with two black counters on the left and two white counters on the right.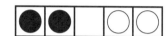

The object is to swap the counters over in the least possible number of moves to finish like this:

The rules for moving are:

(i) A counter may slide into a gap, blacks to the right and whites to the left.

(ii) A counter may jump over just one counter into a gap, a black jumps to the right and a white to the left.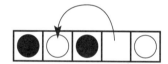

Investigate the minimum number of moves required.
Repeat the exercise for (3, 3), (4, 4) and attempt to generalise.
   Investigate also cases such as (2, 1), (3, 2), (4, 2) and so on, where there is always just one more square than the nunber of counters involved.

2 Using similar rules investigate the minimum number of moves required to 'change over' the counters in the two situations shown. Diagonal moves are forbidden.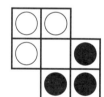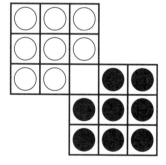

You should be able to show that 46 moves is the minimum in the (8, 8) case.

3 There are 11 identical counters in a pot. Amanda and Bella are playing a game in which the first player can take 1, 2 or 3 counters from the pot. The second player can then take 1, 2 or 3 counters and so on. The player who picks up the last counter loses.
Can Amanda always win if she is the first player?
If so, write down the sequence of moves she must make.
Can Amanda, playing first, always beat Bella when there are 30 counters in the pot at the start?

4 The diagrams show the plans of three American towns of different sizes.

The smallest town consists of four blocks in a 2 × 2 square; the larger towns are 3 × 3 and 4 × 4 squares of blocks.
Starting from the corner A each time, how many different routes are there to C, the opposite corner, when you are allowed to move to the right or up only? Is there a pattern? Can you generalise?

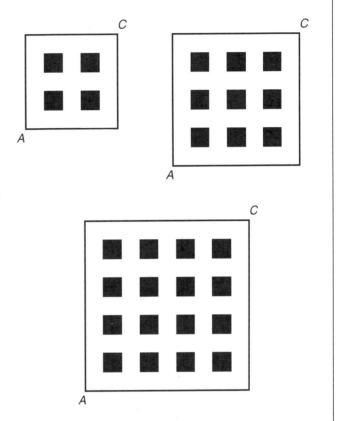

Investigation G

Investigate the game, 'Solitaire', including winning strategies for nominated starting positions for the unoccupied hole on peg-boards with different patterns.

Investigation H

A small toy factory has the choice of making three products A, B or C. It is at present manufacturing A and making £100 000 income annually.

To adapt the machinery to manufacture B would cost £10 000 and for C £20 000; these are one-off sums. It is predicted that manufacturing B would increase sales income by 8% without advertising and by 14% with advertising costing £6000.

It is predicted that manufacturing C would increase sales income by 12% without advertising and by 25% with advertising costing £8000.

Which course of action looks to be the most profitable
(*a*) for 1 year only, (*b*) over a 2-year period?

8. The circle

In this chapter the symmetry properties of a circle are reviewed and the work on angles and tangents introduced in Book 3y is extended.

Chords and symmetry

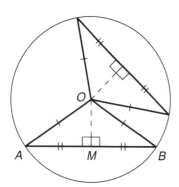

Any triangle formed by joining the ends of a chord to the centre of the circle is **isosceles**, and so by symmetry

    (i) **angle OAB = angle OBA**,

    (ii) **angle OMA = angle OMB = 90°**, and

    (iii) **AM = MB.**

Example 1

In the diagram chord AB = 42 cm and the radius of the circle is 29 cm. Find the distance of AB from the centre O.

The distance required is the *shortest* distance from O to the chord; that is OM, where M is the mid-point of AB.

Using Pythagoras' theorem: $OM^2 + 21^2 = 29^2 \Rightarrow OM^2 = 400$
$$\Rightarrow OM = 20 \text{ cm}$$

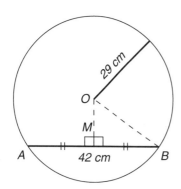

EXERCISE 8.1 (Calculations)

1 A chord of length 18 cm is 12 cm from the centre of a circle of radius r cm. Calculate the value or r.

2 The point P is on the diameter AB of a circle such that AP $= 16$ cm and PB $= 4$ cm. Calculate the length of the chord passing through P and perpendicular to AB.

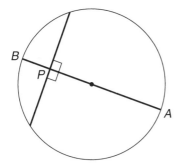

3 An equilateral triangle with sides of length x cm is inscribed in a circle, centre O, of radius 10 cm. Show that each side is 5 cm from O and find the value of x.

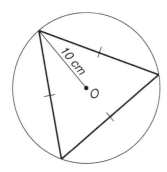

4 Two parallel chords of a circle, of radius 13 cm, are of lengths 12 cm and 24 cm. Given that the chords are on opposite sides of the centre, calculate the distance between them.

5 In a circle of radius 6.5 cm several chords of length 12 cm are drawn.

(_a_) Explain how you know that the centres of all these chords lie on a circle, and calculate its radius.

(_b_) Check your result by drawing the circle and enough chords to produce the locus of their mid-points.

6 Two circles, with centres A and B, of radii 10 cm and 17 cm respectively, intersect at P and Q, where PQ = 16 cm. How far apart are the centres of the two circles?

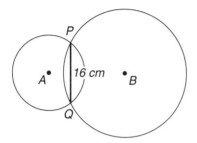

7 P,Q and R are points on the circumference of a circle, with centre C and radius r cm, such that PQ = PR = 13 cm and QR = 10 cm. The point S is on QR such that PCS is a straight line.

(*a*) Draw a diagram to show the data and explain why S must be the mid-point of QR.

(*b*) Calculate the length of PS.

(*c*) Show that CS = $(12 - r)$ cm.

(*d*) Calculate the value of r.

8 Two concentric circles (with the same centre) have radii 6 cm and 10 cm. The line ABCD cuts the first circle at B and C and the second at A and D. Given that BC = 8 cm, show that AB = $4(\sqrt{5} - 1)$ cm.

9 Prove, using congruent triangles, that if two chords are equal then

(*a*) they are equidistant from the centre of the circle, C ,

(*b*) the angles, x and y, that they subtend at the centre are equal.

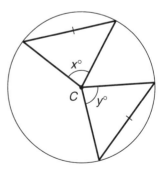

10 A hemispherical bowl, of radius 13 cm, is used to hold water. When the depth of water is 8 cm, calculate

(*a*) the diameter of the circular surface of water,

(*b*) the angle through which the bowl can be tilted before water is lost.

EXERCISE 8.2

1 In each of the following diagrams calculate the value of *x*.

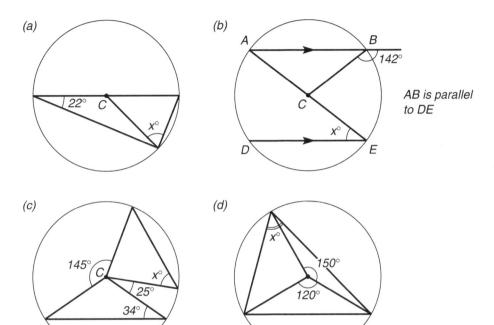

(a)

(b)

AB is parallel
to DE

(c)

(d)

2 A circle, centre O, passes through the points A, B and C. Given
that angle AOB = 120° and angle BOC = 140°, find the angles
of the triangle.

3 A number of chairs are placed at equal intervals around a
circular table. Abi and Ben are sitting diametrically opposite
each other and there are two seats between Ben and Cheri.

(*a*) How do you know that there are an even number of chairs?

The angle that Abi has to turn through to face Cheri is 27°.

(*b*) Calculate how many chairs there are around the table.

(*c*) Deduce the angle that Cheri has to turn through to look
from Ben to Abi.

4 Work out the smaller angle between the hour and the minute
hands of a clock at (*a*) 4 o'clock (*b*) half past six (*c*) 1945.

5 The points on the circumference of a circular clockface to which the hour hand points at 0300, 0600 and 1000 are labelled A, B and C respectively.

(*a*) Write down the angles swept through by the hour hand in moving from (i) A to B (ii) B to C (iii) C to A.

(*b*) Draw a diagram to show the points A, B and C, and the centre O of the clockface, and calculate angles (i) ACB (ii) BAC (iii) CBA.

(*c*) What do you notice about the answers to the corresponding

Tangents and symmetry

1. The tangent-radius property

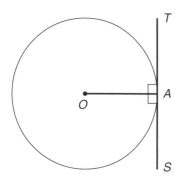

If the page is folded along the line *OA, TA* is mapped onto *SA*. *By* considering symmetry, angle SAO = angle TAO = 90°; that is:

At a point on the circumference of a circle the angle between the tangent and the radius is a right angle.

2. When two tangents are drawn from a point to a circle

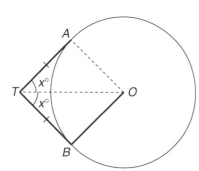

If the page is folded along the line OT, triangle OAT is mapped onto triangle OBT, and so by symmetry:

(i) **AT = BT** and
(ii) **angle ATO = angle BTO**.

Angle in a semi-circle

We also saw in Book 3Y that, when the ends of a diameter are joined to any point on the circumference, a right angle is formed at that point. One proof of this result is given here; another will be seen in Exercise 8.4.

As both triangles ACD and BCD are isosceles we can let angle CAD = angle ADC = $x°$ and angle CDB = angle CBD = $y°$. (*Note*: We cannot assume that all four are equal.)

In triangle ABD: $x + (x + y) + y = 180°$

$$\Rightarrow 2x + 2y = 180°$$

$$\Rightarrow x + y = 90°$$

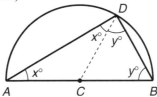

This proves that angle ADB = $90°$, wherever D is on the circumference.

EXERCISE 8.3

1 Find the values of x and y, for the diagrams (a)–(l) on the next page, writing out clearly the steps in your solution. In each diagram C is the centre of the circle.)

2 (These questions refer to the diagrams in question 1.)

(*a*) What type of quadrilateral is that in (e)?

(*b*) (i) How do your results in (f) prove that BC = BT = BD?
(ii) If a circle were to be drawn to pass through C, T and D, where would its centre be?

3 A and B are two points diametrically opposite each other, with B due east of A, on a circular route of radius 5 km. The point C is on the route on a bearing of 030° from A.

(*a*) Show this data in a diagram, which should not be to scale.

(*b*) Write down the bearing of C from B.

Salim walked along the route from A to C but then, to save time, he took a straight-line course from C to B.

(*c*) Calculate the distance he travelled from C to B.

(*d*) Given that he can walk at 5 km/h, calculate the time he saved by taking his 'short cut'.

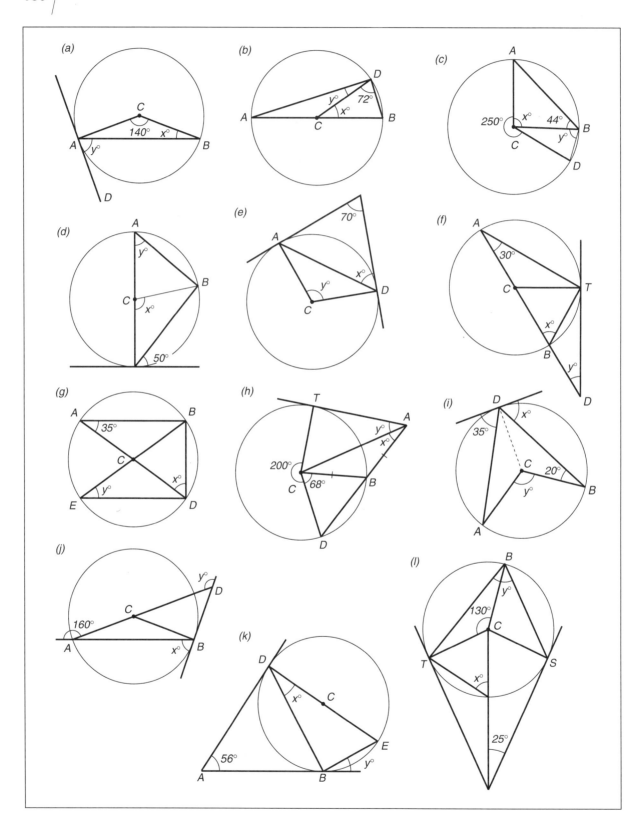

4 A class was asked to find the radius of a circular track laid out on the school playing field, without going inside the track or measuring the circumference. Pupils were allowed to use a 50-m tape besides their own mathematical equipment.

   Sally went to a point outside the circle, used the tape to judge where the two tangents to the circle were, measured their lengths at 28.87 m and found the angle between the tangents to be 120°. What did she find the radius to be, and how far was she from the circumference of the circle?

   Can you suggest another method?

5 For the right-angled triangle shown:

(*a*) Explain why $x + y = 24$.

(*b*) Write down two similar equations involving x and z, and y and z. Hence find x, y and z.

(*c*) Deduce the radius of the inscribed circle shown.

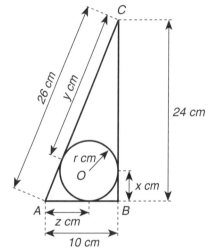

6 A ladder of length 2.5 m rests against a log, whose circular cross-section has radius 1 m, so that it makes an angle of 60° with the ground.

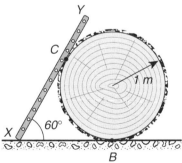

(*a*) What length of ladder is above C, the point of contact with the log?

(*b*) Calculate what angle the ladder needs to make with the ground so that the point C is at the middle of the ladder.

7 A chain fits tightly over two cogs of radii 19 cm and 12 cm as shown in the diagram. Given that the centres of the cogs are 41 cm apart, calculate the length of the straight section AB of chain. (The dotted line, parallel to C_1C_2, may be useful.)

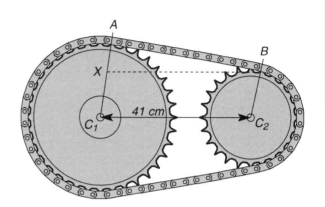

8 The diagram shows a vertical cross-section through the centres of two touching spheres which are standing on horizontal ground. TS is the tangent to the circles at their point of contact.

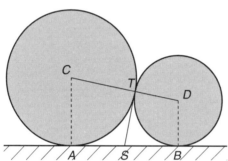

(a) Explain why (i) CTD is a straight line, (ii) AS = TS = SB, (iii) angle ATB must be a right angle.

(b) Given that the radii of the spheres are 6 cm and 13.5 cm, calculate the distance between A and B.

(c) Write down the radius of the circle that can be drawn through A, T and B.

9 Sendip's design for a piece of jewellery is shown in the diagram. The curved part BD is an arc of a circle for which AC, EC and a line through AE are tangents.

(a) Write down in terms of the radius, r cm, of the circle
(i) CD (ii) arc BD (iii) DE.

(b) You should have found that CD = DE. Explain this result, using symmetry.

(c) Given that the total length of wire used in the piece was 43.3 cm, calculate, to 3 significant figures, the value of r.

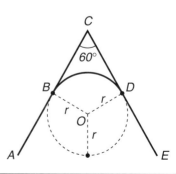

Investigation A

Draw a straight line and mark on the points A, B and C such that
AB = 11.2 cm and BC = 4 cm, and at C draw a line CD perpendicular to AC.

(*a*) Try, by trial and error, to find the point X on CD such that
angle AXB is greatest.

(*b*) Calculate the radius of the circle which passes
through A and B, and also touches the line CD.

(*c*) Now construct the circle and label the point E
in which the circle meets the line.

(*d*) You should find X and E are the same point.
Explain the result.

(*e*) In a game of rugby a try has been scored at the
point C. Where should the goal kicker place the
ball on CD in order to have the best chance of
converting the kick?

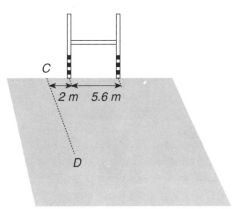

Investigation B

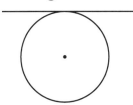

Draw a circle and a tangent as shown.
Find the locus of the centres of circles
that touch both the circle and the tangent.

Investigate other cases where the line is not a tangent. For example:

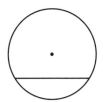   

Now investigate the locus of the centres of circles that touch a fixed circle
and a fixed point C. Two examples are shown but choose some of your own.

   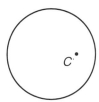

C is the centre of a fixed circle.   C is inside the circle.

Investigation C

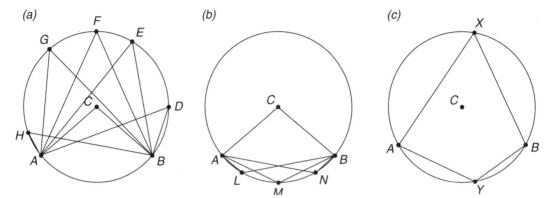

(a)   (b)   (c)

Draw a large circle, centre C, and place two points A and B on the circumference, such that AB is not a diameter, and join these to C. Now mark several points on the circumference, on the same side of AB as C, as shown in diagram (*a*), and join them to A and B.

How are all the angles formed at the circumference related and how are they related to angle ACB? What difference does it make if (i) A and B are moved, (ii) the circle is a different size?

Do the results hold if the points on the circumference are on the opposite side of AB to C, as in diagram (*b*)? Investigate and write up your results.

Diagram (*c*) shows two points on the circumference on opposite sides of AB. How are angle AXB and angle AYB related in this case? Try several cases for different positions of X and Y.

You should have observed some important angle properties of the circle in the above investigation. In the next exercise you will be proving and using your results.

EXERCISE 8.4

1 (*a*) Refer to the diagram and write down,

     (i) in terms of x, angles ADC and ACE,

     (ii) in terms of y, angles BDC and BCE,

     (iii) in terms of x and y, angles ACB and ADB.

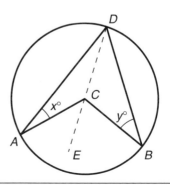

You should have now proved the result that
angle ACB = 2 × angle ADB, that is:

The angle at the centre = twice the angle at the circumference.

(b) When the chord AB is a diameter, what does this theorem
tell you about angle ADB?

(c) In each of the following diagrams calculate the value of x.

(i)

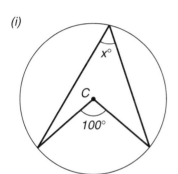

(ii)

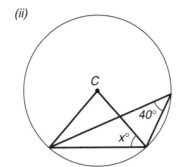

(iii)

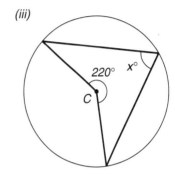

(iv)

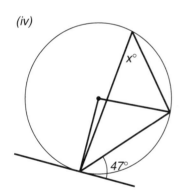

(v)

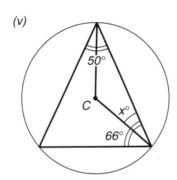

(vi)

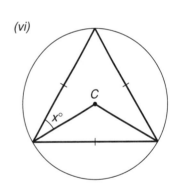

2 (a) Referring to the diagram shown, write out a similar proof
to that in the last question to show that, if C and D are on
opposite sides of the chord AB, then:

The **reflex** angle ACB = twice the angle at the
circumference (angle ADB).

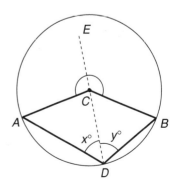

(b) Find x in each of the following diagrams.

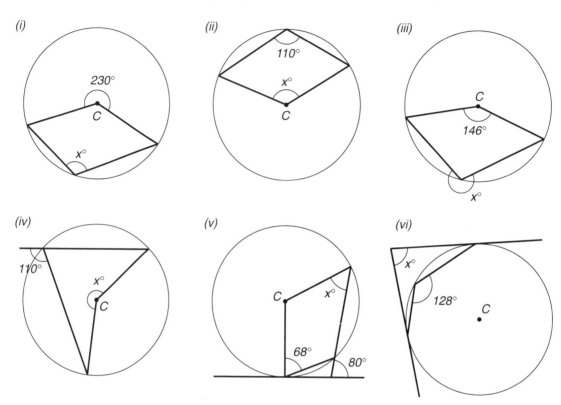

(i)

230°

C

x°

(ii)

110°

x°

C

(iii)

C

146°

x°

(iv)

110°

x°

C

(v)

C

x°

68°

80°

(vi)

x°

128°

C

3 (a) Use the theorem, 'The angle at the centre = twice the angle at the circumference', to prove that $x = y = z$ in each of the cases below.

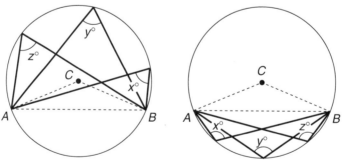

The chord AB divides the circumference into two arcs; the chord AB divides the circle into two segments. If the angles formed by AB at the circumference are in the same segment, then these angles, like x, y and z, are equal, that is:

Angles in the same segment are equal.

(b) Find the value of the letters in each of the following.

(i)

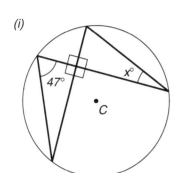

(ii)

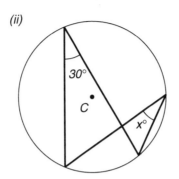

(iii)

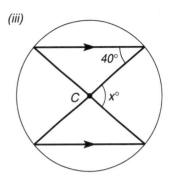

(iv)

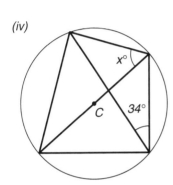

(v)

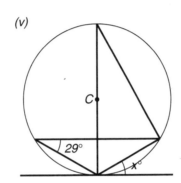

(vi)

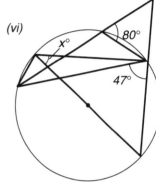

4 (a) Prove that the triangles AXD and BXC are similar.

(b) If AX = 6 cm, BX = 8 cm and DX = 5 cm, deduce CX.

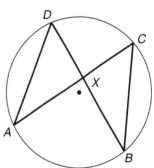

5 In diagram (c) of Investigation C you will have found that angle AXB + angle AYB = 180°. In the diagram angle AXB = $x°$ and angle AYB = $y°$.

(a) Write down, in terms of x, obtuse angle ACB.

(b) Write down, in terms of y, reflex angle ACB.

(c) Complete a proof that $x + y = 180$.

(d) Explain why the sum of the other two angles of the quadrilateral AXBY is also 180°.

If a quadrilateral is such that a circle can be drawn through its vertices, it is called a **cyclic quadrilateral.**

(e) Complete the statement, 'Opposite angles of a cyclic quadrilateral......'

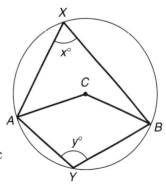

6 Find the value of x in each of the following cases.

(a)

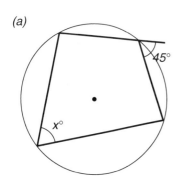

(b)

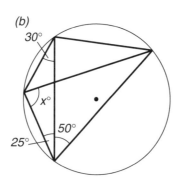

(c)

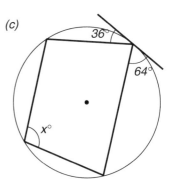

(d)

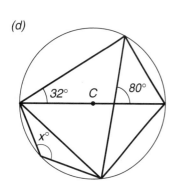

(e)

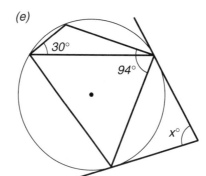

(f)

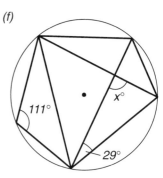

7 (a) For the diagram shown prove that triangles ACE and DBE are similar.

(b) Deduce the length of AE.

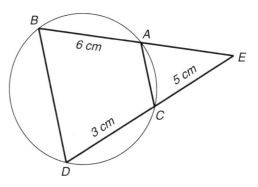

8 State which of the following quadrilaterals are cyclic. For those that are, draw accurately an example of the quadrilateral and construct the circumscribing circle.

(a) a square   (b) a rectangle   (c) a rhombus (not a square)

(d) a parallelogram (non special)   (e) an isosceles trapezium

(f) a kite

9 The diagonals of a cyclic quadrilateral ABCD meet at O; angle BOC = 98° and angle BDC = 49°. Prove that O is the centre of the circle passing through A, B, C and D.

10 The angles of a pentagon are as shown.

(*a*) Calculate the value of *x*.

(*b*) Given that CD = DE, show that a circle can be drawn through the points A, B, C and E.

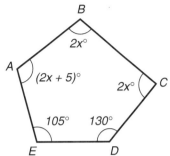

Investigation D

The fact 'The perpendicular bisector of a chord passes through the centre of the circle' is used to find the circle that passes through three non-collinear points.

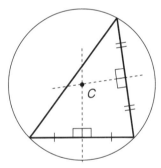

Take four non-collinear points A, B, C and D and draw the perpendicular bisectors of AB and CD. Is the point where they meet the centre of a circle that passes through A, B, C and D? Why does the method work for three points but not generally for four?

Draw a line AB of length 6 cm and mark on it the point X, where AX = 2 cm. Place a point C, not on AB, such that CX = 1 cm. Construct the point D such that CXD is a straight line and A, B, C and D lie on a circle.
Measure XD. How could you have calculated that result ?

There are an infinite number of points that C could be placed at. Describe the locus of D as C takes these positions.

EXERCISE 8.5 *(Miscellaneous)*

1 Find the value of *x* in each of the following cases and give a reason for each step in your calculation.

(a)

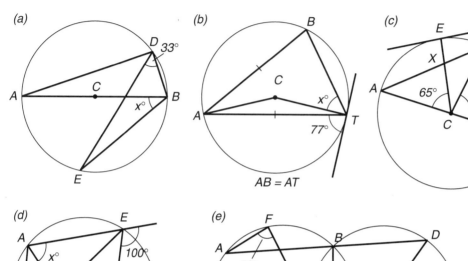

(b)

AB = AT

(c)

(d)

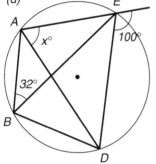

(e)

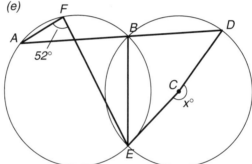

(f)

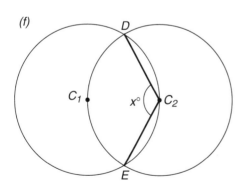

2 In the diagram, O is the centre of the circle, OABC is a rectangle, AC = 6 cm and CD = 2 cm.

(*a*) Find the radius of the circle.

(*b*) Calculate the area of the shaded region ABE.

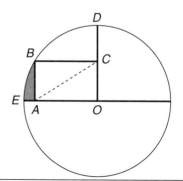

3 Look back to the diagram in Exercise 8.3, question 5.

(*a*) Write down the area of triangle ABC.

(*b*) Write down, in terms of *r*, the area of triangle AOB.

(*c*) By finding the area of triangle ABC in terms of *r*, calculate the value of *r*.

4 Construct a triangle with sides 6 cm, 8 cm and 10 cm.

(*a*) How do you know that the centre of the circle passing through the vertices of the triangle is at the mid-point of the 10-cm side?

(*b*) Construct the circle that touches all three sides.

(*c*) Calculate the radius of this circle.

5 The diagram shows the Big Wheel, of radius 4 m and centre O, at a fair. It is stationary and YOX is horizontal. Amy is in chair A, Latchmi is in chair B and Jamie is in chair C.

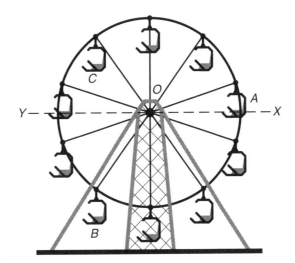

(*a*) State the value of angle AOC.

(*b*) Calculate the angle that Latchmi has to turn through in order to look from Jamie to Amy.

(*c*) Angle AOX = 20°. Calculate (i) the angle that OC makes with the vertical, (ii) angle BOY, (iii) the distance by which a sweet dropped to the ground by Jamie misses Latchmi.

(*d*) When the wheel starts to turn will the answer to (*b*) change?

6 A and B are two coastguard stations 10 km apart with B due east of A. The bearings of a yachtsman C from A and B are 030° and 320° respectively.

(*a*) Calculate angle ACB.

(*b*) If the yachtsman was in distress and the coastguards were told that angle ACB = 70° would they know where he was?

(*c*) Describe how you could construct a scale drawing of the arc of the circle that the yacht was on.

7 A steamer leaves a boarding point A on a lake and travels along part of a circle to another point B, 4 km due east of A. The point D on the trip is due north of A and on a bearing of 300° from B. The bearing from A of another point C on the trip is 050°. Calculate (*a*) the radius of the circle, (*b*) the bearing of C from B.

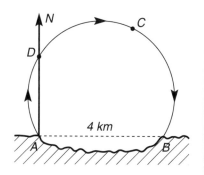

8 In the diagram, in which C is the centre of the circle, calculate (*a*) angle AQP (*b*) angle QAP (*c*) angle BCQ.

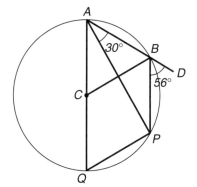

9 In the diagram, in which CT is a tangent and BC = BT, prove that triangle ACT is isosceles.

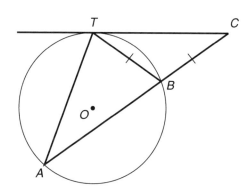

10 (*a*) For the diagram shown write down, in terms of *x*,
      (i) angle PQC (ii) angle PQD (iii) angle PBD.

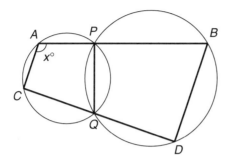

(*b*) What does (iii) tell you about the lines AC and BD?

(*c*) Test this result with several pairs of circles and various
      pairs of lines APQ and CQD.

11 The tangents to a circle at A and B meet at P and
angle BAP = 50°. The diameter BD, when extended,
cuts PA produced at C. Prove that angle CAD is four
times the angle ACD.

12 Three spheres, all of radius 6 cm, with centres A, B and C,
are placed on a horizontal table so that all touch each other.
A fourth equal sphere is placed symmetrically on top of the
three spheres, without disturbing their positions.

(*a*) In the plan (shown) of this arrangement, which is drawn
      on a plane through A, B and C, D is directly below the
      centre of the top sphere.
      (i) State the angles of triangle ABC.
      (ii) Calculate the length of AD.

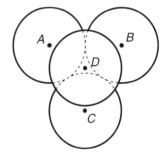

(*b*) Calculate the distance of D below the centre of the top
      sphere.

(*c*) How far is the highest part of the top sphere above the
      ground?

(*d*) Deduce the distance that the lowest part of the top sphere
      is above the ground.

Investigation E

A circle of radius r cm is inscribed in a square S, and square T is inscribed in the circle, as shown. Calculate the areas of S, T and the circle, in terms of r and deduce that $2 < \pi < 4$ ($4 \sin 45° \cos 45° < \pi < 4 \tan 45°$).

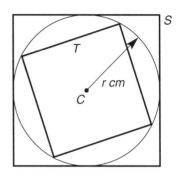

Show that the corresponding inequality for π when the circle is 'sandwiched' between its circumscribed and inscribed regular pentagons is $5 \sin 36° \cos 36° < \pi < 5 \tan 36°$ ($2.38 < \pi < 3.63$).

What inequality would you expect when equilateral triangles are used? Check whether your result is true. Suggest the inequality which would be derived if regular 20-sided figures are used.

This is one way in which an approximation for π can be found. Remember that it is an irrational number; any value we may use in a problem is only an approximation.

Look for other methods or formulae which produce approximations for π

Investigation F

The diagram shows an example of one of the circles, centre E, that Investigation B (page 153) was considering. DB, of length k, is the tangent common to the circles at their point of contact.

Let $OF = R$ and $CE = c$.

(*a*) Show that triangles BOF and ECB are similar.

(*b*) Deduce that $k^2 = Rc$.

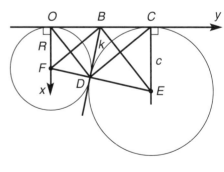

O is now taken as origin and x- and y-axes set as shown in the diagram.

(*c*) Show that the y-coordinate of E is $2k$.

The coordinates of E are therefore $x = \dfrac{k^2}{R}, y = 2k$.

(*d*) Deduce that the equation of the locus of the centres of circles that move so that they touch the fixed circle, centre F, and the fixed line OY has equation $y^2 = 4Rx$.

Extension work – the equation of a circle

A circle is the locus of a point that moves such that it is always the same distance from a fixed point, the centre of the circle. Only the position of the fixed point and the length of the radius, therefore, determine the circle. If the centre and radius are known, the equation of the circle can be found by relating a general point on the circle to this given data.

(1) Circle, centre the origin, radius r

Wherever P is on the locus, it is always true that

$$x^2 + y^2 = r^2,$$

using Pythagoras' theorem, and so this is the equation of this circle.

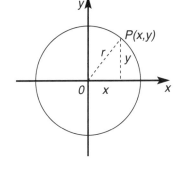

Example 2

(i) The circle with equation $x^2 + y^2 = 4$ has its centre at the origin and a radius of 2.

(ii) The equation $3x^2 + 3y^2 = 6$ represents a circle with its centre at the origin, since it can be written in the form $x^2 + y^2 = r^2$; its radius is $\sqrt{2}$.

(2) Circle, centre (a, b), radius r

Wherever P is on the locus, the length of CN will be $(x - a)$ or $(a - x)$ and the length of PN will be $(y - b)$ or $(b - y)$.
As $CN^2 + PN^2 = PC^2$ is always true, the equation of the circle is

$$(x - a)^2 + (y - b)^2 = r^2$$

If the equation of a curve can be arranged in this way, then it represents a circle, centre (a, b), radius r.

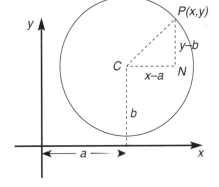

Note: (i) the coefficients of x^2 and y^2 must be the same,
 (ii) there is no term in products of x and y, for example xy, x^2y, and
 (iii) the right hand side of the equation is necessarily positive.

Example 3

The equation $(x - 5)^2 + (y + 2)^2 = 16$ is a circle, centre $(5, -2)$ and radius 4.

Example 4

Find the centre and radius of the circle whose equation is
$2x^2 + 2y^2 - 6x + 10y = 1$.

To arrange in the form above will require dividing through by 2 and
then use of 'completing the square':

$$2x^2 + 2y^2 - 6x + 10y = 1 \Rightarrow x^2 + y^2 - 3x + 5y = 0.5$$
$$\Rightarrow (x - 1.5)^2 + (y + 2.5)^2 = 0.5 + 2.25 + 6.25$$
$$\Rightarrow (x - 1.5)^2 + (y + 2.5)^2 = 9$$

The circle has centre $(1.5, -2.5)$ and radius 3.

EXERCISE 8.6

1 Write down the centre and radius of the following circles.

(a) $x^2 + y^2 = 9$ (b) $4x^2 + 4y^2 = 9$ (c) $y^2 = 2 - x^2$

(d) $(x - 1)^2 + (y - 3)^2 = 1$ (e) $(x + 7)^2 + (y - 2)^2 = 36$ (f) $x^2 + (y + 1)^2 = 8$

(g) $(x - 2)^2 + y^2 = 4$ (h) $(x - 4)^2 + 2y^2 = (1 + y)^2$ (i) $3x^2 + 3(2 - y)^2 = 4.5$

(j) $x^2 + y^2 - 2x + 10y = 10$ (k) $x^2 + y^2 + 6x = -8$ (l) $x^2 + y^2 + y = 3.75$

(m) $2x^2 + 2y^2 - 4x = 0$ (n) $2x^2 + 2y^2 - 4x - 12y + 3 = 0$

How can you tell from the equation (g) that the y-axis is a
tangent to that circle?

2 From the following set of equations choose those that represent
circles and, for each of these, find the centre and radius.

(a) $x^2 + y^2 = 3$ (b) $x^2 - y^2 = 3$

(c) $y^2 = 3 + x^2$ (d) $x^2 + 2y^2 = 4$

(e) $x^2 + (y - 2)^2 = 6$ (f) $x^2 + 2xy + y^2 = 9$

(g) $x^2 + y^2 - 2y + 1 = 0$ (h) $5x^2 + 5y^2 - 10x + 30y = 31$

(i) $y = x^2 + 9$

3 Sketch the circles with equations:

(a) $x^2 + y^2 = 1$ (b) $3x^2 + 3y^2 = 6$ (c) $x^2 + 2x + y^2 = 0$

In each case show the coordinates of the points of intersection
with the axes.

4 Find the equations of the circles shown.

(a)

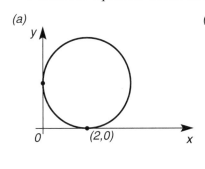

(b)

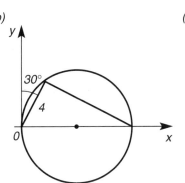

(c)

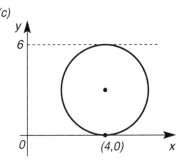

5 Draw a circle with centre (3, 5) and touching the x-axis. Write down the equation of the circle and deduce the coordinates of the points in which it crosses the y-axis.

6 Find the equation of the straight line that passes through the points in which the circle with equation $x^2 + y^2 = 16$ crosses the axes.

7 A circle passes through the points A(−2, 0) and B(4, 0).

(a) The centre lies on the line $x = k$. State the value of k.

The circle also passes through the point C(−2, 8).

(b) Write down the y coordinate of the centre.

(c) Calculate the radius of the circle.

(d) Write down the equation of the circle.

8 A circle *touches* both axes and has a radius of 6.

(a) Write down the equation of the circle.

The point on the circle closest to the origin is P.

(b) Explain why the x and y coordinates of P are equal, and find their values correct to 3 significant figures.

9 A circle C has equation $x^2 - 12x + y^2 - 6y + 36 = 0$.

(a) Find the radius of C.

(b) By putting $y = 0$ in the equation show that the x-axis is a tangent to C.

(*c*) Draw a sketch graph to show the circle.

(*d*) Show, by using trigonometry, that the angle between the two tangents to the circle drawn from O is about 53°.

10 The circle with equation $x^2 - 2x + y^2 - 4y - 3 = 0$, has its centre at the point C and radius of length r.

(*a*) Find the coordinates of C, and the value of r.

The points E and F have coordinates (3, 4) and (5, 2) respectively.

(*b*) Show that E lies on the circle.

(*c*) Find the distances EF and CF, and deduce that EF is a tangent to the circle.

9. Statistics

Information of many different kinds is communicated to us all the time through news bulletins, commercials, newspapers and by general conversation with others around us. Much of the information we gather and exchange is statistical. We need to be selective in our response to the almost continuous barrage of information being conveyed to us. For example, the information from air-traffic control to a pilot or the road signs which appear all the time to a driver or cyclist are vitally important. The advert which claims that eight out of ten cat-owners choose a certain make of catfood is directed at a large audience by a firm who hope that viewers will think, as a result of the commercial, that this is the one catfood they should buy for their cat.

Statistics is often defined as the collection, presentation and analysis of data. In our own studies we use statistical tables and charts in subjects such as Biology, Economics and Geography. In our daily lives we encounter interest rates, pie charts, bar charts, tourist exchange rates and opinion polls to mention just a few.

Sampling

Any statistical survey or investigation requires data about some characteristic of a population. The population may be people of a certain age group of those living in a certain country, district or town. The population could just as well be a species of reptiles in south–east Asia or the goods in a supermarket or the trees on an estate and so on. If all the members of the population are included in the collection of information, the investigation is known as a **census**. Our government holds a census every ten years, which includes all the residents of the UK, the last one being in 1991. This is an immensely time-consuming and expensive operation, and so it is usual for investigations to be conducted on a **sample** or **samples** of the whole population under consideration.

Investigation A

Using bar charts, pie charts and so on, as appropriate, display four different sets of data from the 1991 Census extract of Cardiff. (Public Libraries have this information.)

CARDIFF Communities – 1991 Profiles

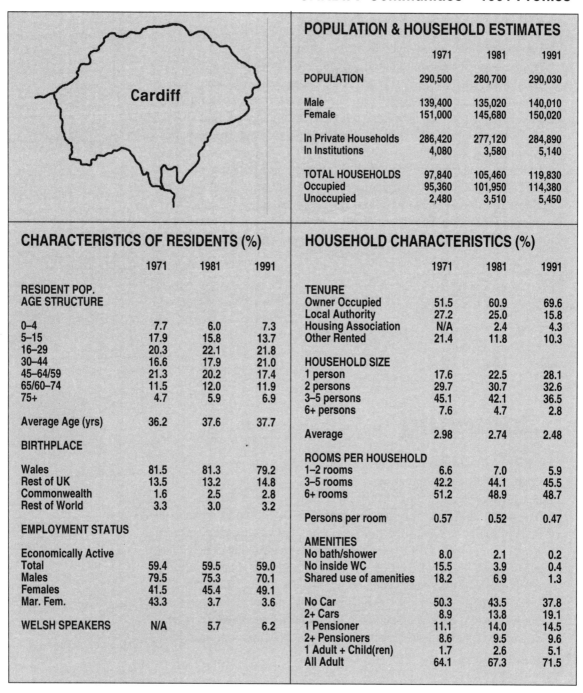

POPULATION & HOUSEHOLD ESTIMATES

	1971	1981	1991
POPULATION	290,500	280,700	290,030
Male	139,400	135,020	140,010
Female	151,000	145,680	150,020
In Private Households	286,420	277,120	284,890
In Institutions	4,080	3,580	5,140
TOTAL HOUSEHOLDS	97,840	105,460	119,830
Occupied	95,360	101,950	114,380
Unoccupied	2,480	3,510	5,450

CHARACTERISTICS OF RESIDENTS (%)

	1971	1981	1991
RESIDENT POP. AGE STRUCTURE			
0–4	7.7	6.0	7.3
5–15	17.9	15.8	13.7
16–29	20.3	22.1	21.8
30–44	16.6	17.9	21.0
45–64/59	21.3	20.2	17.4
65/60–74	11.5	12.0	11.9
75+	4.7	5.9	6.9
Average Age (yrs)	36.2	37.6	37.7
BIRTHPLACE			
Wales	81.5	81.3	79.2
Rest of UK	13.5	13.2	14.8
Commonwealth	1.6	2.5	2.8
Rest of World	3.3	3.0	3.2
EMPLOYMENT STATUS			
Economically Active Total	59.4	59.5	59.0
Males	79.5	75.3	70.1
Females	41.5	45.4	49.1
Mar. Fem.	43.3	3.7	3.6
WELSH SPEAKERS	N/A	5.7	6.2

HOUSEHOLD CHARACTERISTICS (%)

	1971	1981	1991
TENURE			
Owner Occupied	51.5	60.9	69.6
Local Authority	27.2	25.0	15.8
Housing Association	N/A	2.4	4.3
Other Rented	21.4	11.8	10.3
HOUSEHOLD SIZE			
1 person	17.6	22.5	28.1
2 persons	29.7	30.7	32.6
3–5 persons	45.1	42.1	36.5
6+ persons	7.6	4.7	2.8
Average	2.98	2.74	2.48
ROOMS PER HOUSEHOLD			
1–2 rooms	6.6	7.0	5.9
3–5 rooms	42.2	44.1	45.5
6+ rooms	51.2	48.9	48.7
Persons per room	0.57	0.52	0.47
AMENITIES			
No bath/shower	8.0	2.1	0.2
No inside WC	15.5	3.9	0.4
Shared use of amenities	18.2	6.9	1.3
No Car	50.3	43.5	37.8
2+ Cars	8.9	13.8	19.1
1 Pensioner	11.1	14.0	14.5
2+ Pensioners	8.6	9.5	9.6
1 Adult + Child(ren)	1.7	2.6	5.1
All Adult	64.1	67.3	71.5

Sample surveys, as they are called, are very popular. They are used by television companies to determine our viewing preferences, by Gallop and many others to determine our support, or otherwise, for government policies, and by food manufacturers to determine our reaction to some new product which they have introduced. Samples are taken of the manufactured articles coming off a production line to monitor the quality or to identify the number of articles with faults. Sample plots on agricultural land are taken to study the effects of fertilisers or pesticides on crops.

Often we wish to conduct sample surveys of our own and our methods should always apply the good practice followed by any major, responsible survey. Further, we need to be able to recognise and to criticise surveys and their 'conclusions' when insufficient care has been taken so that the results are at best dubious and more often completely misleading and fallacious.

The method of choosing a sample from the population is extremely important. Bias should be minimised. We want a situation in which each member of the population has an equal chance of being selected as one of the sample. A procedure which ensures this is called **random sampling**. The process itself can be long and complicated when the size of the population is large.

We first illustrate how to find a random sample in two different ways when the population is relatively small.

Example 1

A village has 87 residents on the electoral roll. Two students, Ranjit and Frances, each required a random sample of ten residents for their Geography project.

They allocated all of the residents a number from 1–87 so that each resident had a different number.
Ranjit wrote 87 cards, numbered from 1–87, and placed them in a bag. He then asked a friend to pick out ten of the mixed-up cards from the bag to give his sample. Frances used her calculator to generate a list of 2-digit random numbers. She obtained

   09, 45, 89, 81, 66, 37, 75, 09, 17, 50, 93, 23, 07, ...

Frances rejected 89, 93 and the second 09 and she took as her sample

   09, 45, 81, 66, 37, 75, 17, 50, 23, 07

Each of the students then had a random sample of ten residents and all residents, both those selected and those who were not, had been fairly selected or rejected by both approaches.

Example 2

Pancombe is a town with 30 000 people on the electoral roll. The town council has a development grant to build a recreational centre. Suggestions for the centre include a swimming pool, a mini-theatre, a fitness centre, a multi-purpose hall, squash courts, an indoor bowling green and a youth club. Financial restraints mean that only some of these items can be included.

In order to survey the strength of local opinion about what should be included, the council require a sample of 5% of the population, that is 1500 people, to be consulted. The following method was used to select the sample.

The members on the roll were numbered 1, 2, 3, ..., 30 000. As 1500 members were required in the sample, the roll was subdivided into 50 groups, each containing 600 members. A table of random numbers was used to select three members at random from the first group of 600.

The sample was then completed by selecting three members in the remaining 49 groups whose positions corresponded to the members selected at random from the first group.

This method is called **systematic sampling** and it provides a sample which is a fair representation of the population. Simple random sampling on a population of even this size would prove both cumbersome and very expensive.

Example 3

A survey is to be conducted to determine the main out-of-school activities of the 1000 children attending a local comprehensive school. It is decided that the sample should contain 10% of the school population.

In order to ensure that all age groups and both sexes are fairly represented in the sample, the following procedure is adopted.

The school population is tabulated in Years and 10% of each year is shared between boys and girls as shown.

The total sample will contain 49 boys and 51 girls and, in each year, the sample boys and girls will be selected by random sampling in their respective peer group.

This method of sample selection is known as **stratified random sampling**. This method of random selection has the important advantage of ensuring that the sample is representative of the whole population.

Year	Total Boys	Total Girls	Sample size Boys	Sample size Girls
7	70	80	7	8
8	74	76	7	8
9	79	71	8	7
10	68	82	7	8
11	78	72	8	7
12	66	84	7	8
13	50	50	5	5

A note on bias

Bias can occur in any sample but particularly so if
1. an unsound sampling method has been used,
2. the sample is unrepresentative of its population.

Example 4

If you were conducting an investigation into the nation's views on gambling, sampling those leaving a betting shop after a race would almost certainly give a biased sample.

Questionnaires are often used to obtain data from a sample of people. The questions should be straightforward, concise, relevant and not designed to cause offence or create bias. The responses required should be definitive, that is yes/no or with alternative boxes where one only needs to be ticked.

EXERCISE 9.1

1 Show how to obtain a random sample of eight letters from the 26 letters of the alphabet.

2 Postal questionnaires are often used to collect data. Outline the advantages and disadvantages of this method.

3 A survey is planned by the students in a Year 11 class to investigate the incidence of violent scenes in 'News at Ten' on TV. Explain any advantages or disadvantages which could occur by sampling the news programme

(*a*) on the same evening of the week for 5 weeks,

(*b*) from Monday to Friday in a particular week,

(*c*) on one day at random each week for 5 weeks.

4 The students in Year 11 intend to run a survey to investigate the TV viewing patterns of members of their school on sporting activities. How would you choose samples for this? Construct a suitable questionnaire which could be used for the investigation. Should boys and girls be sampled separately? If so, why?

5 Explain the meaning of the term 'a random sample'. A random sample of 12 is required from a school year containing 94 students. By using a set of random numbers

(a) explain carefully how you would select a suitable sample,

(b) explain what changes, if any, you would adopt if the year size was 123.

6 Explain what is meant by the term 'systematic sampling'. A random sample of 1000 is required from a population of 50 000. Explain how a method of systematic sampling could be applied to achieve this.

7 Explain the importance of stratified random sampling when members can be sorted into non-overlapping subsets, called strata, of the whole population.

Explain how this method could be applied to obtain a random sample of 4% of the 1000 members of a Tennis Club, where the strata are: playing male members (250), playing female members (350), social members (300) and life members (100).

8 A survey is planned to investigate the video-viewing habits of unemployed people in a village with just one shop, where videos may be bought or hired. A sample, taken from those who visit this shop, is used to provide the information for the survey. Comment critically on the method used to select this sample and suggest ways in which an alternative and more representative sample could be chosen.

9 Outline briefly the precautions that should be taken when designing a questionnaire to ensure that the replies are as truthful and unbiased as possible.

Further illustrate your answer by showing a questionnaire which you have designed and naming the project for which it was used.

10 Gavin and Sam are investigating whether shops should

(a) stay open to a later time on evenings in the week,

(b) open on Sundays.

Gavin decides to ask the following question to as many people as he can on Saturday morning in the High Street:

'Do you think that shops should be made to keep open until 8.30 p.m. so that people who work in offices and factories can do their shopping after work during the week?'

Sam asks the following question to people in the High Street quite near the Church on Sunday morning.

'Do you think that the shops should open on Sundays so that people who work in offices and factories can do their shopping on Saturdays or Sundays as they wish?'

Comment critically on their choice of samples and on their way of asking questions.

   Construct a single questionnaire which could include both questions and suggest possible samples of the town's population who might be questioned and who would be less biased.

11 A survey is planned to investigate the lunches chosen by the production workers at the staff canteen. It was decided to select and record the menu chosen by every 20th worker on the first Tuesday of each month. Comment on and criticise this procedure for collecting data. Propose a better method of sampling this population.

12 The views of a sample of people living on an estate was needed for a planning enquiry. The person in charge of the sampling visited the estate on a Wednesday morning and questioned an occupant from every fifth house. If no occupant at that house was available, he tried the next house until he found someone at home.

Comment critically on this sampling process.

13 As part of an industrial work experience project, a manufacturer asks a group of pupils from Year 11 in a school to undertake an investigation to determine whether there is a relation between a person's hand-span and length of foot. The students took (i) results from their class, and (ii) a random stratified sample of 30 from the whole school.

For each sample they recorded for each member

(*a*) the hand-span (x cm)

(*b*) the length of the foot (y cm).

They then plotted the pairs (x, y) of the results from (i) and (ii) as separate scatter graphs and wrote up their findings for the manufacturer.

Undertake this project as if you were the participating class from Year 11. Write a suitable report of your findings for the manufacturer.

Investigation B

Many forms of sampling are used in industry and commerce. Research and then write short notes on (*a*) quota sampling, (*b*) cluster sampling, and (*c*) purposive sampling.

Investigation C

What are pilot surveys? Why are they used?

Presenting and processing data

Data may be either quantitative or qualitative and numerical data can be either continuous or discrete.

Example 5

In an international women's 100-metre race, we have

(*a*) the nationality of each runner is a qualitative variable,

(*b*) the number of runners taking part is an integer, that is a discrete variable,

(*c*) the time taken by each runner to complete the race is a continuous variable in the interval 10–13 s, say.

At this point we revise briefly and then extend the work covered in Book 3y on measures of central position and dispersion by considering some examples.

Discrete variables

Consider the following set of discrete data collected from the records of the Fire Service.

The number of emergency calls each hour received by a City Fire Station over a 12-hour period was

  6, 5, 3, 14, 9, 15, 3, 5, 12, 7, 12, 5.

We use this data in the following work to illustrate the methods used in finding measures of central position and dispersion for discrete data.

  Each example is preceded by a short general description of the measure being discussed.

The median

The median is obtained by writing all of the members in order of size and then selecting the middle member when the total frequency is odd, or the two middle members when the frequency is even. In the first case the median is the middle member, and in the second case the median is the mean of the two middle members.

Example 6

We arrange the Fire Station data in ascending order, that is:

3, 3, 5, 5, 5, 6, 7, 9, 12, 12, 14, 15

and note that there are 12 members, that is the frequency is 12. The middle members in order of size are 6 and 7 (underlined). The median number of calls per hour is the mean of 6 and 7, that is

$$\text{median} = \frac{6+7}{2} = 6.5 \text{ calls/hour}$$

Interquartile range

First the data is arranged in size order, smallest first. The **lower quartile** of a distribution is the point at which one-quarter of the members are below and three-quarters are above it. The **upper quartile** has one-quarter above and three-quarters of the members below it.

The **interquartile range** (IQR) = upper quartile − lower quartile. The IQR provides us with a measure of dispersion of the data. Note that 50% of the members are in the IQR.

Example 7

The 12 members in size order can be divided into four equal parts each containing three members; this makes the lower quartile 5 and the upper quartile 12.

In this case then, IQR = 12 − 5 = 7.

The mode

The mode is the member that occurs most often in the data.

Example 8

The number of calls per hour which occurred most often was 5. Hence the mode number of calls = 5 per hour.

The mean

The mean is the common average obtained by dividing the sum of all the members in the list by the frequency.

Example 9

The mean number of calls $= \dfrac{\text{sum of all calls}}{\text{frequency}}$

$\phantom{\text{The mean number of calls}} = \dfrac{96}{12}$

$\phantom{\text{The mean number of calls}} = 8$ calls per hour

The mean is the most important measure of central position for a set of discrete data and for frequency distributions. Unlike the median and the mode, neither of which are used much in extensions of the current work, the **mean**, together with a measure of dispersion called the **standard deviation**, is used widely in the analysis of distributions.

The standard deviation

The standard deviation of a list of N numbers

$x_1, x_2, \ldots x_N$

is found by using the following four steps:

1. Determine the mean of the numbers $\bar{x}$ by using

$$\bar{x} = \frac{x_1 + x_2 + \ldots + x_N}{N}$$

2. Take each of the N numbers in turn and subtract it from $\bar{x}$ to get the N numbers $(\bar{x} - x_1), (\bar{x} - x_2), \ldots (\bar{x} - x_N)$.

3. Square each of these numbers, add the squares and then divide by N. That is, you are finding the mean of these squares, called the **variance** of the N numbers.

4. Take the square root of the variance. This square root is the **standard deviation**.

Example 10

In calculations of the standard deviation, the working should be tabulated. Continuing then from Example 9, where the mean, $\bar{x}$, is 8, we have:

The variance $= \dfrac{200}{12} = 16.67$.
The standard deviation $= \sqrt{16.67} = 4.08$.

No. of calls (x)	($\bar{x} - x$)	$(\bar{x} - x)^2$
3	5	25
3	5	25
5	3	9
5	3	9
5	3	9
6	2	4
7	1	1
9	−1	1
12	−4	16
12	−4	16
14	−6	36
15	−7	49
	Total	200

The working in these calculations of the mean and the standard deviation can be shortened by writing the data as a frequency distribution as shown in Example 11.

Example 11

No. of calls x	Frequency f	fx	x^2	fx^2
3	2	6	9	18
5	3	15	25	75
6	1	6	36	36
7	1	7	49	49
9	1	9	81	81
12	2	24	144	288
14	1	14	196	196
15	1	15	225	225
	$\Sigma f = 12$	$\Sigma fx = 96$		$\Sigma fx^2 = 968$

The Σ notation is extremely useful, for example, Σf means the sum of all the frequencies, and similarly Σfx and Σfx^2 represent the totals as shown.

The mean $= \dfrac{\Sigma fx}{\Sigma f} = \dfrac{96}{12} = 8.$

The variance $= \dfrac{\Sigma fx^2}{\Sigma f} - \left(\dfrac{\Sigma fx}{\Sigma f}\right)^2 = \dfrac{968}{12} - 64 = 16.67.$

The standard deviation $= \sqrt{(16.67)} = 4.08.$

This alternative formula for the variance, $\dfrac{\Sigma fx^2}{\Sigma f} - \left(\dfrac{\Sigma fx}{\Sigma f}\right)^2$,

is important and should be memorised because it saves considerable time and avoids complicated calculations.

Investigation D

By reading the manual of your calculator, find out how to use the Σx and Σx^2 buttons as well as how you can find the mean and the standard deviation of a list of numbers directly from your calculator. Once you are familiar with these additional facilities on your calculator (or computer) use them to check the answers obtained in Examples 9 and 10. Remember the Σ sign is a shorthand way of writing, or saying, 'the sum of all the … '.

$\displaystyle\sum_{r-1}^{n} x_r$ means the sum of all the n numbers from x_1 to x_n, that is, $x_1 + x_2 + x_3 + \ldots + x_n$.

Continuous variables

The values taken by a continuous variable are often placed in class intervals to form a **frequency distribution**. It is essential that the class intervals are defined so that no value can fall in two intervals. As with the work on discrete variables, we consolidate and extend the work on continuous variables by illustrative examples.

The frequency distribution below has been tabulated from data collected by a biologist and recorded in her fieldbook about the lengths of 100 mackerel landed by fishermen in a trawl. The length of each fish was measured to the nearest millimetre and the frequency distribution was made up, as shown.

Note: The class intervals are defined so that there are no overlaps and no gaps.

Length of fish (L cm)	Frequency (f)
$27 \leq L < 29$	2
$29 \leq L < 31$	4
$31 \leq L < 33$	8
$33 \leq L < 35$	21
$35 \leq L < 37$	30
$37 \leq L < 39$	18
$39 \leq L < 41$	12
$41 \leq L < 43$	5
	$\Sigma f = 100$

Example 12

Histogram with equal class intervals

The data could be displayed by the histogram in which the *area* of each rectangle is proportional to the frequency.

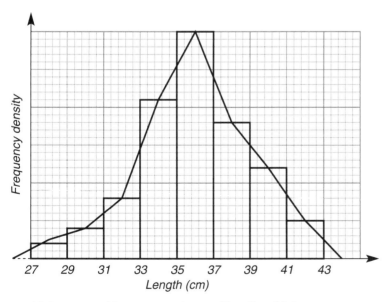

Histogram and frequency polygon of lengths of fish

The **frequency polygon** is obtained by joining the mid-points of the top side of each rectangle.

Example 13

Histrogram with unequal class intervals

The given data could be reclassified, as shown in the table, so that we have unequal class intervals.

Length	$27 \leq L < 35$	$35 \leq L < 37$	$37 \leq L < 39$	$39 \leq L < 43$
Frequency	35	30	18	17
Height of rectangle in histogram	$\dfrac{35}{8}$	$\dfrac{30}{2}$	$\dfrac{18}{2}$	$\dfrac{17}{4}$

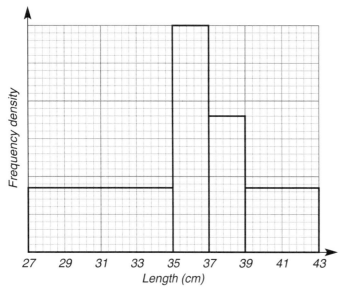

Histogram of length of fish

Example 14

Cumulative frequency curve (ogive)

The data can be reclassified as a cumulative frequency distribution.

L	$27 \leq L < 29$	<31	<33	<35	<37	<39	<41	<43
C.f.	2	6	14	35	65	83	95	100

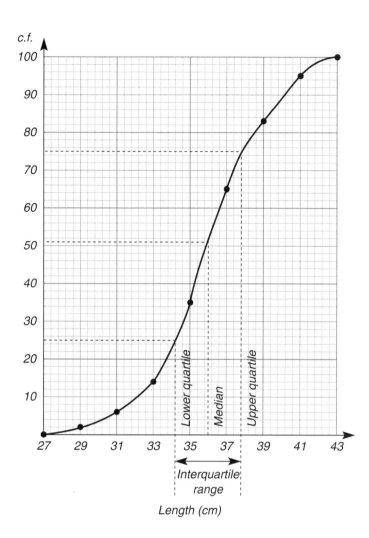

The cumulative frequencies are plotted at the top end of each interval.

Median = 36 cm
IQR   = (37.4 − 34.2) cm
        = 3.2 cm

Mean and standard deviation

The method used to calculate the mean and the standard deviation of continuous data, represented by a frequency distribution, is similar to that shown in Example 11, the only difference being that, with continuous data, *each class interval is represented by its mid-interval value*.

Example 15

Interval in which fish of length L cm lies	Mid-interval value m	Frequency f	fm	m^2	fm^2
$27 \leq L < 29$	28	2	56	784	1 568
$29 \leq L < 31$	30	4	120	900	3 600
$31 \leq L < 33$	32	8	256	1024	8 192
$33 \leq L < 35$	34	21	714	1156	24 276
$35 \leq L < 37$	36	30	1080	1296	38 880
$37 \leq L < 39$	38	18	684	1444	25 992
$39 \leq L < 41$	40	12	480	1600	19 200
$41 \leq L < 43$	42	5	210	1764	8 820
		$\Sigma f = 100$	$\Sigma fm = 3600$		$\Sigma fm^2 = 130\ 528$

$$\text{Estimate of mean} = \frac{\Sigma fm}{\Sigma f} = \frac{3600}{100} = 36.$$

$$\text{Estimate of variance} = \frac{\Sigma fm^2}{\Sigma f} - \left(\frac{\Sigma fm}{\Sigma f}\right)^2$$

$$= \frac{130\ 528}{100} - 36^2$$

$$= 9.28$$

Estimate of standard deviation $= \sqrt{(9.28)} = 3.046$.

The 100 mackerel have a mean length of 36 cm with a standard deviation of about 3 cm.

When making calculations from a frequency distribution, we can only give estimates of the mean and the standard deviation of the members in the distribution because some of the accuracy of the data is lost when placed in class intervals. The calculations shown in Example 15 can be shortened and made more elegant by a process known as **coding**.

Example 16

Mid-interval value m	Frequency f	New variable			
		x	fx	x^2	fx^2
28	2	−3	−6	9	18
30	4	−2	−8	4	16
32	8	−1	−8	1	8
34	21	0	0	0	0
36	30	1	30	1	30
38	18	2	36	4	72
40	12	3	36	9	108
42	5	4	20	16	80
Totals	100		−22 + 122		332

We have then $\Sigma f = 100$, $\Sigma fx = 122 - 22 = 100$, $\Sigma fx^2 = 332$.

The variables m and x are related by the equation $m = 34 + 2x$.

Estimate of mean of $x = \dfrac{\Sigma fx}{\Sigma f} = \dfrac{100}{100} = 1$.

Using the equation, mean of $m = 34 + 2 \times 1 = 36$.

Variance of $x = \dfrac{\Sigma fx^2}{\Sigma f} - \left(\dfrac{\Sigma fx}{\Sigma f}\right)^2$

$= \dfrac{332}{100} - \left(\dfrac{100}{100}\right)^2$

$= 2.32$.

Standard deviation of $x = \sqrt{(2.32)} = 1.523$.

Since $m = 2x + 34$, the m values are on a scale which is twice the x values, so the m values are twice as spread out.
Hence the standard deviation of the m values is 2×1.523, which gives the result as 3.046, the same as we obtained by the method requiring heavier calculation.

The method of coding data, as shown in Example 16, can reduce quite substantially the complexity of arithmetic in calculations of the mean and the standard deviation of a frequency distribution.

Linearly transformed data

A set of data, X, is used to form a new set of data, Y, by a linear transformation such as $y = ax + b$, where a and b are fixed numbers, called **constants**. The mean and standard deviations are given by:

The mean of $Y = a \times$ (mean of X) + b, that is $\bar{y} = a\bar{x} + b$.
The standard deviation of $Y = a \times$ (the standard deviation of X),
that is, $s_y = a\, s_x$, where s_x, and s_y are the standard deviations.

Example 17

Find the mean and the standard deviation of the set of numbers

$$A = \{1, 2, 3, 4, 5, 6, 7, 8, 9\}$$

Hence write down the mean and the standard deviation (SD) of

$$B = \{22, 23, 24, 25, 26, 27, 28, 29, 30\}$$
$$C = \{15, 30, 45, 60, 75, 90, 105, 120, 135\}$$
$$D = \{-7, 7, 21, 35, 49, 63, 77, 91, 105\}$$

By inspection, the mean of $A = 5$.

The standard deviation of $A = \sqrt{\left[\frac{2(16 + 9 + 4 + 1)}{9}\right]} = 2.58$.

Members of sets A and B are related by $b = a + 21$.
The mean of B is $21 + 5 = 26$, the SDs of A and B are equal ($= 2.58$).

Members of sets A and C are related by $c = 15a$.
The mean of C is $15 \times 5 = 75$ and the SD of C is $15 \times 2.58 = 38.7$.

Members of sets A and D are related by $d = 15a - (a + 21)$
$$= 14a - 21.$$

The mean of $D = 14 \times 5 - 21 = 49$.
The SD of $D = 14 \times$ (SD of A) $= 14 \times 2.58 = 36.12$.

EXERCISE 9.2

1 The pie chart, of radius 5 cm, shows the proportions of the ingredients in a cake which contained 2 lb of flour. Calculate

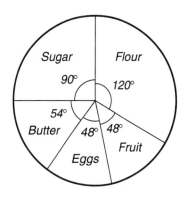

(*a*) the amount of sugar in the cake,

(*b*) the total mass of the cake.

A similar cake of total mass 13.5 lb was made and the cakes were represented by similar pie charts.

(*c*) Find the radius of the larger pie chart.

2 Calculate the mean and the standard deviation of the five numbers: 3, 4, 9, 10, 14.

Deduce the mean and the standard deviation of

(*a*) 12, 16, 36, 40, 56

(*b*) 12, 13, 18, 19, 23

3 A market gardener grew 50 conifer cuttings and the heights (*h* cm) after a year are given by the cumulative frequency distribution, shown in the table.

h	$0 < h < 20$	<30	<40	<50	<80	<120
C.f.	2	6	16	32	44	50

Determine the median and the interquartile range.
Draw a histogram to display the frequency distribution.

4 The lengths of 30 copper pipes were each measured to the nearest cm and recorded in the table.

Length (cm)	107	109	111	113
Frequency	4	12	9	5

Calculate (*a*) the median, (*b*) the mean, (*c*) the standard deviation of the lengths.

5 Yvonne was asked to count the contents of a sample of 50 boxes of matches at the DIY store where she works. Her results were:

No. of matches	42	43	44	45	46	47	48
Frequency	10	6	20	6	5	2	1

Find the mean and the standard deviation.
Yvonne was asked to phone through her results to Ann at another store for checking. Unfortunately Ann recorded the frequencies so that they were the reverse of Yvonne's table. Find the mean and the standard deviation of Ann's distribution and comment on the answers.

6 Find the mean and the standard deviation of the three lists of marks:

(a) 4, 5, 5, 6, 8, 8, 9, 11

(b) 7, 8, 8, 9, 11, 11, 12, 14

(c) 12, 15, 15, 18, 24, 24, 27, 33

Comment on any connections you have found.

7 The masses of some Bramley apples from my garden were recorded as shown.

Mass (m grams)	Frequency	Mass (m grams)	Frequency
$120 \leq m < 130$	1	$160 \leq m < 170$	15
$130 \leq m < 140$	4	$170 \leq m < 180$	12
$140 \leq m < 150$	7	$180 \leq m < 190$	8
$150 \leq m < 160$	10	$190 \leq m < 200$	0
		$200 \leq m < 210$	3

Find the mean mass and the standard deviation.

8 Two new varieties, V_1 and V_2, of tomato plants were compared by recording the number of tomatoes on the first truss of a plant, with the following results:

	No. of tomatoes on first truss of 12 plants
V_1	1, 2, 2, 4, 4, 5, 7, 8, 9, 10, 10, 10
V_2	3, 4, 5, 5, 6, 6, 6, 6, 7, 7, 8, 9

Find the standard deviation in each case. Based on this evidence would you feel able to recommend either variety in preference to the other. Write your answer in the form of a short report.

9 On a particular date, an ornithologist obtained the following discrete distribution from observation of 100 starlings' nests:

No. of eggs	0	1	2	3	4	5	6	7	8 or more
No. of nests	2	2	5	25	30	25	9	2	0

Calculate (*a*) the mean number of eggs per nest, (*b*) the standard deviation, (*c*) the interquartile range.

10 The marks awarded by an army initiative test are on a scale from 10 to 50 with all marks being whole numbers. The marks awarded to 30 recruits were:

38	35	32	16	48	45
25	21	34	18	11	23
23	27	16	49	13	18
30	28	24	40	27	30
27	26	28	43	19	33

Using class intervals of 10–14, 15–19, 20–29, 30–49, construct a frequency distribution and draw a histogram to represent these data.

Estimate the median of the distribution and compare this answer with the actual median, found from the original 30 marks.

11 The cumulative frequency curve of a distribution, when drawn, is the same as the line $y = 2x$ from $x = 0$ to $x = 50$. Given that the frequency is 100, find a frequency distribution which could give this cumulative frequency curve.

12 The marks scored by 200 pupils in each of two English examinations are given in the table as frequency distributions.

Mark range	1–25	26–50	51–75	76–100
Exam 1 frequency	38	79	66	17
Exam 2 frequency	21	58	89	32

(*a*) Using the same axes, draw the frequency polygons.

(*b*) Using the same axes, draw the ogives (c.f. curves).

(*c*) Determine the mean and the standard deviation of each distribution.

13 The masses, in kg, of 100 eighteen-year-old men on their entry to university are given in the table of cumulative frequencies.

Mass (kg)	≤60	≤80	≤100	≤120	≤140	≤160	≤180	≤200	≤220
C.f.	0	3	10	25	44	72	88	99	100

Draw the C.f. curve (the ogive) and hence estimate (*a*) the median, (*b*) the interquartile range, (*c*) the probability that a man selected at random from this group has a mass between 128 kg and 182 kg.

14 The ten members of an archery club each took five shots at a fixed target with a new type of crossbow. The distance that each shot landed from the bull was recorded to the nearest cm, as shown in the data table.

72	64	61	51	21	51	2	44	73	5
83	78	51	91	83	41	81	59	66	65
43	61	90	51	49	80	57	79	92	84
63	71	48	89	11	61	12	58	49	28
75	65	42	78	84	25	47	62	81	36

(*a*) Complete the cumulative frequency distribution started below for these data.

Distance from bull	≤9.5	≤19.5	≤29.5	. . .	≤99.5
C.f.	2	4	7		50

(*b*) By drawing a suitable graph, estimate the median and the range of values in which the middle 40% of the shots lie.

15 Make up a frequency table for the data in question 14 and use it to find estimates of the mean and the standard deviation of the 50 shots.

16 Draw accurate histograms to illustrate the data given in the following tables for distributions (*a*) and (*b*).

(*a*) Ages of 30 passengers on a charter flight:

Age	$0 \leq x < 10$	$10 \leq x < 20$	$20 \leq x < 35$	$35 \leq x < 60$
Frequency	2	6	12	10

(*b*) Heights of 36 French-bean plants:

Height (*h* cm)	$0 \leq h < 20$	$20 \leq h < 30$	$30 \leq h < 35$	$35 \leq h < 50$
Frequency	6	10	14	6

17 Find estimates for the mean and the standard deviation of the distributions in question 16.

18 The marks of ten students in an Electronics exam and in a CDT exam are shown in the table.

Electronics	68	53	69	75	57	66	79	71	63	59
CDT	58	47	74	86	41	52	68	83	61	65

Plot the pairs of marks obtained as a scatter graph and draw in a line of best fit.

Jo scored 50 for CDT but she was absent for the Electronics exam. Use the line you have drawn to find a suitable estimated mark for Jo in the exam she missed.

19 The following pairs of values (x, y) were observed in a series of five trials in an investigation concerning quality control.

x	5	9	13	31	48
y	19	24	29	53	73

By plotting each of the five pairs show that a relation of the form $y = ax + b$ appears to approximately fit these data and estimate a value for a and for b.

20 Gareth is a racing driver and he agreed to take part in an investigation between speed and stopping distance, the distance covered after a random signal to brake as hard as possible has been given. The following results were obtained.

Speed (km/h)	50	60	70	80	90	100
Stopping distance (m)	46	66	90	118	148	183

It is suspected that the distance, d metres, is related to the speed, v km/h, by the equation $d = A + Bv^2$. By drawing a graph of d against v^2, verify this and hence determine values for the constants A and B. Hence find an estimate of the distance that Gareth would need to stop from a speed of 30 km/h.

Why does it appear from the relation, $d = A + Bv^2$, that Gareth needs time to stop from a standstill? Explain this apparent contradiction.

21 Draw a sketch of a scatter graph which shows (*a*) positive correlation, (*b*) negative correlation. In each case suggest two sets of data which could give rise to such a graph.

22 An experiment gave rise to pairs of values (x, y) as shown.

Values of x	1	2	3	4	5	7	8
Values of y	30	26	22	20	16	12	8

Plot these pairs of values as a scatter graph and add a line of best fit.
Hence express the relation between x and y in the form $y = mx + c$ giving estimates of the constants m and c.

Investigation E

When numerical data are recorded at fixed intervals of time, for example in total weekly sales figures, a **time series** is formed. Investigate time series and how **moving averages** can assist in analysing a time series.

Investigation F

Investigate the accuracy of the national weather forecast for
(*a*) tomorrow, (*b*) the day after tomorrow. Keep records over a month at least. Are any patterns evident? For example, is the forecasting more accurate when the wind is in a particular direction?

Investigation G

The percentage of trains which run to time, together with those which are late, is often given in a large station. Write up plans for a survey which could check the accuracy of the information supplied by the railway management and how you would conduct this survey at a large station.

The normal distribution

As larger and larger sizes of samples are taken, the frequency polygons of many distributions associated with natural phenomena tend to be bell-shaped curves. These are shown over the page, together with the histograms.

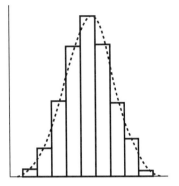 

The fishermen catching a particular species year after year, such as
the mackerel in Examples 12 and 13, would expect adult fish to have
a mean length of about 35 cm with a standard deviation of about
5 cm. They would not expect many to be longer than 45 cm or shorter
than 25 cm.

In the same way, we should not expect to meet many 7-foot men,
even at Twickenham among the 55 000 people attending an
international.

The shape of any normal distribution is dependent only on its mean
and its standard deviation.
The mean gives the position of the axis of symmetry and the standard
deviation determines the spread about the mean.

Irrespective of the shape, the *area* under a normal curve always has
certain properties. A normal distribution curve has:

1. 68% of its area within 1 standard deviation of the
    mean.

2. 95% of its area within 2 standard deviations of the
    mean,

3. 99.7% of its area within 3 standard deviations of the
    mean.

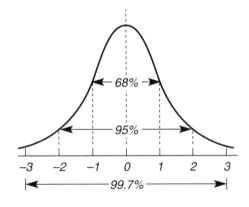

In order to facilitate calculations, all statisticians use the
standard normal curve, which has mean 0 and standard
deviation 1; this gives the total area between the curve
and the *x*-axis as 1. A set of tables is available from
which the area *A*, shown in the diagram on the next page,
can be determined. We give a summary of the table
which is sufficient for all of our calculations at this stage.

x	0.0	0.1	0.2	0.3	0.4	0.5	0.6	0.7	0.8	0.9	
A	0.000	0.040	0.079	0.118	0.155	0.192	0.226	0.258	0.288	0.316	
x	1.0	1.1	1.2	1.3	1.4	1.5	1.6	1.7	1.8	1.9	
A	0.341	0.364	0.385	0.403	0.419	0.433	0.445	0.455	0.464	0.471	
x	2.0	2.1	2.2	2.3	2.4	2.5	2.6	2.7	2.8	2.9	3.0
A	0.477	0.482	0.486	0.489	0.492	0.494	0.495	0.497	0.497	0.498	0.499

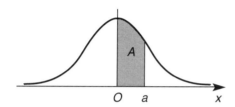

The normal probability curve with the area denoted by A

The unit on the x-axis is 1 standard deviation.
The value of A gives the probability that a member of the
distribution lies in the interval $0 \leq x \leq a$.

Example 18

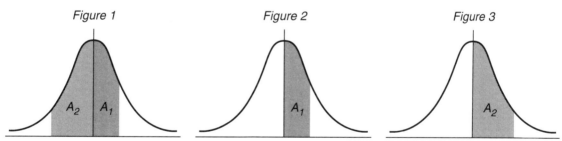

Because of the symmetrical property of the normal curve, the area
shown in figure 1 is the sum of the areas shown in figures 2 and 3.

Example 19

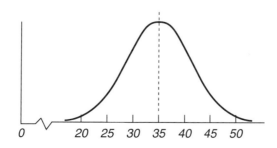

The diagram shows the normal distribution of a species of fish whose mean is 35 cm with a standard deviation of 5 cm.

The standard normal distribution has mean 0 and standard deviation 1, and we need to adjust the data for the fish to this scale, The mean moves to 0 and the scale factor on the x-axis is 5 (from the standard deviation).

A fish of length u cm is equivalent to a length $\dfrac{u-35}{5}$

on the x-scale. For example a fish of length 40 cm is at a distance of 1 standard deviation from its mean. The transformation which brings data u from a normal distribution into line with the data x of the standard normal distribution is

$$x = \frac{u - \text{mean}}{\text{standard deviation}}.$$

Once this has been done, the standard tables can be used.
For example, let us suppose that a fish is taken at random.
The probability that this fish is longer than 40 cm has the same probability as the standard normal variate, x, being greater than 1.

From the tables, we have

$$P\,(u < 40) = P\,(x < 1) = 0.5 + 0.341 = 0.841.$$
$$P\,(u > 40) = P\,(x > 1) = 1 - P\,(x < 1) = 1 - 0.841 = 0.159.$$

Similarly the probability that a fish taken at random is less than 28 cm is given by:

$$P\,(u < 28) = P(x < \frac{28 - 35}{5})$$
$$= P\,(x < -1.4)$$
$$= P\,(x > 1.4) \text{ (from the symmetry of the curve)}$$
$$= 1 - 0.5 - 0.419 = 0.081$$

Further, the probability that a fish taken at random has a length between 28 cm and 40 cm is given by

$$P\,(28 < u < 40) = P\,(-1.4 < x < 1) = 1 - 0.159 - 0.081 = 0.76$$

When solving questions using the normal tables, it is advisable to draw a sketch diagram and shade the region required.

Investigation H

Here are two distributions which are not normal but which often occur in practice.

(a)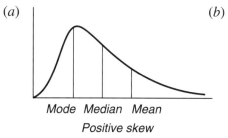

Mode Median Mean

Positive skew

(b)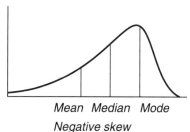

Mean Median Mode

Negative skew

Find two sets of data for (a) and (b) which could result in the type of distribution shown.

EXERCISE 9.3

1 For the standard normal distribution with variable x, find the value of

(a) P $(x > 2)$ (b) P $(x < -1.5)$ (c) P $(-1.5 < x < 2)$

2 The variable y is normally distributed with mean 20 and standard deviation 4. Find the value of

(a) P $(y > 30)$ (b) P $(y > 22)$ (c) P $(22 < y < 30)$

3 The variable z is normally distributed with mean 1000 and standard deviation 100. Find the value of

(a) P $(820 < z < 980)$ (b) P $(920 < z < 1060)$

4 In separate diagrams, sketch the normal distributions which have:

	Mean	Standard deviation
(a)	16	2
(b)	−16	2
(c)	16	16

In each case, mark on your axis, 3 standard-deviation steps either side of the mean.

5 For each normal distribution for the variable x below, give the set of values of x within which you would expect (a) 68% (b) 95% (c) 99.7% of the whole distribution to lie (on both sides of the mean).

	Mean	Standard deviation
(i)	80 miles	12 miles
(ii)	5 m	15 cm
(iii)	120 kg	7 kg

Draw a sketch to illustrate your answers in each case.

6 The word-processing speeds of operators at an agency are normally distributed with a mean of 120 words per minute and standard deviation of 15 words per minute.
Show this distribution in a sketch graph.
Find the percentage of these operators who are faster than 126 words per minute or slower than 108 words per minute.
   A director employs two operators from the agency who were selected at random. Find the probability that

(a) one and only one of the operators is faster than 108 words per minute

(b) both are faster than 126 words per minute.

7 The following facts are known about the normal distribution of a variable x.

$$P(x < 56) = 0.977$$
$$P(x > 26) = 0.977$$

Find the mean and the standard deviation.
Hence find $P(40 < x < 50)$.

8 A normal distribution has mean 1.2 m and the probability that a member chosen at random is less than 0.9 is 0.115. Find

(a) the standard deviation of the distribution

(b) the probability that a member x chosen at random is in the interval $1 < x < 1.5$.

Probability revisited

From previous studies, we know that the probability of an event happening (or occurring) is measured on a scale from 0 to 1. If the probability is 0, the event never happens; if the probability is 1, the event always happens. If the event happens sometimes, then we could make observations over an extended period, counting the number of times the event occurred (often called a **success**) out of the total number of observations (often called **trials**).

$$\text{Probability} = \frac{\text{number of successes}}{\text{total number of trials}}$$

By this practical approach, reasonable estimates of the probability of an event can be obtained when the number of observations, or trials, is large.

Example 20

Tom, Dick and Harry play the following game with three pennies. They each spin a penny. Tom wins if three heads or three tails result, Dick wins if just two heads result and Harry wins if just one head results.

The boys play the game 120 times of which Tom wins 33, Dick wins 40 and Harry wins the rest.

From these results the respective winning relative frequences (or probabilities) are $\frac{33}{120}, \frac{40}{120}$ and $\frac{47}{120}.$

Assuming the pennies and the spinning to be unbiased, the tree diagram gives the probabilities we should expect by taking $\frac{1}{2}$ as the probability of a head when a penny is spun.

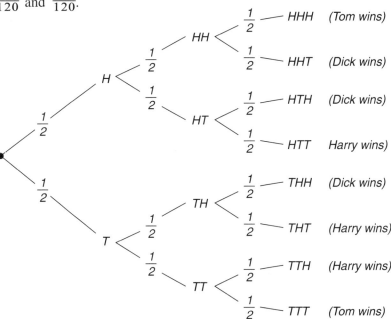

$\frac{1}{2}$	HHH	(Tom wins)
$\frac{1}{2}$	HHT	(Dick wins)
$\frac{1}{2}$	HTH	(Dick wins)
$\frac{1}{2}$	HTT	Harry wins)
$\frac{1}{2}$	THH	(Dick wins)
$\frac{1}{2}$	THT	(Harry wins)
$\frac{1}{2}$	TTH	(Harry wins)
$\frac{1}{2}$	TTT	(Tom wins)

Tree diagram to show theoretical probabilities

	Tom	Dick	Harry
Probabilities from 120 trials	0.275	0.333	0.392
Theoretical probabilities	0.25	0.375	0.375

We see that the probabilities obtained by experiment fit reasonably closely and we would expect the experimental probabilities to get closer in value to the theoretical values as the number of trials increases.

There are many practical two-stage situations where it is not possible to start with exact theoretical probabilities and the relative frequency approach, using a large number of trials, can provide a reliable working value of the probability of success or failure, or whether an event happens or not.

On the other hand, there are many two-stage situations where we know the probability of success, as in games of chance.

Example 21

The probability of obtaining a double when two dice are thrown can be found by counting the possible successful events (6) in the total sample space of 36 simple events.

P (a double when two dice are thrown) $= \frac{6}{36} = \frac{1}{6}$.

Mutually exclusive events

If two events, A and B, from a sample space are mutually exclusive then:

P (A or B) = P (A) + P (B), (the event 'A and B' cannot happen)

Using set notation, this law can be written as:

P (A $\cup$ B) = P (A) + P (B)

Complementary events

In particular, the event A and its complement A', often called 'not A', are mutually exclusive and P (A) + P (A') = 1.

Example 22

When two dice are thrown the event D, 'a double is obtained', and the event T, 'the sum of the scores on the two dice is odd', are mutually exclusive events because if D occurs, then T cannot occur and vice versa.

By counting we find that $P(D) = \frac{6}{36}$ and $P(T) = \frac{18}{36}$.

The probability of obtaining a double or an odd sum is:

$$P(D \cup T) = \frac{6}{36} + \frac{18}{36} = \frac{24}{36} = \frac{2}{3}$$

because the events D and T are mutually exclusive.

Independent events

Two events are independent if the probability of either one of them is the same whether the other occurs or not.
For two events A and B this rule may be expressed in the form

$$P(A \text{ and } B) = P(A)\,P(B),$$

where neither $P(A)$ nor $P(B)$ is zero.
$P(A \text{ and } B)$ is written in set notation as $P(A \cap B)$. Also it is important to note that if $P(A \cap B) = P(A)\,P(B)$, then the events A and B are independent, as long as neither $P(A)$ nor $P(B)$ is zero.

Example 23

The probabilities that two hockey penalty shooters, Rachel and Sarah, score a goal with a single flick are 0.85 and 0.65 respectively. The probabilities are independent.

When each has a single shot, we can show the four possible outcomes and the respective probabilities on a tree diagram:

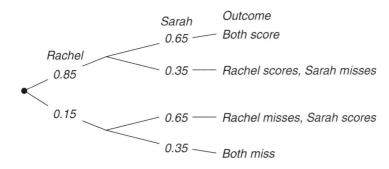

From the tree diagram, we see that, for example,

$$P(\text{both miss}) = (1 - 0.85)(1 - 0.65) = 0.0525$$

Example 24

A bag contains six apples of the same size but two are green and four are red.

An apple is chosen at random from the bag and eaten. A second apple is now chosen at random from the bag (now containing 5 apples). Find the probability that this apple will be red.

This problem is harder because we do not know which type of apple was eaten, it could have been red or green and both possibilities need to be considered.

The tree diagram shows the possibilities after 2 apples have been selected:

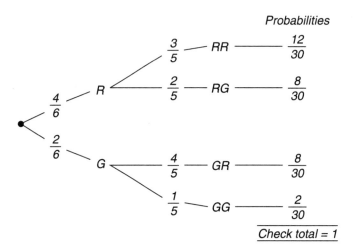

The possible successful events are either RR or GR and we can trace these through the tree diagram.
We then have:

$$P\,(RR) + P\,(GR) = \tfrac{4}{6} \times \tfrac{3}{5} + \tfrac{2}{6} \times \tfrac{5}{5} = \tfrac{2}{3}$$

This is an example of **conditional** probability.

Unrelated events

For any two events, A and B, with probabilities of occurring, P (A) and P (B), we have the rule:

$$P\,(A \cup B) = P\,(A) + P\,(B) - P\,(A \cap B)$$

Example 25

There are five cards, each having a different integer from the set
$\{1, 2, 3, 4, 5\}$ written on it. The cards are shuffled and a card is
selected at random. A second card is selected at random from the four
cards left.
The event A is 'the first integer chosen is smaller than the second'.
The event B is ' the sum of the two integers is even'.
Find P (A), P (B), P (A $\cap$ B), P (A $\cup$ B).

In all there are $5 \times 4 = 20$ simple events possible.

Of these, $(4, 5)$, $(3, 5)$, $(3, 4)$, $(2, 5)$, $(2, 4)$, $(2, 3)$, $(1, 5)$, $(1, 4)$, $(1, 3)$,
$(1, 2)$ are members of event A.

Hence P (A) $= \frac{10}{20} = 0.5$, as would be expected.

Also $(5, 1)$, $(5, 3)$, $(4, 2)$, $(3, 1)$, $(3, 5)$, $(2, 4)$, $(1, 5)$, $(1, 3)$ are the
members of event B.

Hence P (B) $= \frac{8}{20} = 0.4$.

The events which are in both A and B are $(1, 3)$, $(1, 5)$, $(2, 4)$, $(3, 5)$.

Hence P (A $\cap$ B) $= \frac{4}{20} = 0.2$.

Using the formula P (A $\cup$ B) $=$ P (A) $+$ P (B) $-$ P (A $\cap$ B), we have:

$$P (A \cup B) = 0.5 + 0.4 - 0.2 = 0.7$$

In this case, the result can easily be verified by counting the 14
members of the event A $\cup$ B.

EXERCISE 9.4

1 A dice is thrown and a penny is spun. Find the probability that
(*a*) a 2 and a head turn up, (*b*) a 2 or a head turn up, but not
both, (*c*) neither a head nor a 2 turn up.

2 For two events, A and B, we know that P (A) $= \frac{1}{3}$ and P (B) $= \frac{2}{5}$.

(*a*) Find the probability of either A or B occurring if the events
are mutually exclusive.

(*b*) Find the probability of both A and B occurring if the two
events are independent.

3 A yellow bag contains 4 red balls and 3 white balls only. A blue bag contains 2 red balls and 5 white balls only. The yellow bag is twice as likely to be selected as the blue bag.

A bag is selected and a ball is taken at random from this bag. Find the probability that the ball is red.

4 Three children in a class all have a birthday next week but they did not say which day. Assuming that any day is equally likely for all three, find the probability that

(*a*) no birthday will be on Tuesday,

(*b*) all will have their birthday on Saturday,

(*c*) no two birthdays are on the same day.

5 Mr and Mrs Robin and their teenage children, Chris and Sarah, are all at home in the evening. Sarah records the number of phone calls each member of the family received over a long period as part of a coursework project. On any particular evening, she found that Mr Robin, Mrs Robin and Chris would receive 15%, 20% and 25% of the calls respectively and that she would receive the rest.

If the phone rings twice tonight, find the probability that

(*a*) both calls are for Sarah,

(*b*) the first call is for Chris and the second for his father,

(*c*) neither call is for Mrs Robin.

The phone rang three times last night and the first two calls were for Mrs Robin.

(*d*) Find the probability that the third call was also for Mrs Robin.

6 The letters of the word LONDON are printed on the faces of a cube, one letter on each face. The cube is rolled twice. By using a tree diagram, find the probability that

(*a*) the letter obtained on the first role was N and on the second roll was O,

(*b*) the letters obtained on the first and second rolls are the same.

7 The letters of the word EXETER are printed on six cards, one letter on each card. Two cards are selected at random, and without replacement, from the six.

(*a*) Find the probability that the two cards have different letters.

Three cards are selected at random, and without replacement, from the six.

(*b*) Find the probability that there is an E on just two of the cards.

8 Repeat question 7 when the sampling is with replacement.

9 A bag contains a very large number of blue, green and yellow beads in the ratio 2 : 3 : 5 respectively. Three beads are drawn at random. By using a tree diagram, find the probability that

(*a*) all three beads are green,

(*b*) all three beads are the same colour,

(*c*) at least two of the three beads have the same colour.

10 Mr and Mrs Richards have two sons, Alan and Ben, and two daughters, Cindy and Delia. Mrs Richards takes photographs of each child separately, all possible pairs of the children, all possible groups of three children and one photograph of all four children.

(*a*) How many photographs are there in this set?

A photograph from the set is taken at random. Find the probability that this photograph includes

(*b*) Alan,

(*c*) both Cindy and Delia,

(*d*) at least one girl.

11 Each day in Nodland is either cool, warm or hot. The weather today is independent of the weather yesterday and the probability of each type of weather is given in the table over the page.

	Weather		
	Cool	Warm	Hot
Probability	$\frac{1}{2}$	$\frac{1}{3}$	$\frac{1}{6}$

Damian takes a 2-day holiday to Nodland. Find the probability that (a) no days are hot, (b) just one day is hot.

Samantha visits Nodland for 3 days. Find the probability that (c) all the days are cool, (d) at least one day is warm.

12 In a group of girls, 24 are wearing blazers and 22 are wearing white socks. There are ten girls wearing both and nine wearing neither.

(a) Find the number of girls in the group.

A girl is chosen at random, find the probability that

(b) she is wearing white socks and a blazer,

(c) she is wearing white socks or a blazer, but not both.

Two girls are chosen at random, find the probability that

(d) one is wearing a blazer and no white socks and the other is wearing white socks and no blazer.

13 The probability of getting promotion at the first attempt is 0.75. If the first attempt fails, the probability of getting promotion at the second attempt is 0.3 and no third attempt is allowed. Find the probability of failing to get the promotion.

14 The events A and B have probabilities of occurring of 0.6 and 0.25 respectively. Given that P (A ∪ B) = 0.725, explain why the events A and B are not mutually exclusive.

Find P (A ∩ B).

Explain why the events A and B are not independent.

15 It is known that 6% of a large batch of eggs are bad. A boy selects 12 eggs at random. Find the probability that he has selected (*a*) all good eggs, (*b*) at least one bad egg.

16 A card is drawn at random from a normal pack of 52 playing cards. The event K is a king being drawn. The event H is a heart being drawn. Find P (K), P (H) and P (K ∩ H).

Deduce that the events K and H are independent.

Find also P (K ∪ H).

17 A high-jumper is allowed a maximum of three attempts and her probability of a successful jump is $\frac{2}{5}$. Find the probability that she has a successful jump

(*a*) on the second attempt,

(*b*) on the third attempt.

(*c*) What is the probability that she fails?

18 A bag contains seven balls, three white and four red. A ball is selected at random from the bag, its colour is noted and it is then replaced. The process is repeated until three balls have been selected. Find the probability that the three balls (*a*) are all red, (*b*) contain one ball of one colour and two balls of the other colour.

19 Repeat question 18 when the sampling is without replacement.

20 Shenah and Manuel travel from different towns to the same school. The probabilities that Shenah and Manuel are late for school on any day are 0.1 and 0.2 respectively. Find the probability that

(*a*) Shenah is not late on five consecutive days,

(*b*) Manuel is late on Monday and Tuesday and on time on the other three school days next week,

(*c*) one, and only one, out of Shenah and Manuel, will be late on Friday.

10. Sketching the graphs of functions

Drawing the graph of a function from a table of values by plotting and joining up points on graph paper has been extensively covered in the course. Often, however, we do not need this fine detail; the general shape and position of the curve are sufficient. In this chapter we shall be looking at ways of producing such sketch graphs, using only a few critical points. The sketches of simple functions can often be used to help draw the graphs of more complex functions, as we shall see later in the chapter.

First, work on the linear and quadratic functions will be revised through the graphical work.

The linear function

The graph of $y = mx + c$ is a straight line whose gradient is m. Except in the case when $m = 0$, we can find the points in which it crosses the axes and then join them using a ruler. The sketch graph is as informative as a plotted graph in this case.

Example 1

Sketch the graph of $y = 2x - 3$.

When $x = 0$, $y = -3$.

When $y = 0$, $2x - 3 = 0 \Rightarrow x = 1\frac{1}{2}$.

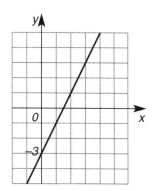

EXERCISE 10.1

In all sketches give the coordinates of the points of intersection with the axes.

1 Sketch the graphs of the straight lines with the following equations.

   (a) $y = 2x + 5$ (b) $y = -3x + 1$ (c) $x = 4y - 2$ (d) $2x + 3y = 12$

   State the gradient of each line.

2 Form the equation of each of the following lines.

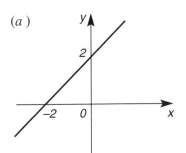   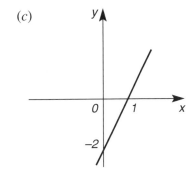

3 State which of the following equations corresponds to the graph shown.

   (a) $y = 2x + 6$ (b) $y = -2x + 6$

   (c) $3y + 2x = 18$ (d) $3y = 2x + 18$

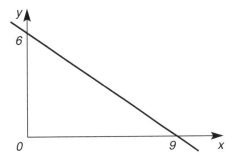

4 (a) On one set of axes sketch the lines with equations:

   (i) $y = 2x$ (ii) $y = 2x + 5$ (iii) $y = 2x - 4$ (iv) $2y = 4x + 2$

   (b) Describe transformations which would map line (i) onto each of the other lines.

5 For each part below sketch the pair of lines and describe how they are related.

   (a) $y = 4x + 1$, $y = 4(x - 1) + 1$ (b) $y = 4x + 1$, $y = 4x + 2$

   (c) $y = 4x + 1$, $y = -4x + 1$ (d) $y = 4x + 1$, $y = -(4x + 1)$

6 (a) Find the coordinates of the points A, B and C in the diagram.

(b) Find the equation of the line which is parallel to AC and passes through B, and give the coordinates of the points of intersection with the axes.

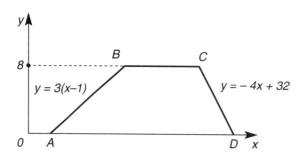

7 (a) On one set of axes sketch the graphs of (i) $y = 2x + 5$ and (ii) $2y + x = 10$.

(b) Find the coordinates of the following points: A, in which line (i) meets the x-axis; B, in which line (ii) meets the x-axis; and C, where the two lines meet.

(c) Calculate the values of: AB^2, BC^2 and AC^2.

(d) What does this tell you about the two lines?

(e) Write down the gradients of the two lines and verify that their product is -1.

Investigation A

In the last question you should have found that the two lines were at right angles and that the product of the gradients of the two lines was -1. Draw, on squared paper, other pairs of lines which meet at right angles, find their gradients and investigate whether they too multiply to give -1. If you think this is a general result, try to prove it.

The quadratic function

As the quadratic function has been covered in some detail the graphs of such functions can be readily drawn. A good sketch graph of the curve with equation $y = ax^2 + bx + c$ can be drawn by noting that:

1. It always crosses the y-axis at $(0, c)$.

2. If it crosses the x-axis, the x coordinates can be found by solving $ax^2 + bx + c = 0$.

3. There is always a line of symmetry, parallel to the y-axis, which passes through the vertex.

Note: If a is positive, the vertex of the parabola is downwards – it is '∪' shaped; if a is negative, the vertex is upwards – it is '∩' shaped.

Example 2

Sketch the graph whose equation is $y = x^2 - 4x + 3$.

1. The curve crosses the y-axis where $x = 0 \Rightarrow y = +3$.

2. The curve meets the x-axis where
   $y = 0 \Rightarrow x^2 - 4x + 3 = 0$.
   As $b^2 > 4ac$, there are two solutions which can be found by one of the methods given in Chapter 4. (Check that $x = 1$ or $x = 3$.)

3. The line of symmetry must have equation $x = 2$, as it must be halfway between the intercepts on the x-axis, and so the lowest point is $(2, -1)$.
   With this information a good, detailed sketch can be drawn.

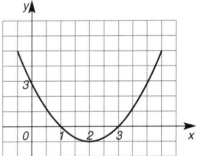

Example 3

Sketch the graph whose equation is $y = x^2 + 4x + 5$.

1. The curve passes through $(0, 5)$.

2. As $b^2 < 4ac$, there are no solutions of $x^2 + 4x + 5 = 0$ and so the curve does not cross the x-axis.

3. The lowest (or highest, if a is negative) point, and hence the line of symmetry, can be found by 'completing the square':
   $x^2 + 4x + 5 = (x + 2)^2 + 1$ and so the minimum value of y is $+1$ and occurs when $x = -2$. The sketch can then be drawn.

Even when the curve crosses the x-axis, if the x coordinates are irrational, the sketch is more easily drawn by finding the lowest (or highest) point as in the last example.

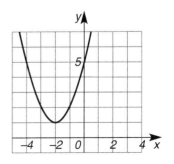

EXERCISE 10.2

1 The equation of a curve is $y = x^2 - 3x - 10$.

(a) By putting $x = 0$, find where the curve crosses the y-axis.

(b) By putting $y = 0$ and solving the resulting equation, find where the curve crosses the x-axis.

(c) Using your results to (b) deduce:
(i) the equation of the line of symmetry,
(ii) the coordinates of the lowest point on the curve.

(d) Using this information only, sketch the curve.

2 For the curve whose equation is $y = -x^2 + 6x + 8$,

(a) state the coordinates of the point of intersection with the y-axis,

(b) rearrange $-x^2 + 6x + 8$ in the form $q - (x - p)^2$ and deduce the coordinates of the vertex of the parabola,

(c) sketch the curve.

3 The graph of a quadratic function is the parabola whose equation is $y = x^2 + 3x + 5$.

(a) Write down the coordinates of the point of intersection with the y-axis.

(b) Without plotting the curve, how do you know that it does not meet the x-axis?

(c) Rewrite the equation in the form $y = (x + p)^2 + q$ and hence deduce the coordinates of the lowest point.

(d) Sketch the curve.

4 The graphs shown are all of quadratic functions.

(i)

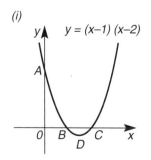

$y = (x-1)(x-2)$

(ii)

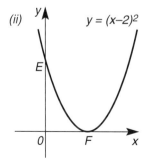

$y = (x-2)^2$

(iii)

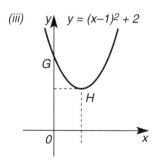

$y = (x-1)^2 + 2$

(iv)

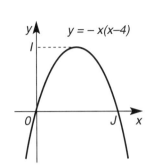

y = − *x*(*x*−4)

(v) *y* = *k* (*x* + 1)(*x* + 3)

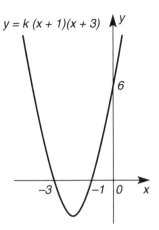

(vi)

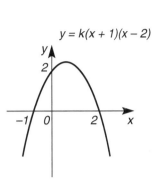

y = *k*(*x* + 1)(*x* − 2)

(*a*) Write down the equation of the line of symmetry for each curve.

(*b*) For curves (i)–(iv), give the coordinates of *A, B, C, D, E, F, G, H, I* and *J*.

(*c*) For curves (v) and (vi), state the value of *k*.

5 (*a*) Sketch the graph of $y = x^2 - 6x - 27$ showing the coordinates of the points of intersection with the axes.

(*b*) Use your graph to solve the inequation $x^2 - 6x - 27 > 0$.

6 The graph of a function has equation $y = 2x^2 + 5x - 3$.

(*a*) Write down the coordinates of the points of intersection with the *y*-axis.

(*b*) Show that $y = (2x - 1)(x + 3)$ and deduce the points of intersection with the *x*-axis.

(*c*) Use symmetry to find the coordinates of the lowest point on the curve.

(*d*) Show that $y = 2(x + 1\frac{1}{4})^2 - 6\frac{1}{8}$. How does this give the coordinates of the lowest point on the curve?

(*e*) Sketch the curve.

7 The graphs given are parabolas. Use the data given in the sketches to find the equations of the curves and hence find the coordinates of the point A.

(a)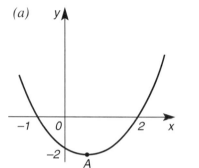

(b)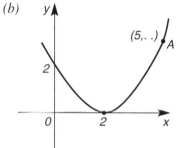

(c)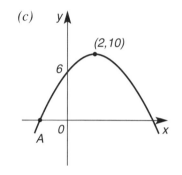

Investigation B

Draw the graph of the function whose equation is $y = x^2 - 6x + 9$.
You should find that the x-axis is a tangent to the curve. Now write down several more quadratic functions whose graphs you think will just touch the x-axis; check by plotting the curves or using a computer or graphical calculator.
Find the relationship that exists between a, b and c if the curve with equation $y = ax^2 + bx + c$ touches the x-axis.

Other functions

During the course you have met many functions; you should be able to sketch or at least recognise the graphs of many of these. In the next exercise you will be reminded of some and be encouraged to think about others that you may not have met before.

EXERCISE 10.3

1 (a)

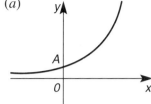

(b)

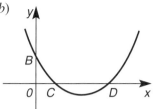

(c)

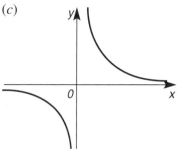

(d)

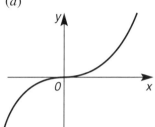

(e)

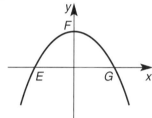

(f)

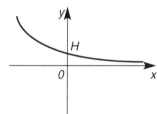

(g)

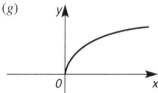

(h)

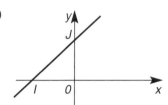

Each of the graphs can be associated with one of the equations:

(i) $y = (x-1)(x-3)$ (ii) $y = 2x + 5$ (iii) $y = x^3$ (iv) $y = 2^x$

(v) $y = \sqrt{x}$ (vi) $y = 1 - x^2$ (vii) $xy = 1$ (viii) $y = 3^{-x}$

Match them up and deduce the coordinates of the points A, B, . . . , J.

2 (a) For the curve with equation $y = \dfrac{1}{x^2}$, write notes so that you can explain to your partner how you know that (i) the curve is always above the x-axis, (ii) the curve gets closer to the x-axis as x becomes very large, and (iii) the curve is very steep if x is close to 0.

(b) Sketch on the same set of axes the graphs of the functions

(i) $y = \dfrac{1}{x}$ (ii) $y = \dfrac{1}{x^2}$

(c) Using a computer compare the graphs of $= \dfrac{1}{x}$, $y = \dfrac{1}{x^2}$, $y = \dfrac{1}{x^3}$, $y = \dfrac{1}{x^4}$.

3 (a) Sketch the graph of $y = \sin x°$ in the interval $-360 < x < 360$, and add to it the line with equation $y = 0.5$.

(b) Write down the calculator solution of $\sin x° = 0.5$.

(c) Use (a) and (b) to find the values of x for which $\sin x° > 0.5$ in the given interval.

(d) By considering the effect of squaring numbers less than 1 sketch the graph of $y = \sin^2 x°$ [$\sin^2 x°$ is the notation used to mean $(\sin x°)^2$].

(e) Check your result in (d) by using a computer or graphical calculator. Hence, or otherwise, describe the differences between the graphs of $y = \sin x°$ and $y = \sin^2 x°$.

4 The curve C has equation $y = (x + 2)(x - 1)(x - 3)$.

(a) By putting $x = 0$, find where it crosses the y-axis.

(b) By putting $y = 0$ and solving the resulting equation, find where the curve crosses the x-axis.

(c) Check that the value of y when $x = 2$ is -4. How do you know that y must be negative for all values of x between 1 and 3?

(d) Complete the table, which gives the sign of y in the intervals on the x-axis determined by (b).

x	$x < -2$	$-2 < x < +1$	$+1 < x < +3$	$x > 3$
sign of y	$y < 0$		$y < 0$	

(e) Does y increase slowly or rapidly as x increases from 3 to infinity?

(f) Does y decrease slowly or rapidly as x decreases from -2 to infinity?

(g) Sketch the graph of $y = (x + 2)(x - 1)(x - 3)$.

5 By following a similar programme to that in question 4 sketch the graphs of

(a) $y = (x + 3)(x - 1)(2x - 5)$ (b) $y = x(1 - x)^2$

(c) $y = (x - 2)^3$ (d) $y = x(1 - x^2)(x - 3)$

In the rest of the chapter it is convenient to use the notation of functions; if you are not familiar with this, you should work through the following section.

The notation of functions

When we draw the graph of $y = x^2 + 1$ we are giving a picture in two dimensions of a one-dimensional mapping of numbers, $x \mapsto x^2 + 1$. The equations of many curves can be expressed as mappings like this one.

A **function**, **f**, is a mapping in which every element has one and only one image and we denote the image of x by $f(x)$ ['f of x']. For example, the function f which maps x onto $x^2 + 1$, written as $f: x \mapsto x^2 + 1$, is equally defined by the statement $f(x) = x^2 + 1$. For a particular value of x, $f(x)$ is evaluated by replacing x by the given value.

Example 4

For the function $f: x \mapsto 2x^2 - x + 7$,

(a) $f(3) = 2(3)^2 - (3) + 7 = 18 - 3 + 7 = 22$

(b) $f(-1) = 2(-1)^2 - (-1) + 7 = 2 + 1 + 7 = 10$

(c) $f(x + 2) = 2(x + 2)^2 - (x + 2) + 7$
$= 2x^2 + 8x + 8 - x - 2 + 7 = 2x^2 + 7x + 13$

(d) $f(x) + 5 = (2x^2 - x + 7) + 5 = 2x^2 - x + 12$

(e) $2f(x) = 2(2x^2 - x + 7) = 4x^2 - 2x + 14$

(f) $f(3x) = 2(3x)^2 - (3x) + 7 = 18x^2 - 3x + 7$

The graph of the function f has equation $y = f(x)$, since the points on the graph have coordinates $[(x), f(x)]$; the images $f(x)$ are the y coordinates of the points.

EXERCISE 10.4

1 Given that $f(x) = 5x + 7$,

(a) find (i) $f(2)$ (ii) $f(-5)$ (iii) $f(0)$,

(b) show that $f(x - 1) = 5x + 2$.

2 For the function f defined by $f : x \mapsto (x - 4)(2x - 3)$,

(a) evaluate (i) $f(-1)$ (ii) $f(0)$ (iii) $f(1\frac{1}{2})$ (iv) $f(4)$ (v) $f(4\frac{1}{2})$,

(b) write down expressions for (i) $f(-x)$ (ii) $f(2x)$ (iii) $f(x + 4)$,

(c) find x if $f(x) = 0$.

3 The function f is defined as $f : x \mapsto x^2$. Write down, in terms of x,

(a) $f(x)$ (b) $f(x - 1)$ (c) $f(3x)$

(d) $f(x) - 3$ (e) $4f(x)$ (f) $f(2x + 5)$

4 For the function $g : x \mapsto \frac{1}{x}$, simplify $g(3x + 1) + 1$.

5 The functions f and g are defined as $f : x \mapsto bx + a$, $g : x \mapsto ax + b$. Given that $f(-1) = g(3)$, find the ratio $a : b$.

6 Given that $f(a) = b$, where $f : x \mapsto \dfrac{x + 2}{x}$, $(x \neq 0)$, express a in terms of b.

7 The function f is defined as $f : x \mapsto ax^2 + bx + c$, where a, b and c are constants. Given that $f(0) = 1$ and $f(2x + 1) = 4f(x)$,

(a) find the values of a, b and c,

(b) hence verify that $f(-3) = 4$.

8 The graph of the function $f : x \mapsto x^2 + 1$ is shown; its equation is $y = x^2 + 1$.
Write down the equations of the graphs of

(a) $f(x - 1)$

(b) $f(x) - 1$

(c) $3f(x)$ and then sketch each curve.

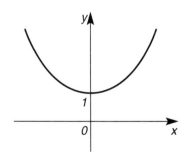

Transformations and curve sketching

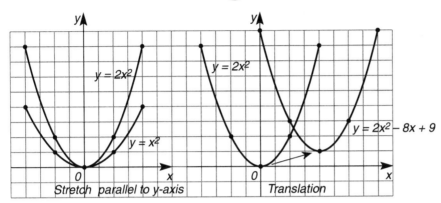

Stretch parallel to y-axis   Translation

In Book 3y and in this chapter we have seen that the graph of the general quadratic function, $x \mapsto ax^2 + bx + c$ is similar to the graph of the simpler function $x \mapsto ax^2$ but with its vertex no longer at the origin; the actual translation being dependent on the values of a, b and c. The graph of $y = f(x)$, where $f(x) = ax^2$, is itself a transformation, a stretch parallel to the y-axis of scale factor a, of the graph of $y = f(x)$, where $f(x) = x^2$, and so the graph of any quadratic function is a transformation, or combination of transformations, of the graph of $y = x^2$. We shall, in the next exercise, explore in more detail how the graph of $y = f(x)$ is transformed when $f(x)$ is replaced by:

    (*a*) $f(x) + a$ (*b*) $f(x + a)$ (*c*) $af(x)$ (*d*) $f(ax)$

EXERCISE 10.5

1 (*a*) Given that $f(x) = 2x^2$, copy and complete the tables, which correspond to the functions:

    (i) $y = f(x)$ (ii) $y = f(x) + 5$

x	−3	−2	−1	0	1	2	3
$f(x)$		8			2		

x	−3	−2	−1	0	1	2	3
$f(x) + 5$	23			7	5		

    (iii) $y = f(x) - 2$

x		−3	−2	−1	0	1	2	3
$f(x) - 2$			6					16

(*b*) Draw the graphs of (i), (ii) and (iii) on the the same diagram. How are (ii) and (iii) related to (i)?

2 (*a*) Sketch, on separate diagrams, the graphs of
(i) $y = f(x)$, where $f(x) = 2x$, (ii) $y = g(x)$, where $g(x) = x^2$.
(iii) $y = h(x)$, where $h(x) = \frac{1}{x}$.

(*b*) On the appropriate diagram in (*a*) add the graphs of
(i) $y = f(x) + 3$ (ii) $y = g(x) + 3$ (iii) $y = h(x) + 3$.

(*c*) Describe a transformation that would map the graphs in (*a*) onto the corresponding graph in (*b*).

(*d*) Investigate the effect, on the graphs of the functions in (*a*), of replacing $f(x)$ by $f(x) + a$, $g(x)$ by $g(x) + a$, and $h(x)$ by $h(x) + a$, in the cases when $a = -2, \frac{1}{2}, 8$.

(*e*) Complete the following statement: To draw the graph of $y = f(x) + a$ we can draw the graph of $y = f(x)$, the simple function, and translate by ... units parallel to the ... axis.

(*f*) Use your answer to (*e*) to sketch the following curves, showing the coordinates of the points of intersection with the axes, where appropriate. (Try to use a graphical calculator or computer to check your results.)

(i) $y = \sin x° + 1$　(ii) $y = -0.5 + \cos x°$　(iii) $y = x^2 - 1$

(iv) $y = \frac{1}{x} + 2$　　　(v) $y = 2^x - 1$　　　(vi) $y = \frac{1}{x^2} - 4$

3 In the diagram graph (i) has equation $y = f(x)$, where $f(x) = x(x - 1)$.

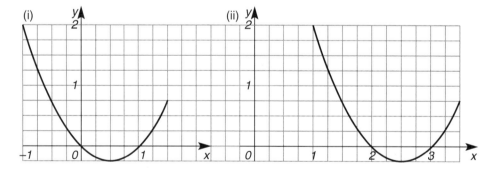

(*a*) Describe the transformation that maps graph (i) onto graph (ii).

(*b*) One of the following equations is that of graph (ii):

$y = (x + 2)(x + 3)$; $y = (x - 2)(x - 3)$; $y = (x + 2)(x + 1)$;
$y = x(x - 1) + 2$

By considering points on the graph decide which is the correct one.

(c) Write down, in terms of x, expressions for:

(i) f$(x-2)$ (ii) f$(x+1)$ (iii) f$(x+2)$

(d) Using your answers to (b) and (c), write the equation of graph (ii) in the form $y =$ f$(...)$.

4 (a) Sketch the graph of $y =$ f$(x) = x^2$.

(b) Complete the statements:
(i) $y =$ f$(x-2) = \ldots$ (ii) $y =$ f$(x+1) = \ldots$

(c) Add the graphs of $y =$ f$(x-2)$ and $y =$ f$(x+1)$ to that of $y =$ f(x).

(d) Describe the effect of replacing x by $x + a$ for this function f.

(e) By replacing x by $x + a$ for various values of a investigate whether the same effect is seen in the graphs of the functions:

(i) $g : x \mapsto x^3$ (ii) $h : x \mapsto \frac{1}{x}, (x \neq 0)$

5 (a) Sketch the graph of the function $y =$ f$(x+2) = (x+2)^3$ by using the appropriate translation of the graph of $y =$ f$(x) = x^3$.

(b) Use similar reasoning to sketch the graphs of

(i) $y = \sin(x-30)°$ (ii) $y = (x+10)^2$ (iii) $y = \dfrac{1}{(x-8)^2}$

6 The diagram shows the graphs of $y =$ f$(x) = (x+1)(x-2)$ and $y = 2$f$(x) = 2(x+1)(x-2)$.

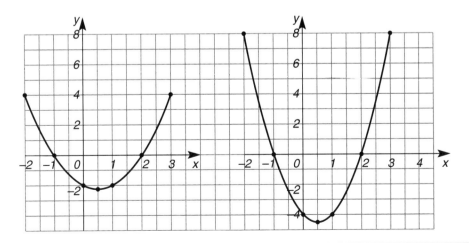

(a) Copy the graphs and add those of

    (i) $y = 3f(x)$ (ii) $y = \frac{1}{2} f(x)$

    (iii) $y = -2f(x)$ (iv) $y = -f(x)$

(b) Which points are common to all curves?

(c) Write down the y coordinate corresponding to $x = \frac{1}{2}$ for each of the six curves.

(d) If (p,q) is a point on the graph of $y = f(x)$, what is the corresponding point on each of the curves in (a)?

(e) Draw the graphs of the functions: (i) $y = g(x) = (x - 2)^2$
(ii) $y = h(x) = \sin x°$ (iii) $y = m(x) = x^3$,

Investigate the effect on the graphs of replacing g(x) by $a[g(x)]$, h(x) by $a[h(x)]$ and m(x) by $a[m(x)]$ in the cases:
$a = \frac{1}{3}, 2, 3, -1$.

(f) For any function f describe the transformation that the graph of $y = f(x)$ undergoes when f(x) is replaced by $a[f(x)]$. In the case when $a = -1$, to what other transformation is this equivalent?

(g) Use these results to sketch the graphs of

    (i) $y = 2 \sin x°$ (ii) $y = \frac{5}{x}$

    (iii) $y = -2(x - 1)(x + 1)$ (iv) $y = -\cos x°$

7 Copy the sketch graph of $y = f(x) = (x - 1)(x - 3)$.

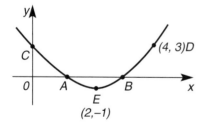

(a) On the same graph sketch the curve with equation
$y = f(2x) = (2x - 1)(2x - 3)$, by considering where it crosses the axes.

(b) Considering the graph in (a) as a transformation of the given graph, write down the coordinates of the images of the points A, B, C, D and E.

(c) Describe this transformation.

(d) Repeat the exercise for $y = f(\frac{1}{2}x) = (\frac{1}{2}x - 1)(\frac{1}{2}x - 3)$.

(e) Draw the graphs of the functions:

(i) $g(x) = \sin x°$ (ii) $h(x) = x(x + 1)$ (iii) $j(x) = \dfrac{1}{x - 1}$

Investigate the effect on the graphs of repacing x by ax in the cases: $a = \frac{1}{3}, 2, 3, -1$.

(f) Describe the transformation that the graph of $y = f(x)$ undergoes when x is replaced by ax. In the case when $a = -1$, to what other transformation is this equivalent?

8 (a) Sketch the graphs of (i) $y = (x - 1)^3$ (ii) $y = \sin x°$
(iii) $y = (x + 1)^2 + 3$.

(b) By considering the effect of replacing x by $2x$, sketch the graphs of (i) $y = (2x - 1)^3$ (ii) $y = \sin 2x°$
(iii) $y = (2x + 1)^2 + 3$.

Summary of results

1. The effect on the graph, $y = f(x)$, of replacing $f(x)$ by $f(x) + a$ is to translate it by a units in the y direction.

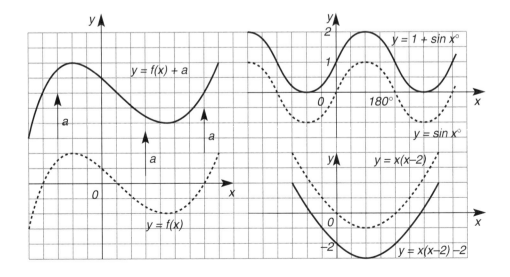

2. The effect on the graph, $y = f(x)$, of replacing $f(x)$ by $f(x + a)$ is to translate it by $-a$ units in the x direction.

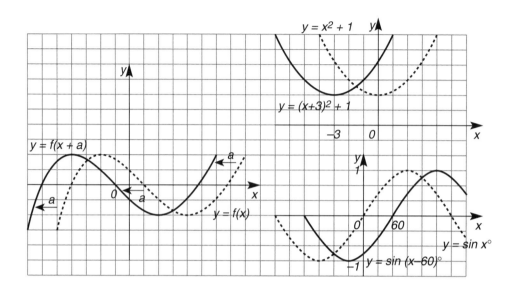

3. The effect on the graph, $y = f(x)$, of replacing $f(x)$ by $af(x)$ is to stretch it by a scale factor of a units in the y direction.

Note: If $a = -1$, this is a reflection in the x-axis

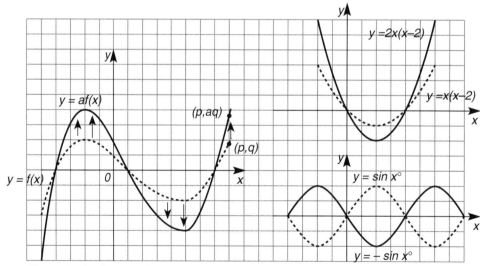

The point (p,q) on $y = f(x)$ moves to
the point (p,aq) on $y = a\,f(x)$

4. The effect on the graph, $y = f(x)$, of replacing $f(x)$ by $f(ax)$ is to stretch it by a scale factor of $\frac{1}{a}$ units in the y direction.

   Note: If $a = -1$, this is a reflection in the y-axis

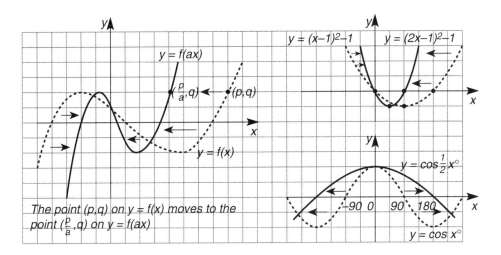

EXERCISE 10.6 (Miscellaneous)

1 For each of the following pairs of equations describe fully how the second graph is related to the first.

(a) (i) $y = x^2$ (ii) $y = (x + 5)^2$

(b) (i) $y = \frac{1}{x}$ (ii) $y = 2 + \frac{1}{x}$

(c) (i) $y = \cos x°$ (ii) $y = 3 \cos x°$

(d) (i) $y = x^4$ (ii) $y = -x^4$

2 Draw sketch graphs of the following, giving the coordinates of any points of intersection with the axes.

(a) $y = -x^3$ (b) $y = \dfrac{1}{x - 2}$ (c) $y = \sin \frac{1}{2}x°$

3 Describe the transformation, or succession of transformations in the correct order, that would map the graph of $y = x^2$ onto the graph of each of the following. Hence draw each parabola and state the coordinates of its vertex.

(a) $y = x^2 + 5$ (b) $y = (x + 5)^2$ (c) $y = (x - 4)^2 + 1$

(d) $y = 1 - x^2$ (e) $y = -2 + 7(x + 3)^2$

4 The curve with equation $y = x^2$ undergoes the following two transformations, in order:

(i) a translation of 3 units parallel to the y-axis,

(ii) a stretch of 2 units parallel to the y-axis.

(a) Draw the final curve and give its equation.

(b) Repeat (a) for (ii) followed by (i).

5 Sketch the graphs of the following by considering them as the result of applying two transformations to the graph of a simple function.

(a) $y = 2 - x^3$ (b) $y = -(x^3 + 2)$

(c) $y = 3 + 2 \sin x°$ (d) $y = 1 - \dfrac{1}{x}$

6 The diagram shows the graph of a function f.

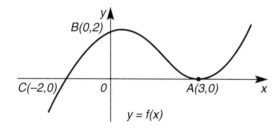

$y = f(x)$

On separate diagrams sketch the graphs of

(a) $y = f(x - 2)$ (b) $y = f(2x)$ (c) $y = f(-x)$

In each case give the coordinates of the points onto which A, B and C are mapped.

7 For each of the following curves choose the equation with which it could be associated.

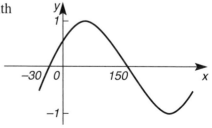

(a) (i) $y = \sin(x - 30)°$

(ii) $y = \sin(x + 30)°$

(iii) $y = 30 + \sin x°$

(b)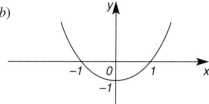

(i) $y = x^2 - 1$

(ii) $y = (x - 1)^2$

(iii) $y = (x + 1)^2$

(c)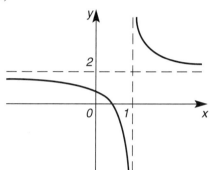

(i) $y = \frac{1}{x} + 2$

(ii) $y = \dfrac{1}{x + 2}$

(iii) $y = \dfrac{1}{x - 1} + 2$

(iv) $y = \dfrac{2}{x - 1}$

8 Sketch the curves with equations:

(a) $y = -x^2$ (b) $y = -x^3$ (c) $y = -\sin x°$

(d) $y = -\cos x°$ (e) $y = -2^x$ (f) $xy = -1$

9 Sketch, in separate diagrams, in the interval $0 < x < 360$, the graphs of $y = \sin x°$ with each of the following curves. Show the coordinates of the points of intersection with the axes.

(a) $y = 2 \sin x°$ (b) $y = \sin 2x°$

(c) $y = 1 + 2 \sin x°$ (d) $y = 1 - \sin x°$

10 (a) Draw a sketch graph of $y = \frac{1}{x^2}$ and deduce that of
$y = -\frac{1}{x^2}$.

(b) By adding a suitable straight line to the second sketch deduce the number of roots of the equation $x + 1 = -\frac{1}{x^2}$.

11 The graph of $y = x^2$ is labelled. Give the equations of the other curves shown.

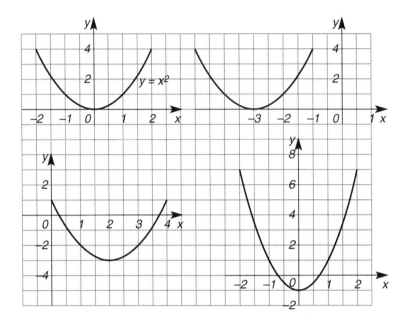

12 Sketch the graph of $y = (x-1)(x-2)$.
This curve C is mapped to the curve C_1 under the translation defined by $\begin{pmatrix} -3 \\ -1 \end{pmatrix}$. Sketch C_1 and give its equation.

13 (*a*) (i) Draw a sketch graph of the curve C, whose equation is $y = \frac{1}{x}$.

    (ii) Translate the graph by 2 units parallel to the *x*-axis. Write down the equation of this curve C_1.

    (iii) Translate the curve C_1 by 1 unit parallel to the *y*-axis. Write down the equation of this curve.

(*b*) Show that $\frac{2x+3}{x+1} = 2 + \frac{1}{x+1}$ and hence sketch the graph

of $y = \frac{2x+3}{x+1}$.

14 The diagram shows the sketch of $y = x^3 - 3x^2$.

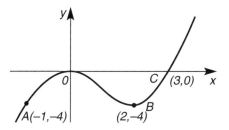

(a) By translating this curve deduce a sketch graph of
$y = (x-2)^3 - 3(x-2)^2$, showing the coordinates of the
images of A, B and C.

(b) Show that $(x-2)^3 - 3(x-2)^2 = x^3 - 9x^2 + 24x - 20$,
and hence

  (i) deduce the solutions of the equation
$x^3 - 9x^2 + 24x - 20 = 0$,

  (ii) sketch the graph of $y = x^3 - 9x^2 + 24x - 16$.

Investigation C

Sketch the graphs of $y = \sin x°$ and $y = \cos(x - 90)°$. Write down
what you notice about them. Now sketch and compare the graphs
of $y = \cos x°$ and $y = \sin(x - 90)°$. Is there a similar result?
Investigate for other relationships between sine and cosine.

Investigation D

By drawing the graphs of the functions $f : x \rightarrow \cos x°$ and
$g : x \rightarrow \cos(-x)°$ show that $\cos x° = \cos(-x)°$ for all values of x.
Test, using your calculator, the result for several values of x. This
demonstrates a case where $f(x) = f(-x)$. Write down a few more
functions for which this is true.
Investigate whether a similar result holds for $\sin x°$ and $\sin(-x)°$.
Some functions are described as 'odd', some as 'even'. Find out
what is meant by such functions and produce examples of each
together with their graphs.

Extension work

Using the graph of y = f(x) to sketch the graph of $y = \dfrac{1}{f(x)}$

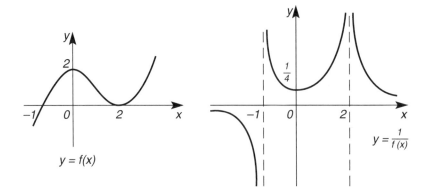

We have already seen some simple 'reciprocal curves', for example those with equations $y = \dfrac{1}{x}$ and $y = \dfrac{1}{x^2}$. However, curves whose equations are of the form $y = \dfrac{1}{f(x)}$, where f(x) is a little more complicated than x or x^2, tend to be more complex, as can be seen in the sketch above. It is a good idea to first sketch the curve with equation $y = f(x)$, especially if this is one of the more standard curves.

It is useful to remind ourselves of the properties of reciprocals.

EXERCISE 10.7

1 (a) What can be said about $\dfrac{1}{k}$ when k is (i) positive (ii) negative?

(b) Sketch the graph of $y = f(x)$, where $f(x) = x^2 + 1$.

How do you know that the graph of $y = \dfrac{1}{f(x)}$ is above the x-axis?

(c) Sketch the graph of $y = f(x) = (x - 1)(x - 2)$.

For what values of x is the graph of $y = \dfrac{1}{f(x)}$

(i) above the x-axis (ii) below the x-axis?

2 (*a*) What can be said about the value of $\dfrac{1}{k}$ if

    (i) $k > 1$,   (ii) $k = 1$,

    (iii) $0 < k < 1$,   (iv) $-1 < k < 0$,

    (v) $k = -1$ (vi) $k < -1$?

(*b*) Explain, using the graph in 1(*b*), how we know that the graph of

$$y = \frac{1}{x^2 + 1}$$ only lies in the interval $0 < y \le 1$.

(*c*) Explain, using your graph in 1(*c*), why the graph of

$$y = \frac{1}{(x-1)(x-2)}$$ does not pass through the region $-4 < y < 0$.

3 (*a*) As k increases from zero, describe what happens to $\dfrac{1}{k}$.

(*b*) Does a curve with equation $y = \dfrac{1}{f(x)}$ ever cross the x-axis?

(*c*) Describe what happens on the graphs of $y = \dfrac{1}{x^2 + 1}$ and $y = \dfrac{1}{(x-1)(x-2)}$ as x tends to infinity.

4 (*a*) As k gets closer to zero what happens to $\dfrac{1}{k}$?

(*b*) What happens on the graph of $y = \dfrac{1}{f(x)}$ for those values of x in which $y = f(x)$ meets the x-axis ?

(*c*) On the graph of $y = \dfrac{1}{(x-1)(x-2)}$ what happens when $x = 1$ and $x = 2$?

We shall use the results of Exercise 10.7 to sketch the graphs of the two 'reciprocal' curves considered.

Example 5

To sketch the graph of $y = \dfrac{1}{x^2 + 1}$ use the sketch of $y = x^2 + 1$.

The new curve will lie in the interval $0 < y \leq 1$, with $(0, 1)$ being the maximum point on the curve. Also there must be symmetry in the y-axis.

The scale on the y-axis for $y = \dfrac{1}{x^2 + 1}$ has been enlarged to show the mapping more clearly; if it were superimposed on the graph of $y = x^2 + 1$ it would not make much of an impact!

Note: A line to which a curve approaches as x or y tend to infinity is called an **asymptote**; in this example the x-axis is an asymptote to the curve.

If the graph of $y = f(x)$ meets the x-axis, then the graph of $y = \dfrac{1}{f(x)}$ will be a discontinuous curve; there will be asymptotes parallel to the y-axis.

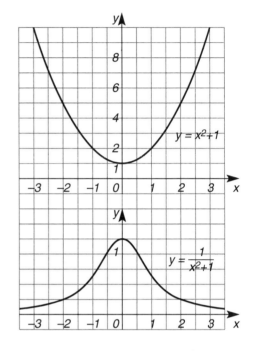

Example 6

The graph, C, of $y = (x - 1)(x - 2)$ meets the x-axis at $(1, 0)$ and $(2, 0)$; the graph, C', of $y = \dfrac{1}{(x - 1)(x - 2)}$ has asymptotes $x = 1$ and $x = 2$.

For $x < 1$: C is positive and decreasing,
        C' is positive and increasing.
For $x > 2$: C is positive and increasing,
        C' is positive and decreasing.
For $1 < x < 2$: C is negative with a lowest
        y value of $-\frac{1}{4}$,
        C' is negative with a maximum
        y value of -4.

Note: The symmetry in the line $x = 1\frac{1}{2}$ has been preserved.

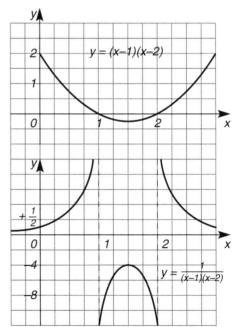

Now look back to the two curves given at the start of this extension work.

Check that you could derive the graph of $y = \dfrac{1}{(x + 1)(x - 2)^2}$ from the graph of $y = (x + 1)(x - 2)^2$.

EXERCISE 10.8

In questions 1–6 try to check your curves by generating them on a computer or graphical calculator.

1 (a) Draw the line $y = x$ and use it to sketch the curve C_1 with equation $y = \dfrac{1}{x}$. Describe the form of symmetry that C_1 possesses.

(b) Sketch the graph of $y = x^3$ and use it to sketch the curve C_2 with equation $y = \dfrac{1}{x^3}$.

(c) The curves C_1 and C_2 look quite similar.
   (i) Do they have any points in common?
   (ii) If the curves were drawn on the same axes, for what values of x would C_1 be above C_2?

2 (a) Sketch the graphs of (i) $y = x - 3$, (ii) $y = x + 3$, (iii) $y = \frac{x}{2}$ and (iv) $y = 2x + 1$, showing their intercepts on the axes.

(b) Using these graphs sketch the graphs of
   (i) $y = \dfrac{1}{x - 3}$, (ii) $y = \dfrac{1}{x + 3}$, (iii) $y = \dfrac{2}{x}$ and (iv) $y = \dfrac{1}{2x + 1}$.

(c) Check these graphs by considering them as transformations of the graph of $y = \dfrac{1}{x}$.

3 (a) Sketch the graph of $y = \sin x°$, in the interval $0 \le x \le 360$.

(b) Check that the graph of $y = \dfrac{1}{\sin x°}$, in the same interval, has the form shown in the diagram and write down the coordinates of A and B.

(c) Sketch the graph of $y = \dfrac{1}{\cos x°}$ in the same interval.

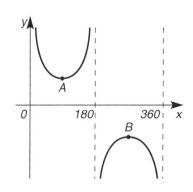

4 (*a*) Draw the graphs of (i) $y = x^2$ (ii) $y = x^2 + 1$ (iii) $y = x^2 - 1$.

(*b*) Copy the graphs of $y = \dfrac{1}{x^2}$ and $y = \dfrac{1}{x^2 + 1}$ (this can be seen in Example 5 above) and sketch the graph of $y = \dfrac{1}{x^2 - 1}$.

(*c*) One way to classify the graph of a quadratic function is by the number of intersections it has with the x-axis. Investigate how this number affects the form of the graph of the reciprocal function.

5 The diagram shows the graph of the function f, where $f : x \mapsto x^2(3 - x)$. Sketch the graph of $y = \dfrac{1}{f(x)}$.

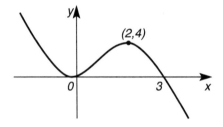

11. Area under a graph

During the course you will have found the area of many shapes. This chapter is primarily concerned with calculating or, in the case of curves, estimating the area of a region enclosed by a graph, the x-axis and two lines parallel to the y-axis. But first the following general revision exercise will remind you of the various methods that have been used to find the area enclosed between straight-line boundaries.

EXERCISE 11.1

1 The points A (6, 0) and B (8, 4) are joined to a third point C to form a triangle.

(a) Make a sketch of the triangle when the coordinates of C are (i) (3, 0), (ii) (3, 4), (iii) (6, 6), and write down the area of each triangle.

(b) Show, using the method indicated in the diagram, that the area of the triangle, when the coordinates of C are (3, 2), is 8 square units.

(c) Calculate the area of the triangle when C has coordinates (1, 1).

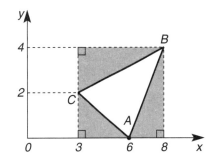

2 In the diagram BC is parallel to AD. Calculate the area enclosed by the four sides when:

(a) the coordinates of A, B, C and D are (3, 0), (4, 2), (8, 2) and (10, 0) respectively,

(b) the equations of the lines AB, BC and DC are $2y = 7(x-1)$, $y = 7$ and $x + y = 14$ respectively.

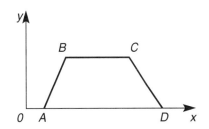

3 Calculate the area of a regular pentagon ABCDE, given that the coordinates of A and B are (1, 0) and (6, 0) respectively.

4   The diagram shows the plan of a field enclosed within five straight hedges. The farmer marks out three lines and measures the distances shown. Calculate the area of his field in hectares. (1 hectare $= 10\,000$ m^2)

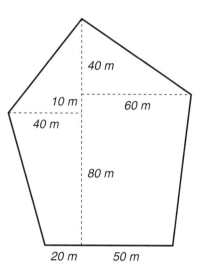

5   In the triangle shown AB is parallel to CD, AB $= 6$ cm, CD $= 18$ cm and the area of trapezium ABDC $= 48$ cm^2. Calculate the area of triangle OAB.

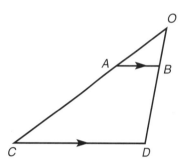

6   A plot of land has the dimensions (in metres) shown in the diagram.

(*a*) Show that BC $= 65$ m.

(*b*) Calculate, in m^2, the total area of the land.

(*c*) For triangle ABC evaluate $\sqrt{\{s(s-a)(s-b)(s-c)\}}$, where *a*, *b* and *c* are the lengths of the sides of the triangle and $s = \frac{1}{2}(a+b+c)$. What has this found?

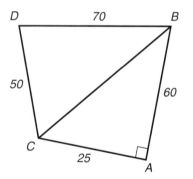

Area under a straight-line graph

The area 'under a graph' is the area of the region between the graph and the *x*-axis. When the graph consists only of straight lines, the region between the graph and the *x*-axis from one *x* value to another can be split into simple shapes, such as triangles, rectangles and trapezia, and so its area can be calculated easily.

Example 1

The region shown can be split into
triangle P, and trapezia Q and R.

Area of triangle $P = \frac{1}{2} \times 4 \times 5 = 10$

Area of trapezium $Q = \frac{1}{2} \times (5 + 6) \times 3 = 16\frac{1}{2}$

Area of trapezium $R = \frac{1}{2} \times (5 + 8) \times 6 = 39$

Total area under the graph is $65\frac{1}{2}$ square units.

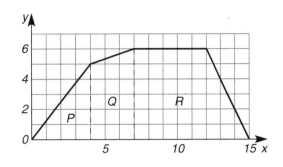

EXERCISE 11.2

1 Find the area under each of the following graphs.

(a)

(b)

(c)

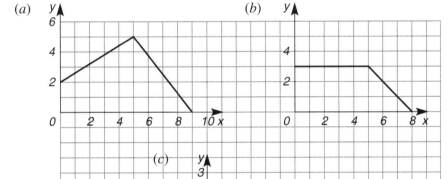

(d)

(e)

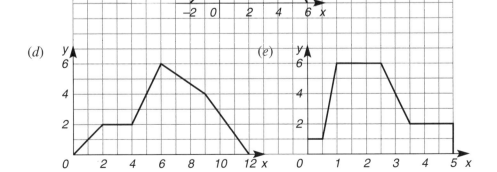

2 Find the exact area of the shaded regions in each of the following graphs.

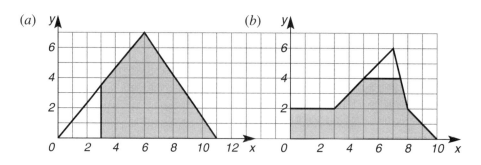

Interpretation of the area under a graph

When the axes represent physical quantities we saw in Book 3y how the gradient could represent a physical quantity too. For example, on a distance–time graph for motion in a straight line, the **gradient** could be seen dimensionally to represent $\dfrac{\text{distance}}{\text{time}}$, that is **speed**;

on a speed–time graph, the gradient represents $\dfrac{\text{speed}}{\text{time}}$, that is **acceleration.**

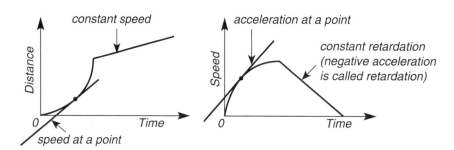

Similarly, area may also represent some feature.

Example 2

If a car travels at a constant speed of 20 m/s for 10 s, the distance the car travels, in metres is clearly 200.

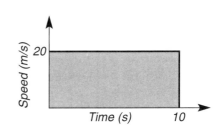

The speed–time graph for this motion is shown in the diagram; from this we can see that the area under the graph is 200.

On a speed–time graph area represents distance.

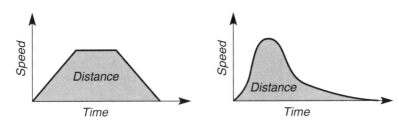

To find out what the area under the graph represents we need to multiply the dimensions given on the two axes. For example:

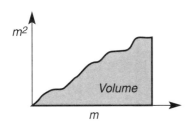 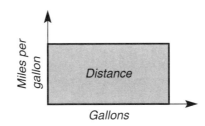

Area represents $\text{m}^2 \times \text{m}$
$= \text{m}^3$ (volume)
(See Exercise 11.6, question 8.)

Area represents $\dfrac{\text{miles}}{\text{gallons}} \times \text{gallons}$
$= \text{miles (distance)}$

The dimensions are found as above and the area of the relevant region will give the numerical value of that quantity.

Example 3

The three stages in a journey are shown in the speed–time graph. In the first part there is an acceleration of 4 m/s^2 (gradient of line) and the distance travelled is $(\frac{1}{2} \times 2 \times 8)$ m $= 8$ m. In the second part, showing a constant speed, the distance travelled is (3×8) m $= 24$ m. In the third stage there is a retardation (negative acceleration) of 1.6 m/s^2, and the distance travelled is $(\frac{1}{2} \times 5 \times 8)$ m $= 20$ m. The total distance travelled, 52 m, could have been found in one move by finding the area of the trapezium to give $\frac{1}{2} \times (10 + 3) \times 8$ m $= 52$ m.

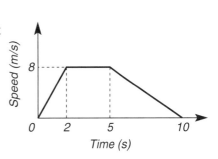

EXERCISE 11.3

1 The speed–time graph for a journey of 6 seconds is shown.

(a) Find, in m, the distance travelled

(i) in the first second, (ii) in the first five seconds.

(b) Find the average speed for the whole journey.

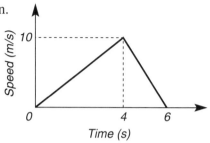

2 The speed–time graph for a journey from A to B, where AB = x km, is shown.

(a) Show that x = 3.5.

(b) Find the time taken to reach halfway between A and B.

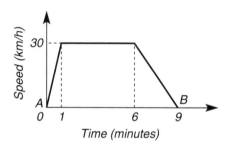

3 Find the value of V in the diagram, given that the total distance covered on the journey that this speed–time graph represents is 165 m.

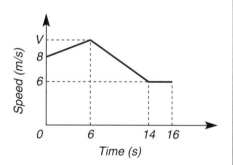

4 Describe fully the journey represented in the diagram. You should include the relevant accelerations and distances for the three stages.

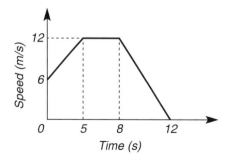

5 The acceleration in the first part of the journey is 0.8 m/s^2 and the total distance travelled is 104 m.

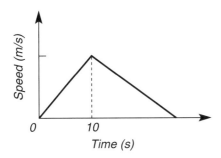

Find

(*a*) the average speed for the journey,

(*b*) the distance travelled between 9 s and 12 s.

6 Given that the average speed for the journey represented is 9.4 m/s and the acceleration in the final stage is 0.6 m/s^2, find

(*a*) the values of *V* and *T*,

(*b*) the time taken by a person who covers the same distance, starting from rest, with a constant acceleration of 0.5 m/s^2.

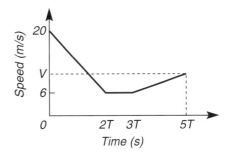

7 A lift starts in the basement of a building and moves without stopping to the top floor. For the first 6 s it accelerates uniformly at 1.5 m/s^2, for the next 12 s it travels at constant speed, and then it decelerates for 4 s until it stops. Draw a speed–time graph for the motion and hence find the distance to the top floor.

8 A car starts from rest and is accelerated uniformly to a speed of *V* m/s in 10 seconds. This speed is then maintained for 30 seconds before the car is brought to a stop by applying the brakes to produce a uniform deceleration which is numerically equal to twice the acceleration.

(*a*) Sketch the speed–time graph.

(*b*) Calculate the time during which the car is decelerating.

(*c*) Given that the total distance travelled is 600 m, calculate the value of *V*.

9 A particle moves, from rest at the point P, with an acceleration of 10 m/s^2 for 3 s, then over the next 5 s its speed decreases uniformly to 5 m/s, after which it continues at this steady speed until it reaches the point Q.

(*a*) Sketch the speed–time graph for the first 10 s.

(*b*) Can you suggest a situation that this data might model?

(*c*) Calculate the distance travelled in the first 10 s.

(*d*) Given that the distance PQ is 500 m, find the total time taken to reach Q.

10 The speed–time graph for a particle moving in a straight line is a straight line passing through the origin. Given that the particle covers 48 m in the first 4 s of its motion,

(*a*) find the speed at the end of each of the first 6 seconds,

(*b*) find the distance covered in each of the first 6 seconds,

(*c*) sketch the distance(s)–time (t) graph for the motion and give its equation.

Investigation A

In a small business it is assumed that employees can make 100 articles in about 10 hours. However, the employers do not assume a constant flow of finished articles, but use a simple model, assuming a linear decline in the rate at which the articles are produced. The graph of 'number produced per hour against time' is shown.

Find a formula for the number (*n*) produced in *T* hours, by considering the area under the graph from $t = 0$ to $t = T$, and show that the profit *P* (£) made by the business on each person's work, given that employees are paid £8 per hour and the articles are sold at £1.20 each, is related to *T* by $P = 16T - 1.2T^2$. Investigate this profit for values of *T* up to $T = 10$.

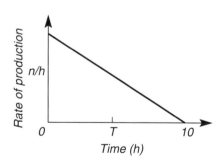

Area under a curve and the trapezium rule

When the graph is a curve then, at this stage, we cannot find the exact area, we can only estimate it. In this section we shall look at some methods for doing this:

1. by counting squares;
2. by considering the curve as a series of steps;
3. by considering the curve as a series of straight lines.

Out of the latter will emerge the **trapezium rule,** which is the method that will be used in most of the exercises that follow.

1. Counting squares

Clearly, counting squares is easy, and quite accurate but does have the following drawbacks: (*a*) it depends on the accuracy with which the points are plotted and the curve drawn; (*b*) it is difficult to estimate part squares; (*c*) it is time consuming. Care needs to be taken too in calculating what area each square on the graph paper represents if the scales are different.

Example 4

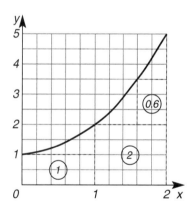

A good estimate for the area under $y = x^2 + 1$, from $x = 0$ to $x = 2$, using the graph shown, where each small square represents an area of 0.1 square units, would be about 4.6 [3.6 + (10 × 0.1)], which is remarkably accurate.

It is a good idea to have a crude estimate before we calculate; this might alert us to errors in the calculations. If we draw a sketch of $y = x^2 + 1$ we can see immediately that the area must lie between 2 and 10 by considering the 'lower' and 'upper' rectangles – but we may feel that does not tell us a lot! By inserting the chord PQ we can find the 'tighter' band from 2 to 6.

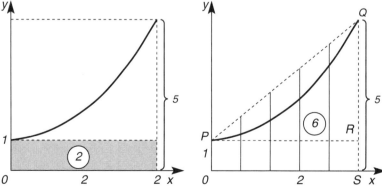

area rectangle OPRS < area under curve < area trapezium OPQS

2 < area under curve < 6

The following methods use these ideas to produce better estimates, without the need to plot the curve accurately.

2. Estimating the area under a curve by using a series of rectangles

Example 5

(*a*) Using 'lower' rectangles   (*b*) Using 'upper' rectangles

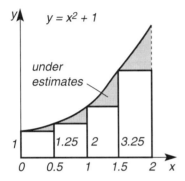   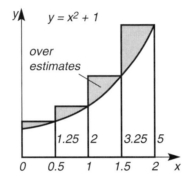

Area of lower rectangles
$= 0.5 + 0.625 + 1 + 1.625 = 3.75$
For this curve this estimate is clearly too low.

Area of upper rectangles
$= 0.625 + 1 + 1.625 + 2.5 = 5.75$
For this curve this estimate is clearly too high.

$3.7 <$ area under curve < 5.75

The required area lies between these two values. In this example four rectangles were used; by increasing the number of rectangles better estimates can be found. For example: five rectangles result in $3.92 <$ area < 5.52; 10 rectangles give $4.12 <$ area < 5.08.

Check these results and try other numbers of rectangles; the computer program, given in Investigation B, could be used.

The following 'mid-ordinate' approach, where the rectangle is centred on the middle of a strip, will often give a better degree of accuracy.

Example 6

If we take four rectangles as before, they will be centred on 0.25, 0.75, 1.25 and 1.75, with corresponding y values (ordinates) of 1.0625, 1.5625, 2.5625 and 4.0625 respectively.

Area $= 0.5 \times [1.0625 + 1.5625 + 2.5625 + 4.0625]$
     $= 4.625$

For this function we can see how the over-estimates and under-estimates are tending to balance each other.

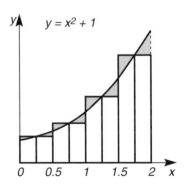

EXERCISE 11.4

1 (a) On graph paper plot the curve with equation $y = x^2$ for $x = 0$ to
$x = 5$. Estimate the area under the curve by counting squares.

(b) Show, by calculating the area of five 'lower rectangles',
that this area is greater than 30. (*Note:* The first one will
have zero area.)

(c) How do you know that the area is below 62.5?

(d) Calculate an estimate for the area using (i) five 'upper
rectangles', and (ii) five 'mid-ordinate rectangles' centred
on x values of 0.5, 1.5, …, 4.5.

(e) Given that the exact answer for the area is $41\frac{2}{3}$, calculate the
percentage error in your anwers from (a), (d) (i) and (ii).

(f) Explain how, if it is possible, you could improve the
estimates you have found.

Investigation B

The following BASIC program can be used to estimate the area under
a curve; before using it, see if you can interpret each step and decide
which of the previous methods it is using.

```
 10 area = 0
 20 INPUT"Y = ", a$
 30 INPUT "Lower limit", a
 40 INPUT "Upper limit", b
 50 INPUT "Number of steps", n
 60 h = (b - a)/n
 70 FOR X = a + h TO b STEP h
 80 Y = EVAL(a$)
 90 area = area + Y*h
100 NEXT
110 PRINT "area = " , area
120 PRlNT "Press G to change the number
    of steps or <Escape> to exit"
130 G = GET
140 area = 0, GOTO 50
```

Try this out by typing in at line 20 "$x\char94 2 + 1$", with $a = 0, b = 2$ and
(i) $n = 4$, (ii) $n = 5$, (iii) $n = 10$ to check the answers in Example 5.
Then use larger values of n and investigate how close to $4\frac{2}{3}$ you can reach.
    Use the program to find a better estimate to the area required in
Exercise 12.4. See how close to $41\frac{2}{3}$ you can get. Investigate other functions.

Investigation C

Amend the program given in Investigation B so that it calculates the area using the 'mid-ordinate' approach and compare the results with those found using other methods.

3. Estimating the area under a curve by using trapezia – The trapezium rule

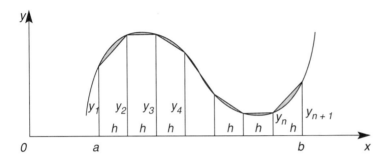

If we require to find the area under a curve from $x = a$ to $x = b$ this interval is divided up into a number (n) of strips, of equal width (h), and trapezia formed as in the diagram. In using the summation of the areas of these trapezia as an estimate to the area under the curve, the curve is, therefore, being considered as a series of straight lines. Using the notation y_1, y_2 ... to indicate the y values of the vertices of the trapezia on the curve, the estimate of the area under the curve is:

$$\tfrac{1}{2}(y_1 + y_2)h + \tfrac{1}{2}(y_2 + y_3)h + \tfrac{1}{2}(y_3 + y_4)h + \ldots\ldots + \tfrac{1}{2}(y_n + y_{n+1})h$$

There is a common factor of $\tfrac{1}{2}h$ and then, as all the y values occur twice except the first and the last, we have the result known as the **trapezium rule**.

Estimate of the area $= \tfrac{1}{2}h\,[y_1 + y_{n+1} + 2(y_2 + y_3 + \ldots\ldots + y_n)]$.

This is better learnt in words:

> Estimated area $=$ half the width of a strip $\times$ (the sum of the first and last y values together with twice all the other y values)

The shaded regions indicate the error in using the method and it is often clear whether it will give an under-estimate or over-estimate. For most curves this method usually gives a good degree of accuracy without large numbers of strips.

Example 7

We shall estimate the area under the curve $y = x^2 + 1$ from $x = 0$ to $x = 2$, using four strips, and compare the result with those found earlier using the rectangle methods.

x	0	0.5	1	1.5	2
y	1	1.25	2	3.25	5

6.5

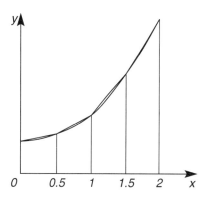

$$\text{Estimate} = \tfrac{1}{2} \times 0.5 \times [1 + 5 + 2(6.5)]$$
$$= 4.75$$

It is clear from the diagram that this is an over-estimate.
(Check that with five strips the estimate is 4.72.)

EXERCISE 11.5

1 Estimate the shaded area under each of the curves, using the trapezium rule with the data shown.

(*a*)

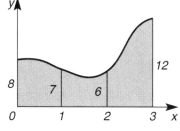

(*b*)

$y = 1 - \dfrac{1}{x}$

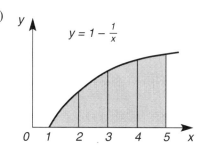

(*c*) $y = 4 + 3x - x^2$

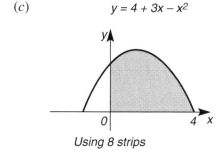

Using 8 strips

(*d*) $y = 2^x$

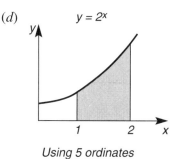

Using 5 ordinates

2 Estimate the area under each curve using the trapezium rule, with y values corresponding to the x values labelled.

(a)   (b)

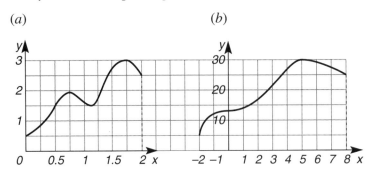

3 The diagram shows part of the curve with equation $y = 3x^2 - x^3$.

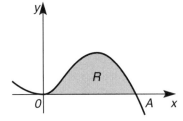

(a) Write down the coordinates of A.

(b) Use the trapezium rule, with six strips, to estimate the area of region R. (*Note*: The first and last y values used are both 0 here.)

4 (a) Calculate a 3 significant figure estimate, using the trapezium rule, for the area under $y = \frac{4}{x}$ between $x = 1$ and $x = 2$, using four strips as shown.

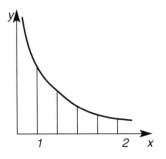

(b) Given that the exact area is 2.77 (3 s.f.), calculate the percentage error in the estimate.

(c) Explain why trying to find the area from $x = 0$ to $x = 2$ would cause a problem.

5 The diagram shows the plan of a field. Using the lines drawn on the plan, estimate, using the trapezium rule, the area of the field, giving your answer in (a) m², (b) hectares. (1 cm represents 50 m)

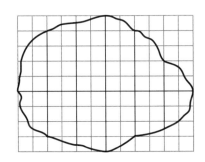

6 The diagram shows the cross-section of a tunnel. Given that the equation of the curved section is $y = \frac{1}{2}(16 - x^2)$ and the units are in metres, estimate

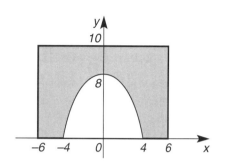

(a) the area under the curved section, using y values calculated at 1-m intervals of x,

(b) the cross-sectional area of the shaded brickwork.

7 At a particular point on the River Dart, where the river is 4.5 m wide, a group of geography students were asked to estimate the cross-sectional area of the river. Their results for the depth of the river, at intervals of 0.5 m from one bank, are shown in the table.

Distance from bank (m)	0	0.5	1	1.5	2	2.5	3	3.5	4	4.5
Depth (cm)	24.6	22	18.6	17.5	17.4	28.7	25.4	28.9	20.9	12

(a) Using all the data found, calculate, using the trapezium rule, an estimate (in cm^2) for the cross-sectional area.

(b) One of the group measures the speed of the current at the centre of the river as 0.8 m/s. Using a simple model that the river is flowing evenly at 0.8 m/s, estimate the volume, in m^3, of water passing this point each hour.

(c) Explain why the model used in (b) is likely to be unrealistic. Suggest a way of improving the estimate.

8 (*a*) A class were asked to estimate the area under the curve
with equation $y = \sqrt{(9 - x^2)}$, from $x = 0$ to $x = 3$, using the
trapezium rule with six strips. What should the answer be?

(*b*) The teacher then told them that the equation of a circle,
centre the origin, is $x^2 + y^2 = r^2$, where r is the radius, and
asked them to use their answer in (*a*) to deduce an estimate
for π. How is this possible and what should it be?

(*c*) Find the estimate for π when ordinates are evaluated at
intervals of 0.25.

Investigation D

Find out from a more advanced book, about Simpson's Rule for
estimating area, and write a few notes on the process.

In the following questions the area under the graph represents a
particular quantity.

EXERCISE 11.6

1 A particle moving in a straight line has speed $(6t^2 + 4)$ m/s
at t seconds after it starts from the point O.

(*a*) Complete the table.

t (s)	0	0.5	1	1.5	2	2.5	3
Speed (m/s)	4			17.5			58

(*b*) Using these data, estimate the distance travelled in the 3 seconds.

(*c*) Is the actual distance more or less than your estimate?
Give a reason.

2 The following data were collected
about the speed of an electric
train over a continuous interval of
1 minute.

Time (s)	0	10	20	30	40	50	60
Speed (m/s)	0	9	17	24	30	32	33

(*a*) Estimate the distance travelled in the minute.

(*b*) Is it reasonable to suggest that the estimate will be on the low side?

3 The speed of a car (v m/s) is recorded after a time (t s) and shown in the table.

t (s)	0	1	2	3	4	5	6	7	8
v (m/s)	0	5	7.6	8.0	6.2	4.9	4.6	3.8	2.5

(a) Without drawing a graph estimate, using the trapezium rule, the distance travelled in the 8 seconds.

(b) Show the information on graph paper and estimate:
  (i) by counting squares, the distance travelled in the 8 seconds,
  (ii) the maximum speed reached during this time,
  (iii) the acceleration of the car after 4 seconds.

4 The speed (v m/s)–time (t s) graph for a car in the first minute after it sets off is shown.

(a) Describe, fully, the motion of the car.

(b) Estimate the distance travelled in the minute, using the trapezium rule with speeds measured at every 5 seconds.

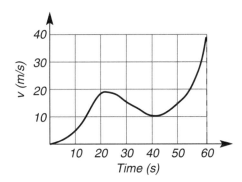

5 It is known that all light bulbs of a certain type have a life expectancy of between 0 and 6 years. The area under the curve $y = \frac{1}{36} x (6 - x)$, $0 \le x \le 6$, between $x = a$ and $x = b$, gives the probability that a light bulb chosen at random will last between a and b years.

Estimate, using the trapezium rule with six intervals, the probability that a light bulb chosen at random will last between 2 and 5 years, giving your answer to 3 significant figures.

6 Every 15 minutes, from 0800 to 1000, the number of cars passing a 'black spot' in a one-minute interval are recorded. The results are shown in the table.

Time	0800	0815	0830	0845	0900	0915	0930	0945	1000
Number/min	46	54	60	72	50	42	38	30	22

Estimate the number of cars that passed between 0800 and 1000.

7 The flow (f), at time t minutes, in litres/minute, of water into a tank can be modelled by $f = \dfrac{8}{t^2 + 1}$.

Make a table of values of f and t from $t = 0$ to $t = 8$, in 1-minute intervals, and estimate how much water is in the tank at the end of the 8 minutes, given that there was 12 litres at the start.

8 The area A, in units of 1000 m^2, of the surface of the water in a reservoir at different levels, l metres, above the lowest point in the reservoir are shown in the table.

l (m)	0	5	10	15	20	25	30	35	40
A (10^3m^2)	0	17	30	42	58	80	88	95	100

(a) Use the trapezium rule, and using all the data given, to estimate the volume of water below 40 m.

(b) Also estimate the volume of water lost, if the level drops from 40 m to 25 m.

9 The diagram shows the speed–time graph for a car over a one-minute period. The equation of the curved part is $v = k\,t\,(30 - t)$, where k is a constant.

(a) Describe the journey.

(b) Show that $k = 0.1$.

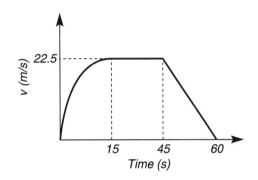

(c) Estimate the distance travelled in the first 15 s, using the trapezium rule with five strips, and hence estimate the total distance travelled in the minute.

(d) Find the time at which the car is first travelling at 20 m/s.

(e) Estimate the distance the car travels between this time and when it next has a speed of 4.5 m/s.

12. Vectors and matrices

Vectors: a revision

Although these topics were covered extensively in Book 4y a general review is included for revision purposes.

Vectors and translations

A convenient way of representing the translation shown is to use the 'column vector' $\begin{pmatrix} 3 \\ -2 \end{pmatrix}$. A translation is defined by the distance moved and by the direction of the movement, and these two values can be easily calculated if the column vector is known.

Example 1

For the translation shown above, the distance moved is 3.61 units (3 s.f.), found using Pythagoras' theorem, and the direction of the movement is at $x°$ below the horizontal, where $\tan x° = \frac{2}{3}$ and so $x = 33.7$ (3 s.f).

If the point P, with coordinates (1, 5) is subjected to two translations $\mathbf{T}_1$ and $\mathbf{T}_2$ in succession, where $\mathbf{T}_1$ is represented by $\begin{pmatrix} 3 \\ -2 \end{pmatrix}$ and $\mathbf{T}_2$ is represented by $\begin{pmatrix} 6 \\ 3 \end{pmatrix}$, the effect can be seen in the diagram. The image P' of P has coordinates (10, 6) and so the single translation $\mathbf{T}_3$ that maps P onto P' is $\begin{pmatrix} 9 \\ 1 \end{pmatrix}$.

As $\begin{pmatrix} 3 \\ -2 \end{pmatrix} + \begin{pmatrix} 6 \\ 3 \end{pmatrix} = \begin{pmatrix} 9 \\ 1 \end{pmatrix}$, we talk of 'adding vectors' when the effect of two vectors is required.

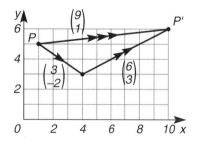

EXERCISE 12.1

1 For each translation given below, find (i) the length, (ii) the direction.

(a)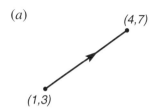

(b)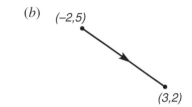

(c) $\begin{pmatrix} 4 \\ 0 \end{pmatrix}$ (d) $\begin{pmatrix} -1 \\ 3 \end{pmatrix}$

2 A translation **T** maps the point $(-1, 5)$ onto the point $(3, 3)$.

(a) Write down the column vector of the translation.

(b) State the coordinates of the image of the point $(3, 3)$.

(c) What point is mapped onto $(-2, 4)$?

(d) A second translation **S** has column vector $\begin{pmatrix} 5 \\ 2 \end{pmatrix}$. Find the image of the point $(6, 2)$ under the translation 'S followed by **T**'

(e) Write down the column vector of the single translation equivalent to 'S followed by **T**'

3 (a) Find the lengths of each of the translations given by

(i) $\begin{pmatrix} 3 \\ 4 \end{pmatrix}$ (ii) $\begin{pmatrix} 2 \\ 8 \end{pmatrix}$ (iii) $\begin{pmatrix} 3 \\ 4 \end{pmatrix} + \begin{pmatrix} 2 \\ 8 \end{pmatrix}$

(b) Explain why your answer to (iii) is not the sum of the answers to (i) and (ii).

4 Write down the column vectors for the translations which map the following.

(a) A onto C   (b) B onto E   (c) E onto D   (d) D onto A

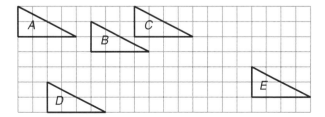

5 The diagram represents an automatic stacking system in a warehouse. To move the robot stacker from the position shown to pallet E5 it would be programmed with the vector $\begin{pmatrix} -3 \\ 0 \end{pmatrix}$; to then raise the lift to load goods in A5 would require the vector $\begin{pmatrix} 0 \\ 4 \end{pmatrix}$ to be added. The single vector $\begin{pmatrix} -3 \\ 4 \end{pmatrix}$ instructs the robot to move from its base to the pallet A5. To move from the loading bay to D3, to transfer these goods to B4 and then return to base, the program would be $\begin{pmatrix} -5 \\ 1 \end{pmatrix} + \begin{pmatrix} 1 \\ 2 \end{pmatrix} + \begin{pmatrix} 4 \\ -3 \end{pmatrix}$.

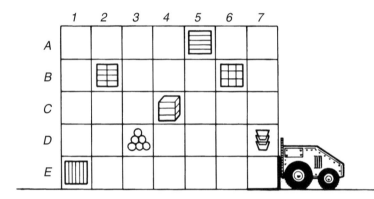

(*a*) Write down the vector program that the stacker needs in order to move from its base, transfer the following pallets, and then return to base.

(i) E1 to B3　(ii) B6 to A2　(iii) C4 to D6　(iv) A5 to E7

(*b*) For each of the following programs, write down the destination pallet and the *single* vector which would have produced the same effect.

(i) From D3: $\begin{pmatrix} 2 \\ 0 \end{pmatrix} + \begin{pmatrix} -1 \\ 3 \end{pmatrix}$

(ii) From A5: $\begin{pmatrix} -3 \\ -3 \end{pmatrix} + \begin{pmatrix} -1 \\ 2 \end{pmatrix}$

(iii) From E1: $\begin{pmatrix} 4 \\ 2 \end{pmatrix} + \begin{pmatrix} -4 \\ -2 \end{pmatrix}$

(iv) From B2: $\begin{pmatrix} 5 \\ -1 \end{pmatrix} + \begin{pmatrix} -3 \\ -2 \end{pmatrix}$

6 A plane is based at airfield B. The diagram shows B and five other places that the plane regularly visits. The journey from B to A can be represented by the column vector $\binom{60}{70}$.

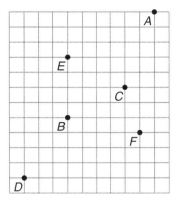

(a) Represent, in the same way, the journeys

    (i) B to C,   (ii) B to A to F,

    (iii) B to F direct,   (iv) C to D.

(b) On one journey from B to A the plane has to visit E on the way. Write down the vector for (i) the direct route from B to A, (ii) the route from B to A through E, and use these to (iii) calculate how much further it is by the longer route, given that the units are miles.

(c) The plane visits another place G, which is in the direction of D from B but twice as far from B. Write down the vector for the journey BG.

Vectors

A vector is any quantity that requires a magnitude *and* a direction to define it. A translation is one example of a vector quantity and all the results that have been noted for a translation will be true for all vectors.

Notation

A vector may be represented numerically or diagrammatically:

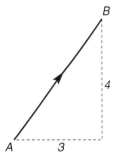

1. In numerical form, as in the column form $\binom{3}{4}$.

2. Diagrammatically as a directed line segment.

In print a vector may be written as $\overrightarrow{AB}$, using the end points of the line, as in 'vector $\overrightarrow{AB} = \binom{3}{4}$', or a small letter may be used, as in 'the vector **a**'. In written work we can indicate the vector by using $\overrightarrow{AB}$ and $\underline{a}$.

Manipulation of column vectors

We have seen that to add column vectors we add corresponding elements in the columns.

Example 2

$$\binom{4}{6} + \binom{3}{5} = \binom{3+4}{6+5} = \binom{7}{11}$$

Similarly, to subtract column vectors we subtract corresponding elements.

Example 3

If $\binom{a}{b} = \binom{10}{5} - \binom{2}{3}$, then $\binom{10}{5} = \binom{a}{b} + \binom{2}{3} = \binom{a+2}{b+3}$

and so $a = 10 - 2 = 8$ and $b = 5 - 3 = 2$.

To multiply a column vector by a number we multiply each element by the number (multiplication is shorthand for repeated addition).

Example 4

$$3\binom{2}{5} = \binom{2}{5} + \binom{2}{5} + \binom{2}{5} = \binom{3 \times 2}{3 \times 5} = \binom{6}{15}$$

EXERCISE 12.2

1 Write as single column vectors:

(a) $3\binom{1}{4}$ (b) $\binom{8}{-5} + \binom{3}{3}$ (c) $\binom{3}{0} - \binom{-1}{2}$

2 Simplify:

(a) $3\binom{2}{6} + 7\binom{3}{-2}$ (b) $2\binom{1}{-3} - 5\binom{6}{-2}$

3 The vector **b** is parallel to, but not the same length as, the vector **a**, where $\mathbf{a} = \binom{4}{3}$.

Which of the following vectors could represent **b**?

(a) $\binom{3}{4}$ (b) $\binom{8}{6}$ (c) $\binom{-4}{-3}$ (d) $\binom{5}{0}$ (e) $\binom{2}{1\frac{1}{2}}$ (f) $\binom{k}{k}$

4 Find of values of u and v given that

$$4\binom{u}{3} + 5\binom{2}{-1} = 2\binom{-1}{v}.$$

5 Given that **a** is parallel to the vector $\binom{2}{1}$ and $3\mathbf{a} + \binom{4}{5} = \binom{16}{k}$, find the value of k and give **a** as a column vector.

6 Given that $c\begin{pmatrix} 3 \\ 1 \end{pmatrix} + k\begin{pmatrix} -1 \\ 4 \end{pmatrix} = \begin{pmatrix} 0 \\ 26 \end{pmatrix}$, find the values of c and k.

7 The points A, B and C lie on a straight line. The coordinates of A are (4, 5), B is on the x-axis and $\overrightarrow{CA} = \begin{pmatrix} 12 \\ 6 \end{pmatrix}$.

(*a*) Write down the coordinates of C.

(*b*) Find the equation of the line AC.

(*c*) Hence, or otherwise, find the coordinates of B.

(*d*) Show that $\overrightarrow{BA} = 5\ \overrightarrow{CB}$.

8 The points A, B and C have coordinates (−4, −6), (2, 2) and (11, 14) respectively.

(*a*) Write down the column vectors for (i) $\overrightarrow{AB}$, (ii) $\overrightarrow{AC}$.

(*b*) Explain how the results in (*a*) show that A, B and C are collinear. (Collinear means 'lie on a straight line'.)

(*c*) Deduce the ratio AB:BC.

9 The points A, B, C, D and E are defined by $\overrightarrow{OA} = \begin{pmatrix} 3 \\ 4 \end{pmatrix}$, $\overrightarrow{OB} = \begin{pmatrix} 2 \\ 1 \end{pmatrix}$ $\overrightarrow{OC} = \begin{pmatrix} 4 \\ -3 \end{pmatrix}$, $\overrightarrow{OD} = \begin{pmatrix} 5 \\ 5 \end{pmatrix}$ and $\overrightarrow{OE} = \begin{pmatrix} 6 \\ 8 \end{pmatrix}$, where O is the origin.
Match each point to one of the following statements:

(*a*) The point lies on the circle $x^2 + y^2 = 5$.

(*b*) The distance of the point from the origin is $5\sqrt{2}$.

(*c*) The line from the origin to this point is parallel to $\overrightarrow{OA}$.

(*d*) The line from the origin to this point is perpendicular to $\overrightarrow{OC}$.

(*e*) The vector from this point to (12, 1) is parallel to $\overrightarrow{OB}$.

Addition of vectors represented diagrammatically

Vectors are 'added' geometrically by placing them 'nose to tail', as in the diagram.

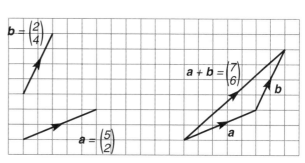

The effect of multiplying a vector by a number

As the vector 3**a** is shorthand for **a** + **a** + **a** it can be represented by placing three vectors **a** 'nose to tail' as in the diagram.

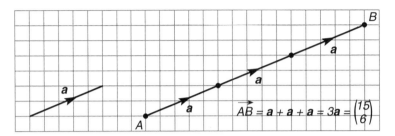

3**a** is a vector in the same direction as **a** but three times its length.

Special case: The vector −**a** is of the same length as **a** but in the opposite direction to **a**. Draw the vectors $\mathbf{a} = \binom{5}{2}$ and $-\mathbf{a} = \binom{-5}{-2}$, if you are in any doubt.

Subtraction of vectors

As **a** − **b** = **a** + (−**b**), the effect of subtracting vector **b** from the vector **a** can be represented by finding the effect of adding −**b** to **a**.

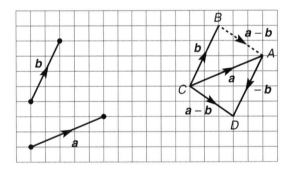

In the diagram $\overrightarrow{CD}$ shows the result of placing **a** and −**b** nose to tail. It is clear that $\overrightarrow{BA}$ also represents **a** − **b** and so, in practice, this presents a quicker method for finding **a** − **b**, in that it does not require −**b** to be drawn.

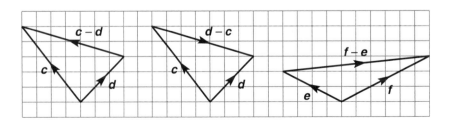

Representing vectors in terms of given vectors

We are often presented with a vector diagram in which some of the vectors are defined and others are left to be found. This can be resolved by using the three results that have been diagrammatically illustrated previously.

Example 5

In the diagram, D is the mid-point of AB, $\vec{CA} = \mathbf{a}$ and $\vec{CB} = \mathbf{b}$.

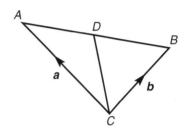

We can write the vector $\vec{CD}$ in terms of $\mathbf{a}$ and $\mathbf{b}$ as follows:

$$\vec{CD} = \vec{CB} + \vec{BD} = \mathbf{b} + \vec{BD}, \text{ but } \vec{BD} = \tfrac{1}{2}\vec{BA} = \tfrac{1}{2}(\mathbf{a} - \mathbf{b})$$
$$\Rightarrow \vec{CD} = \mathbf{b} + \tfrac{1}{2}(\mathbf{a} - \mathbf{b}) = \tfrac{1}{2}(\mathbf{a} + \mathbf{b})$$

Example 6 (Harder)

In the triangle OAB, OX $= 2$XA and Y is the mid-point of AB. $\vec{OA} = 3\mathbf{a}$ and $\vec{OB} = \mathbf{b}$,

(a) Express $\vec{BX}$ in terms of $\mathbf{a}$ and $\mathbf{b}$.

(b) Express (i) $\vec{BA}$ (ii) $\vec{BY}$, in terms of $\mathbf{a}$ and $\mathbf{b}$.

(c) Given that OC $= c$OY, show that $\vec{OC} = \tfrac{1}{2}c(3\mathbf{a} + \mathbf{b})$.

(d) Given that BC $= k$BX. express $\vec{BC}$ in terms of k, $\mathbf{a}$ and $\mathbf{b}$.

(e) By writing down a relationship between $\vec{OC}$, $\vec{OB}$ and $\vec{BC}$ show that $\tfrac{1}{2}c(3\mathbf{a} + \mathbf{b}) = 2k\mathbf{a} + (1 - k)\,\mathbf{b}$.

(f) Deduce the values of c and k.

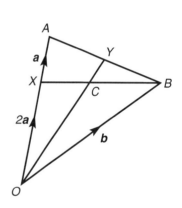

(a) $\vec{BX} = \vec{BO} + \vec{OX} = -\mathbf{b} + 2\mathbf{a}$ (or $2\mathbf{a} - \mathbf{b}$)

(b) (i) $\vec{BA} = \vec{BO} + \vec{OA} = 3\mathbf{a} - \mathbf{b} \Rightarrow$ (ii) $\vec{BY} = \tfrac{1}{2}(3\mathbf{a} - \mathbf{b})$

(c) $\vec{OY} = \vec{OB} + \vec{BY} = \mathbf{b} + \tfrac{1}{2}(3\mathbf{a} - \mathbf{b}) = \tfrac{1}{2}(3\mathbf{a} + \mathbf{b}) \Rightarrow \vec{OC} = \tfrac{1}{2}c(3\mathbf{a} + \mathbf{b})$

(d) $\vec{BC} = k(2\mathbf{a} - \mathbf{b})$

(e) $\vec{BC} = \vec{BO} + \vec{OC} \Rightarrow k(2\mathbf{a} - \mathbf{b}) = -\mathbf{b} + \tfrac{1}{2}c(3\mathbf{a} + \mathbf{b})$
$$\Rightarrow \tfrac{1}{2}c(3\mathbf{a} + \mathbf{b}) = \mathbf{b} + k(2\mathbf{a} - \mathbf{b}) = 2k\mathbf{a} + (1 - k)\,\mathbf{b}$$

(f) For this vector equation to be true, each side must have the same coefficients for $\mathbf{a}$ and $\mathbf{b}$, that is

$$1\tfrac{1}{2}c = 2k \text{ and } \tfrac{1}{2}c = 1 - k$$

Solving these simultaneous equations, $2k = 3(1 - k) \Rightarrow k = \tfrac{3}{5}$ and $c = \tfrac{4}{5}$.

EXERCISE 12.3

1 In each of the diagrams find, in terms of **a**, **b** or **a** and **b**, the vectors listed.

(a) ACBD is a parallelogram.

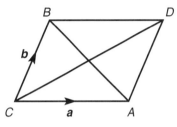

(i) $\overrightarrow{BD}$ (ii) $\overrightarrow{DA}$ (iii) $\overrightarrow{CD}$ (iv) $\overrightarrow{BA}$

(b) C and D are the mid-points of EA and EB, $\overrightarrow{CD} = $ **a**, $\overrightarrow{EC} = $ **b**.

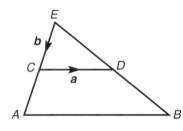

(i) $\overrightarrow{EA}$ (ii) $\overrightarrow{ED}$ (iii) $\overrightarrow{EB}$ (iv) $\overrightarrow{AB}$

(c) O is the centre of the circle.

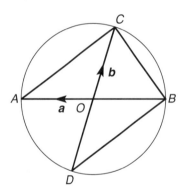

(i) $\overrightarrow{OB}$ (ii) $\overrightarrow{BC}$ (iii) $\overrightarrow{DB}$

As OA and OC are radii, why are $\overrightarrow{OA}$ and $\overrightarrow{OC}$ given as different vectors?

(d) In the rectangle OADB, $\overrightarrow{OA} = $ **a**, $\overrightarrow{OB} = $ **b**, E is the mid-point of AD and $\overrightarrow{BC} = \frac{1}{4}\overrightarrow{BD}$.

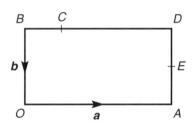

(i) $\overrightarrow{OC}$ (ii) $\overrightarrow{OE}$ (iii) $\overrightarrow{CE}$ (iv) $\overrightarrow{BE}$

2 Copy the diagram and add the points C, D, E, F, G and H such that (i) $\overrightarrow{OC} = \frac{1}{2}(a + b)$, (ii) $\overrightarrow{OD} = a - b$, (iii) $\overrightarrow{OE} = 2b - a$, (iv) $\overrightarrow{OF} = a + \frac{1}{2}b$, (v) $\overrightarrow{BG} = 2a$, (vi) $\overrightarrow{GH} = \overrightarrow{AB}$.

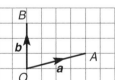

Write down, in terms of **a** and **b**, the vectors
(vii) $\overrightarrow{OH}$, (viii) $\overrightarrow{OG}$.

3 Given that $\overrightarrow{AB} = \mathbf{a}$ and $\overrightarrow{CD} = \mathbf{b}$, find, in terms of $\mathbf{a}$, $\mathbf{b}$, or $\mathbf{a}$ and $\mathbf{b}$:

(i) $\overrightarrow{DE}$ (ii) $\overrightarrow{CI}$ (iii) $\overrightarrow{GB}$ (iv) $\overrightarrow{AG}$ (v) $\overrightarrow{FH}$

(vi) $\overrightarrow{FE}$ (vii) $\overrightarrow{CE}$ (viii) $\overrightarrow{DA}$

4 The vectors $\mathbf{i}$ and $\mathbf{j}$ are defined by $\mathbf{i} = \begin{pmatrix} 1 \\ 0 \end{pmatrix}$ and $\mathbf{j} = \begin{pmatrix} 0 \\ 1 \end{pmatrix}$ respectively.

(*a*) Write down as single column vectors,
(i) $6\mathbf{i}$ (ii) $4\mathbf{i} + 3\mathbf{j}$ (iii) $\mathbf{i} - \mathbf{j}$.

(*b*) Write down in the form $a\mathbf{i} + b\mathbf{j}$,
(i) $\begin{pmatrix} 0 \\ 7 \end{pmatrix}$ (ii) $\begin{pmatrix} 3 \\ 5 \end{pmatrix}$ (iii) $\begin{pmatrix} -1 \\ 2 \end{pmatrix}$.

(*c*) In the diagram, $\overrightarrow{OA} = \mathbf{i}$ and $\overrightarrow{OB} = \mathbf{j}$. Express, in terms of $\mathbf{i}$, $\mathbf{j}$, or $\mathbf{i}$ and $\mathbf{j}$:

(i) $\overrightarrow{AD}$ (ii) $\overrightarrow{OD}$ (iii) $\overrightarrow{DB}$ (iv) $\overrightarrow{OC}$

(v) $\overrightarrow{CD}$ (vi) $\overrightarrow{CA}$ (vii) $\overrightarrow{AE}$ (viii) $\overrightarrow{EC}$

5 The coordinates of the vertices A, B and C of the parallelogram ABCD are $(-1, -2)$, $(3, 4)$ and $(8, 12)$ respectively.

(*a*) Write down $\overrightarrow{BA}$ as a column vector.

(*b*) Deduce the coordinates of the point D.

6 ABCDEF is a regular hexagon.

(*a*) Prove that each of the triangles is equilaterial.

(*b*) Given that $\overrightarrow{AB} = \mathbf{a}$ and $\overrightarrow{BC} = \mathbf{b}$, express in terms of $\mathbf{a}$, $\mathbf{b}$, or

$\mathbf{a}$ and $\mathbf{b}$
(i) $\overrightarrow{ED}$ (ii) $\overrightarrow{FC}$ (iii) $\overrightarrow{EF}$ (iv) $\overrightarrow{FA}$ and hence show that
(v) $\overrightarrow{EA} = \mathbf{a} - 2\mathbf{b}$.

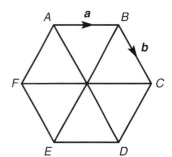

7 In the triangle ABO, D is the point such that AD:DB = 2:3, $\overrightarrow{OA} = \mathbf{a}$ and $\overrightarrow{OB} = \mathbf{b}$.

(a) Express, in terms of $\mathbf{a}$, $\mathbf{b}$, or $\mathbf{a}$ and $\mathbf{b}$ (i) $\overrightarrow{AB}$, (ii) $\overrightarrow{AD}$, and

hence show that (iii) $\overrightarrow{OD} = \dfrac{3\mathbf{a} + 2\mathbf{b}}{5}$.

(b) Given that the coordinates of A are (−2, 4) and those of B are (3, −1), find the coordinates of D.

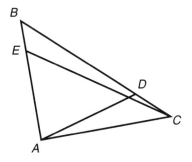

8 In the diagram $\overrightarrow{AE} = 3\mathbf{a}$ and $\overrightarrow{AC} = \mathbf{b}$. D is such that $\overrightarrow{BD} = 3\overrightarrow{DC}$ and E is such that $\overrightarrow{AE} = 3\overrightarrow{EB}$. Write down, in terms of $\mathbf{a}$, $\mathbf{b}$, or $\mathbf{a}$ and $\mathbf{b}$:

(a) $\overrightarrow{AB}$ (b) $\overrightarrow{BC}$ (c) $\overrightarrow{DC}$ (d) $\overrightarrow{AD}$ (e) $\overrightarrow{ED}$

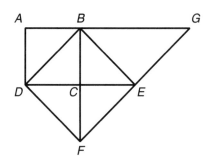

9 In the figure the sides DA and AB of the square ABCD are defined by $\overrightarrow{DA} = \mathbf{a}$ and $\overrightarrow{AB} = \mathbf{b}$. DBEF is also a square and ABG and FEG are straight lines.

(a) Explain why $\overrightarrow{DE} = 2\mathbf{b}$.

(b) Write down the vectors for
    (i) $\overrightarrow{BF}$ (ii) $\overrightarrow{DB}$ (iii) $\overrightarrow{BE}$ (iv) $\overrightarrow{EG}$.

(c) Given that the length of DA is one unit, calculate the area of the complete shape.

10 In the diagram AB, BC and CD are three sides of a regular octagon and BCEF is a square. $\overrightarrow{AB} = \mathbf{a}$ and $\overrightarrow{BC} = \mathbf{b}$.

(a) Show that $\overrightarrow{AD} = (1 + \sqrt{2})\mathbf{b}$.

(b) Express $\overrightarrow{CD}$ in terms of $\mathbf{a}$ and $\mathbf{b}$.

(c) Show that $\overrightarrow{BE} = 2\mathbf{b} - \sqrt{2}\,\mathbf{a}$.

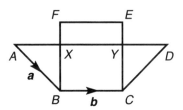

11 In the triangle OAB, $\overrightarrow{OA} = \mathbf{a}$, $\overrightarrow{OB} = \mathbf{b}$ and C and D are the mid-points of AB and OC respectively.

(a) Express $\overrightarrow{OC}$ in terms of $\mathbf{a}$ and $\mathbf{b}$ and show that
$$\overrightarrow{AD} = \tfrac{1}{4}(\mathbf{b} - 3\mathbf{a})$$

The point E divides $\overrightarrow{OB}$ in the ratio 1:2.

(b) Express $\overrightarrow{AE}$ in terms of $\mathbf{a}$ and $\mathbf{b}$.

(c) Deduce that ADE is a straight line and find the ratio AD:DE.

12 In the diagram $\overrightarrow{OA} = \mathbf{a}$, $\overrightarrow{OB} = \mathbf{b}$, C divides AB in the ratio 2:1 and E divides OC in the ratio 3:1, and BEF is a straight line.

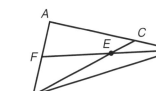

(a) Express $\overrightarrow{OC}$ in terms of $\mathbf{a}$ and $\mathbf{b}$.

(b) Show that $\overrightarrow{OE} = \tfrac{1}{4}\mathbf{a} + \tfrac{1}{2}\mathbf{b}$.

(c) Express $\overrightarrow{BE}$ in terms of $\mathbf{a}$ and $\mathbf{b}$.

(d) By writing $\overrightarrow{BF}$ in the form $c\,\overrightarrow{BE}$, express $\overrightarrow{OF}$ in terms of c, $\mathbf{a}$ and $\mathbf{b}$.

(e) As $\overrightarrow{OF}$ is in the direction of $\mathbf{a}$ it can be written in the form $k\mathbf{a}$. Use the two forms of $\overrightarrow{OF}$ to deduce the values of c and k.

13 In the diagram $\overrightarrow{OA} = 3\mathbf{a}$, $\overrightarrow{OB} = 4\mathbf{b}$, OC = 2CA and OD = 3DB.

(a) Given that $\overrightarrow{CE} = p\overrightarrow{CD}$, express $\overrightarrow{OE}$ in terms of p, $\mathbf{a}$ and $\mathbf{b}$.

(b) Given that $\overrightarrow{AE} = q\overrightarrow{AB}$, express $\overrightarrow{OE}$ in terms of q, $\mathbf{a}$ and $\mathbf{b}$.

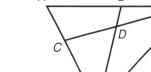

(c) Using your answers for (a) and (b), find the values of p and q.

(d) Deduce that (i) the area of triangle ODE = 3 × area of triangle OCD, (ii) the area of triangle OBE = 2 × area of triangle OAB.

(e) Using the results in (d), show that:
area of triangle DEB = area of quadrilateral ABDC.

Position vectors

Vectors are not fixed in space; in the diagram all the lines represent the vector $\mathbf{a} = \binom{2}{1}$.

For the vector $\overrightarrow{OA}$, where O is the origin, we say that A 'has **position vector a**'. A position vector is therefore fixed in space; there is only one point that has position vector $\mathbf{a}$. If the point P has coordinates (a,b) then we can equally well say that A has position vector $\binom{a}{b}$, since $\overrightarrow{OA} = \binom{a}{b}$.

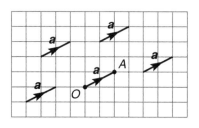

The modulus of a vector, $|\mathbf{a}|$

The magnitude of a vector $\mathbf{a}$, or its length when represented graphically, is called its **modulus** and is denoted by $|\mathbf{a}|$.

EXERCISE 12.4

1 In the diagram O is the origin, and $\mathbf{a}$ and $\mathbf{b}$ are shown. Identify the points with the following position vectors:

(a) $\mathbf{a}$ (b) $2\mathbf{a} - \mathbf{b}$ (c) $3\mathbf{b} + 2\mathbf{a}$

(d) $3(\mathbf{a} + \mathbf{b})$ (e) $4\mathbf{a} + 2(\mathbf{b} - \mathbf{a})$

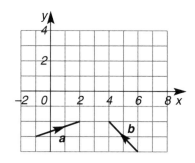

2 The points A and B have position vectors $\mathbf{a}$ and $\mathbf{b}$ referred to an origin O. Find, in terms of $\mathbf{a}$ and $\mathbf{b}$, the position vectors of the following points:

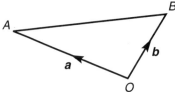

(a) C, where C is the mid-point of AB.

(b) D, where $AD = 3DB$.

3 The points C, D and E have position vectors $2\mathbf{a} - \mathbf{b}$, $4\mathbf{a}$, and $14\mathbf{a} + 5\mathbf{b}$ respectively, relative to an origin O.

(a) Find, in terms of $\mathbf{a}$ and $\mathbf{b}$, the vectors $\overrightarrow{CD}$ and $\overrightarrow{DE}$ and hence show that C, D and E are collinear.

(b) Deduce the ratio CD:DE.

4 Given that $\mathbf{a} = \begin{pmatrix} 3 \\ 4 \end{pmatrix}$, $\mathbf{b} = \begin{pmatrix} -5 \\ 12 \end{pmatrix}$ and $\mathbf{c} = \begin{pmatrix} 7 \\ k \end{pmatrix}$,

    (*a*) find the value of (i) $|\mathbf{a}|$, (b) $|\mathbf{b}|$, (iii) $|\mathbf{a} + \mathbf{b}|$, (iv) $|3\mathbf{a} - \mathbf{b}|$,

    (*b*) find the values of k, if (i) $|\mathbf{c}| = 25$, (ii) $\mathbf{c}$ is parallel to $2\mathbf{a} - 3\mathbf{b}$.

5 In the parallelogram OACB, $\overrightarrow{OA} = \mathbf{a}$ and $\overrightarrow{OB} = \mathbf{b}$.

    (*a*) Find, in terms of $\mathbf{a}$ and $\mathbf{b}$, $\overrightarrow{BA}$ and $\overrightarrow{OC}$.

    (*b*) Given that $|\mathbf{a} + \mathbf{b}| = |\mathbf{a} - \mathbf{b}|$, and $|\mathbf{a}| = |\mathbf{b}|$, what type of parallelogram is OACB?

    (*c*) Given that $|\mathbf{a}| = |\mathbf{b}| = |\mathbf{a} - \mathbf{b}|$, (i) explain why OABC must be a rhombus, (ii) deduce the value of $|\mathbf{a}|$, if $|\mathbf{a} - \mathbf{b}| = 5$ cm.

Using vector methods to solve problems involving forces and velocities

There are many situations where we need to find the net effect of two or more vectors acting simultaneously. In this chapter we shall only consider the effect of two but the methods can be extended to more, as we saw in Book 4y.

Consider a plane that is capable of moving at a speed of 500 m.p.h. If it has to travel from A to B, a distance of 2000 miles, then in still air it would head directly from A to B and reach it in 4 hours. However, we often find planes arriving earlier or later than their estimated time of arrival, due to the effect of the wind. Unless the wind is blowing directly in the directions $\overrightarrow{AB}$ or $\overrightarrow{BA}$, the plane will have to head in some other direction to compensate for the wind velocity. In this case the plane's net, or resultant, velocity, can be found using the addition law for vectors.

Velocity 'vector triangle'

The direction associated with the vector **a** is called the **heading** and the speed associated with this velocity is called the **airspeed**, that is the speed of the plane in still air. The vector **w** represents the wind velocity. The sum **r** of these two, $\mathbf{r} = \mathbf{a} + \mathbf{w}$, gives a velocity vector representing the effective speed of the plane, called the **ground speed**, and its direction of flight known as the **track**.

Example 7

An aircraft that can move at 300 m.p.h. in still air is heading on a bearing of 030° in a wind of speed 80 m.p.h. blowing from 280° in order to travel from A to B. Find (i) the resultant velocity of the plane, (ii) the time of flight, to the nearest 10 minutes, given that AB = 2500 miles.

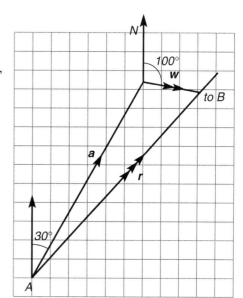

The diagram shows a scale drawing of the vector triangle, using a scale of 1 cm to represent 50 m.p.h.

  (i) The length of **r** gives the resultant speed, the ground speed, as 340 m.p.h.

 (ii) The time taken $= \dfrac{2500 \text{ h}}{340} = 7$ h 20 min (nearest 10 min).

The bearing associated with **r** is about 043° from the drawing.

A calculation method, not requiring the sine and cosine rules is given in Investigation A.

For some questions the velocities can easily be given as column vectors and then the calculation is straightforward.

Example 8

In a river flowing with velocity represented by **c** in the diagram, a boat sets off with a velocity which, if there were no current, would be represented by **a**. In the diagram **i** represents 1 km/h due east and **j** represents 1 km/h due north.
The column vectors for **a** and **c** are

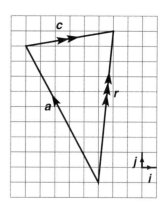

$\mathbf{a} = \begin{pmatrix} -5 \\ 9 \end{pmatrix}$ and $\mathbf{c} = \begin{pmatrix} 6 \\ 1 \end{pmatrix}$.

As $\mathbf{r} = \mathbf{a} + \mathbf{c}$, $\mathbf{r} = \begin{pmatrix} 1 \\ 10 \end{pmatrix}$ and

so $|\mathbf{r}| = \sqrt{101} = 10.0$ km/h (3 s.f.), and the bearing of $\mathbf{r} = 005.7°$ (Read off the answers from the drawing and see how accurate they are.)

Investigation A

In Example 7 the results could be found by calculation. One method would be to use the cosine rule to find the resultant speed and then use the sine rule to find the angle between **a** and **r**. This presents a good opportunity to practise these techniques, but here you are encouraged to take the column vector approach of Example 8 to solve the problem posed in Example 7.

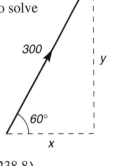

$x = 300 \cos 60°$
$= 150$

$y = 300 \sin 60°$
$= 259.81$

Vector **a**, written as a column vector, is

is $\begin{pmatrix} 300 \cos 60° \\ 300 \sin 60° \end{pmatrix} = \begin{pmatrix} 150 \\ 259.8 \end{pmatrix}$

as shown in the diagram.

Using the same method write down the column vector for **w**.
As **r** = **a** + **w** you can then find the column vector for **r**; it is $\begin{pmatrix} 238.8 \\ 245.9 \end{pmatrix}$.
Use this to find the resultant speed of the plane and the bearing of the track, and compare them with the results found by drawing.

Another common problem involving two vectors can be seen when two forces are acting on a point. We require to find the net effect of these forces; we require the single force, the resultant, equivalant to the two given forces. In practice this is important because the resulting movement will be in the direction of this resultant force.

Example 9

The two forces pulling the barge each have magnitudes 50 N. (The unit of force is a Newton). Find the resultant force.

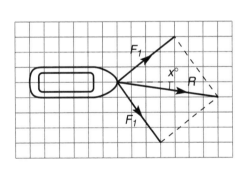

We can either use a scale drawing or calculate using the column vectors.

We can see that $\mathbf{F_1} = k\begin{pmatrix} 4 \\ 3 \end{pmatrix}$ as it is in the direction of $\begin{pmatrix} 4 \\ 3 \end{pmatrix}$ and, as its size is 50, $\mathbf{F_1} = \begin{pmatrix} 40 \\ 30 \end{pmatrix}$.

Similarly $\mathbf{F_2} = \begin{pmatrix} 30 \\ -40 \end{pmatrix}$.

Using vector addition, $\mathbf{R} = \begin{pmatrix} 40 \\ 30 \end{pmatrix} + \begin{pmatrix} 30 \\ -40 \end{pmatrix} = \begin{pmatrix} 70 \\ -10 \end{pmatrix}$.

The magnitude of the resultant force is therefore $\sqrt{(70^2 + 10^2)} = 70.7$ N, and its direction is such that $x = 8.13$.

EXERCISE 12.5

1 In the diagram, **a** represents the velocity of a plane in still air, **w** represents the wind velocity. (Scale: 1 cm represents 50 km/h.)

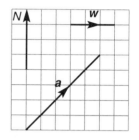

(*a*) Calculate the speeds associated with **a** and **w**.

(*b*) Write down the bearing of (i) the direction in which the plane is heading, (ii) the direction *from* which the wind is blowing.

(*c*) Write down the column vectors for **a** and **w** and hence for the resultant velocity **r**.

(*d*) Deduce the magnitude and direction of the resultant velocity.

2 The vectors **i** and **j** represent velocities of 1 km/h due east and 1 km/h due north respectively. A boy swims in such a way that, if there were no current, his velocity would be 4**j**. The river is flowing with velocity 3**i**.

(*a*) Write down the boy's actual velocity **v** in the form $p\mathbf{i} + q\mathbf{j}$.

(*b*) Calculate the boy's actual speed.

(*c*) Given that the parallel banks of the river run west–east and the banks are 400 m apart, calculate how far downstream from his starting point the boy is when he reaches the other side.

(*d*) If the boy wants to reach a point directly opposite his starting point, he must have an actual velocity in the direction **j**. Let $\mathbf{v} = k\mathbf{j}$.

  (i) Show that the boy must swim so that, if there were no current, his velocity would be $-3\mathbf{i} + k\mathbf{j}$.

  (ii) Given that his speed is 4 km/h, find the value of k, and find the angle to the bank at which he must swim.

3 A pilot wishes to reach a point 500 miles due north of his starting point. There is a wind blowing from the east with speed 60 m.p.h. and the plane has an airspeed of 400 m.p.h.

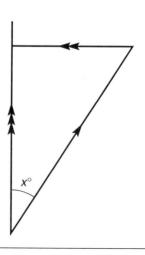

(*a*) Copy the vector diagram and add the 60 and 400 on the correct sides.

(*b*) Show that $x = 8.63$ (3 s.f.).

(*c*) Calculate the actual speed of the plane and deduce the time taken for the journey.

4 In the diagrams, where the scale is such that 1 cm represents 100 km/h, **a** is the velocity a plane would have if there were no wind, **w** is the wind velocity and **r** is the resultant velocity, so that $\mathbf{r} = \mathbf{a} + \mathbf{w}$.

(i) 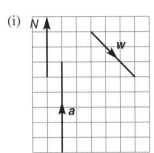   (ii)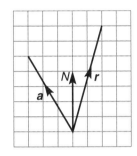

(a) Find, in column vector form, the missing velocity in each case.

(b) Calculate the speed and direction associated with each of these velocities.

(c) In (ii) the plane takes 5h 20 min to reach its destination. How far, to the nearest kilometre, is the journey.

5 Use a scale drawing to solve this problem. An aircraft sets a course of 080° and has an airspeed of 300 knots. Its ground speed and track, representing the resultant velocity, are 340 knots and 100° respectively. Find the wind speed, and the direction from which it is blowing. (A knot is the usual unit for the speed of aircraft and is defined as 1 nautical mile per hour, where 1 nautical mile is 1852 metres.)

6 A plane sets off from airport A to reach airport B, which is on a bearing of 045° from A. The wind has a velocity vector $\binom{30}{0}$, where the units are knots.

(a) Explain why the column vector of the resultant velocity must be of the form $\binom{k}{k}$.

(b) Let the column vector of the velocity the plane would have if there were no wind (vector **a**) be $\binom{c}{d}$. Show that $c + 30 = k$ and $d = k$.

(c) Given that the distance AB = 250 nautical miles, and the journey takes 30 minutes, show that $k = 354$, correct to 3 s.f.

(d) Deduce the airspeed of the plane, correct to 3 s.f.

7 Each of the diagrams shows two forces acting at a point A. The scale is that 1 cm represents 1 newton, so that, in (i) for example, $\mathbf{F_1}$ has the column vector $\binom{3}{1}$.

(i)

(ii)

(a) From the diagrams, by measurement, find the magnitude and direction of the resultant force. (Give the direction measured from the dotted line.)

(b) Write down the column vectors for $\mathbf{F_1}$ and $\mathbf{F_2}$ and deduce that of the resultant force.

(c) Calculate, using your resultant in (b) the magnitude and direction of the resultant force.

8 Find by means of a scale drawing the resultant of each of the sets of forces shown.

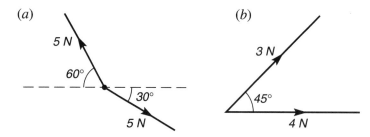

(a)

5 N

60°

30°

5 N

(b)

3 N

45°

4 N

9 The resultant of two forces whose column vectors are $\binom{20}{30}$ and $\binom{15}{k}$ is in the direction given by the column vector $\binom{1}{2}$.

Show that $k = 40$ and deduce the magnitude of the resultant force.

10 The resultant of two forces F_1 and F_2 acting at a point is R.

   (a) If $F_1 = \begin{pmatrix} 5 \\ 6 \end{pmatrix}$ and $R = \begin{pmatrix} 17 \\ -4 \end{pmatrix}$ find the column vector for F_2 and show that F_1 and F_2 are acting at right angles to each other.

   (b) If F_1 has magnitude 5 N and is acting due east, and F_2 has magnitude 4 N and is acting on a bearing of 060°, find the magnitude and direction of R

      (i) by drawing,

      (ii) by calculation, by first forming the column vectors for F_1, F_2 and hence R.

11 Copy the diagram and add to it

   (a) the resultant force acting on the point A,

   (b) a force F_3 which would counterbalance the effect of F_1 and F_2 on A. (A is then said to be in **equilibrium**.)

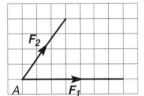

12 A particle of weight 20 N is being supported by two strings as shown in the diagram. The forces in the one string is known to be 10 N.

   (a) Explain how we know that the resultant of the forces in the two strings is 20 N vertically upwards.

   (b) Using all the information given, draw a vector triangle for the forces in the string and their resultant, and hence find the values of x and y.

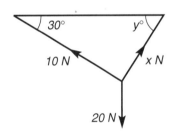

Matrices: a revision

A matrix is a rectangular array of numbers. They can be of any shape, for example $\begin{pmatrix} 3 & 4 \\ 5 & 6 \end{pmatrix}$ is a 2 × 2 matrix; $\begin{pmatrix} 1 & 2 \\ 4 & 5 \\ 7 & 8 \end{pmatrix}$ is a 3 × 2 matrix; and the column vector $\begin{pmatrix} 2 \\ 1 \end{pmatrix}$ can be seen as a special case of a 2 × 1 matrix.

   We used all shapes of matrices in Book 4y, in many situations. Here we shall only consider their use as transformations and so most of the work will relate only to 2 × 2 and 2 × 1 matrices.

   A degree of manipulation of matrices is required and first we shall revise aspects of the algebra of matrices.

Addition and subtraction of matrices

Providing the matrices are of the same shape, or **order**, matrices can be added or subtracted, like vectors, by adding or subtracting corresponding elements.

Example 10

$$\begin{pmatrix} 3 & 5 \\ 4 & 0 \end{pmatrix} + \begin{pmatrix} 6 & -3 \\ -1 & 5 \end{pmatrix} = \begin{pmatrix} 3+6 & 5+(-3) \\ 4+(-1) & 0+5 \end{pmatrix} = \begin{pmatrix} 9 & 2 \\ 3 & 5 \end{pmatrix}$$

$$\begin{pmatrix} 3 & 5 \\ 4 & 0 \end{pmatrix} - \begin{pmatrix} 6 & -3 \\ -1 & 5 \end{pmatrix} = \begin{pmatrix} 3-6 & 5-(-3) \\ 4-(-1) & 0-5 \end{pmatrix} = \begin{pmatrix} -3 & 8 \\ 5 & -5 \end{pmatrix}$$

Multiplication of a matrix by a number

Again, as for vectors, each element in the matrix is multiplied by the number.

Example 11

$$6\begin{pmatrix} 5 & -3 \\ 7 & 2 \end{pmatrix} = \begin{pmatrix} 6\times5 & 6\times(-3) \\ 6\times7 & 6\times2 \end{pmatrix} = \begin{pmatrix} 30 & -18 \\ 42 & 12 \end{pmatrix}$$

Multiplication of matrices

If two matrices are of compatible shapes, they can be multiplied. If **A** and **B** are two matrices, then the product **AB** is possible when the number of columns in **A** is the same as the number of rows in **B**; so if **A** has order $p \times q$, then **B** must be a matrix with q rows. The reason for this can be seen when the process for multiplying matrices is defined.

Example 12

The matrices $\mathbf{A} = \begin{pmatrix} 1 & 2 \\ 3 & 4 \end{pmatrix}$ and $\mathbf{B} = \begin{pmatrix} 5 & 6 \\ 7 & 8 \end{pmatrix}$ are multiplied as follows:

$$\begin{pmatrix} 1 & 2 \\ 3 & 4 \end{pmatrix} \begin{pmatrix} 5 & 6 \\ 7 & 8 \end{pmatrix} = \begin{pmatrix} (1\times5) + (2\times7) & (1\times6) + (2\times8) \\ (3\times5) + (4\times7) & (3\times6) + (4\times8) \end{pmatrix} = \begin{pmatrix} 19 & 22 \\ 43 & 50 \end{pmatrix}$$

The brackets in the intermediate stage are not necessary; they are inserted to emphasise the procedure.

Note: If we form the product **BA** the result is not the same as **AB**.

$$\begin{pmatrix} 5 & 6 \\ 7 & 8 \end{pmatrix} \begin{pmatrix} 1 & 2 \\ 3 & 4 \end{pmatrix} = \begin{pmatrix} (5\times1) + (6\times3) & (5\times2) + (6\times4) \\ (7\times1) + (8\times3) & (7\times2) + (8\times4) \end{pmatrix} = \begin{pmatrix} 23 & 34 \\ 31 & 46 \end{pmatrix}$$

Example 13

$$\begin{pmatrix} 2 & 1 \\ 1 & 4 \end{pmatrix}\begin{pmatrix} 3 & 0 & 2 \\ 5 & -1 & 3 \end{pmatrix} = \begin{pmatrix} 2\times3 + 1\times5 & 2\times0 + 1\times-1 & 2\times2 + 1\times3 \\ 1\times3 + 4\times5 & 1\times0 + 4\times-1 & 1\times2 + 4\times3 \end{pmatrix} = \begin{pmatrix} 11 & -1 & 7 \\ 23 & -4 & 14 \end{pmatrix}$$

Sometimes two matrices will give the same result whichever way they are multiplied, but in general, even if they can be multiplied both ways, **AB** ≠ **BA**, that is matrices are *not* **commutative** under matrix multiplication.

EXERCISE 12.6

1 Write each of the following as a single matrix.

(a) $\begin{pmatrix} 1 & 6 \\ 3 & -2 \end{pmatrix} + \begin{pmatrix} 5 & -4 \\ 5 & 0 \end{pmatrix}$

(b) $\begin{pmatrix} 9 & 0 \\ 8 & -2 \end{pmatrix} - \begin{pmatrix} -6 & 1 \\ -5 & -2 \end{pmatrix}$

(c) $3\begin{pmatrix} 2 & 6 \\ 1 & 2 \end{pmatrix} + 5\begin{pmatrix} 1 & 0 \\ 5 & -4 \end{pmatrix}$

(d) $2\begin{pmatrix} -6 & 3 \\ 3 & -1 \end{pmatrix} - \begin{pmatrix} 4 & -2 \\ 3 & -1 \end{pmatrix}$

(e) $\begin{pmatrix} 4 & 3 \\ 2 & 1 \end{pmatrix}\begin{pmatrix} 1 & 6 \\ 0 & 3 \end{pmatrix}$

(f) $\begin{pmatrix} 8 & -2 \\ 1 & 2 \end{pmatrix}\begin{pmatrix} 3 & 6 \\ -3 & 4 \end{pmatrix}$

(g) $\begin{pmatrix} 3 & 6 \\ 4 & 1 \end{pmatrix}\begin{pmatrix} 2 & 1 & 0 \\ -1 & 5 & 7 \end{pmatrix}$

(h) $\begin{pmatrix} 2 & 1 \\ 1 & -2 \end{pmatrix}\begin{pmatrix} 5 \\ 1 \end{pmatrix}$

(i) $\begin{pmatrix} 6 & 0 \\ 7 & -4 \end{pmatrix}\begin{pmatrix} 5 \\ 6 \end{pmatrix}$

2 Find the value of the letters in the following.

(a) $\begin{pmatrix} 3 & a \\ 4 & 7 \end{pmatrix} - 2\begin{pmatrix} 3 & 2 \\ -1 & a \end{pmatrix} = \begin{pmatrix} b & 6 \\ c & d \end{pmatrix}$

(b) $\begin{pmatrix} 4 & e \\ f & -1 \end{pmatrix}\begin{pmatrix} 2 \\ 3 \end{pmatrix} = \begin{pmatrix} 8 \\ 1 \end{pmatrix}$

(c) $\begin{pmatrix} x & y \\ 2x & -y \end{pmatrix}\begin{pmatrix} 1 \\ 1 \end{pmatrix} = \begin{pmatrix} 4 \\ 20 \end{pmatrix}$

(d) $\begin{pmatrix} x & y \\ 6 & 5 \end{pmatrix}\begin{pmatrix} x \\ 2 \end{pmatrix} = \begin{pmatrix} 3 \\ 4 \end{pmatrix}$

3 The result of multiplying the matrix **A** by itself is denoted by $\mathbf{A}^2$; $\mathbf{A}^3$ means 'multiply $\mathbf{A}^2$ by **A**', etc.

Given that $\mathbf{A} = \begin{pmatrix} 0 & 1 \\ 1 & 0 \end{pmatrix}$, $\mathbf{B} = \begin{pmatrix} 3 & 2 \\ 7 & 5 \end{pmatrix}$, $\mathbf{C} = \begin{pmatrix} 5 & -2 \\ -7 & 3 \end{pmatrix}$:

(a) Find the matrix for $\mathbf{A}^2$ and deduce the matrices for (i) $\mathbf{A}^{17}$ (ii) $\mathbf{A}^{36}$.

(b) Find the single matrices for (i) **AB** (ii) **BA** (iii) $(\mathbf{AC})^2$.

(c) Find the single matrix for (i) **BC** (ii) **CB**.

The unit or identity matrix

In the last question we saw that $\mathbf{A}^2 = \begin{pmatrix} 1 & 0 \\ 0 & 1 \end{pmatrix}$. The matrix $\begin{pmatrix} 1 & 0 \\ 0 & 1 \end{pmatrix}$ has the same effect in matrix multiplication as the number 1 has in numerical multiplication. It is called the **unit** matrix, or when matrices are being considered as transformations, the **identity** matrix, and is often denoted by $\mathbf{I}$.

The inverse of a matrix

If two matrices multiply together to form the unit or identity matrix then each matrix is said to be the **inverse** of the other, and they form $\mathbf{I}$ whichever way they are multiplied; a matrix and its inverse are commutative under multiplication.

In question 3 of the last exercise the matrix $\mathbf{B} = \begin{pmatrix} 3 & 2 \\ 7 & 5 \end{pmatrix}$ is the inverse of the matrix $\mathbf{C} = \begin{pmatrix} 5 & -2 \\ -7 & 3 \end{pmatrix}$ and vice versa, as $\mathbf{BC} = \mathbf{I} = \mathbf{CB}$.

In general, if $\mathbf{A} = \begin{pmatrix} a & b \\ c & d \end{pmatrix}$, where $ad - bc \neq 0$,

then the inverse of $\mathbf{A}$, denoted by $\mathbf{A}^{-1}$, is $\begin{pmatrix} \dfrac{d}{ad\text{-}bc} & \dfrac{-b}{ad - bc} \\ \dfrac{-c}{ad - bc} & \dfrac{a}{ad - bc} \end{pmatrix}$.

Example 14

For the matrix $\mathbf{A} = \begin{pmatrix} 6 & 3 \\ -1 & 2 \end{pmatrix}$, $ad - bc = (6 \times 2) - (3 \times -1) = 15$,

and so $\mathbf{A}^{-1} = \begin{pmatrix} \dfrac{2}{15} & \dfrac{-3}{15} \\ \dfrac{1}{15} & \dfrac{6}{15} \end{pmatrix} = \begin{pmatrix} \dfrac{2}{15} & \dfrac{-1}{5} \\ \dfrac{1}{15} & \dfrac{2}{5} \end{pmatrix}$.

The determinant of a matrix

The value of $ad - bc$ is called the **determinant** of the matrix. If the determinant is zero, then the matrix can have no inverse and the matrix is called a **singular matrix**.

EXERCISE 12.7

1 Find the inverse of the following matrices.

(a) $\begin{pmatrix} 8 & 1 \\ 7 & 1 \end{pmatrix}$ (b) $\begin{pmatrix} 3 & 5 \\ 1 & 2 \end{pmatrix}$ (c) $\begin{pmatrix} 1 & 0 \\ 0 & -1 \end{pmatrix}$ (d) $\begin{pmatrix} 4 & -5 \\ -3 & 4 \end{pmatrix}$

(e) $\begin{pmatrix} 5 & 2 \\ 3 & 3 \end{pmatrix}$ (f) $\begin{pmatrix} 8 & 0 \\ 6 & 2 \end{pmatrix}$ (g) $\begin{pmatrix} -2 & 5 \\ 1 & -2 \end{pmatrix}$ (h) $\begin{pmatrix} -2 & -1 \\ -4 & -3 \end{pmatrix}$

2 State whether the following statements are true or false. If you think it is false produce a counter-example.

(a) A matrix can only have an inverse if it is a square matrix, that is, it has the same number of rows as columns.

(b) The matrix $\begin{pmatrix} 5 & 2 \\ -5 & 2 \end{pmatrix}$ does not have an inverse.

(c) If two matrices multiply to give the **null** or **zero** matrix $\begin{pmatrix} 0 & 0 \\ 0 & 0 \end{pmatrix}$, then one of the matrices must be $\begin{pmatrix} 0 & 0 \\ 0 & 0 \end{pmatrix}$.

(d) If $\mathbf{AB} = \mathbf{BA}$, then $\mathbf{A}$ must be the inverse of $\mathbf{B}$.

3 Given that $\mathbf{A} = \begin{pmatrix} 2 & 0 \\ 1 & -2 \end{pmatrix}$, (a) find $\mathbf{A}^2$, and (b) deduce (i) $\mathbf{A}^{-1}$, (ii) $\mathbf{A}^6$.

4 Find the value of the determinant of each of the following matrices and state which matrices are singular.

(a) $\begin{pmatrix} 4 & 3 \\ 3 & 5 \end{pmatrix}$ (b) $\begin{pmatrix} 6 & 9 \\ 2 & 3 \end{pmatrix}$ (c) $\begin{pmatrix} 1 & 2 \\ -1 & 2 \end{pmatrix}$

(d) $\begin{pmatrix} \frac{3}{5} & -\frac{4}{5} \\ \frac{4}{5} & \frac{3}{5} \end{pmatrix}$ (e) $\begin{pmatrix} 3 & 6 \\ 2 & 4 \end{pmatrix}$

Transformation matrices

This topic was treated very fully in Book 4y but the main features are included as revision.

The point with coordinates (2, 1) can be denoted by the position vector $\begin{pmatrix} 2 \\ 1 \end{pmatrix}$.

The matrix equation $\begin{pmatrix} 1 & 0 \\ 0 & -1 \end{pmatrix} \begin{pmatrix} 2 \\ 1 \end{pmatrix} = \begin{pmatrix} 2 \\ -1 \end{pmatrix}$ can be looked at in the following way: as a result of performing the matrix multiplication the point (2, 1) has moved to the point (2, −1). More generally, the image of the point (x, y) can be found by placing the position vector $\begin{pmatrix} x \\ y \end{pmatrix}$ on the right of the matrix and forming the product $\begin{pmatrix} 1 & 0 \\ 0 & -1 \end{pmatrix} \begin{pmatrix} x \\ y \end{pmatrix} = \begin{pmatrix} x \\ -y \end{pmatrix}$ to give an image $(x, -y)$. This is a transformation of the plane that we should recognise as 'reflection in the x-axis'; we say that $\begin{pmatrix} 1 & 0 \\ 0 & -1 \end{pmatrix}$ is the matrix of this transformation. Before we look at the method for finding the matrix of a given transformation, or identifying the transformation associated with a given matrix, the following exercise reinforces the basics as well as providing some exploratory work.

EXERCISE 12.8

1 The matrix of transformation is $\begin{pmatrix} 0 & -1 \\ -1 & 0 \end{pmatrix}$.

   (a) Find the images of the points (i) (0, 0), (ii) (2, 0), (iii) (–5, 0), (iv) $(k, 0)$ under this transformation, and deduce that the image of the x-axis is a straight line whose equation should be given.

   (b) Prove that points on the y-axis map onto points on the x-axis.

   (c) Show that the points on the line $y = x$ map onto points on the same line.

   (d) What is special about the images of the points on the line $y = -x$?

   (e) Find the images of the points (i) (0, 1), (ii) (2, 5), (iii) (4, 9), (iv) (–1, –1).

   (f) Prove that the image of the line with equation $y = 2x + 1$ is the line with equation $y = \frac{1}{2}(x + 1)$.

   (g) What transformation does this matrix represent?

2 The vertices of a square ABCD have coordinates (2, 0), (4, 2), (2, 4) and (0, 2) respectively. Plot and label these points on squared paper. A transformation has the matrix $\begin{pmatrix} 0 & 1 \\ 1 & 0 \end{pmatrix}$.

   (a) Find the images of the points A, B, C and D under this transformation and, in a separate diagram draw, and label these points A', B', C' and D'.

   (b) Describe the transformation that maps ABCD onto A'B'C'D'.

3 Answer parts (*a*) and (*b*) of the last question for the transformations whose matrices are:

(i) $\begin{pmatrix} 2 & 0 \\ 0 & 2 \end{pmatrix}$ (ii) $\begin{pmatrix} 0 & -1 \\ 1 & 0 \end{pmatrix}$ (iii) $\begin{pmatrix} -1 & 0 \\ 0 & -1 \end{pmatrix}$ (iv) $\begin{pmatrix} \frac{1}{2} & -\frac{\sqrt{3}}{2} \\ \frac{\sqrt{3}}{2} & \frac{3}{5} \end{pmatrix}$

4 On squared paper draw the triangle with vertices A, B and C whose coordinates are (3, 0), (5, 2) and (1, 6) respectively.

(*a*) Find the images of the points A, B and C under the transformation whose matrix is $\mathbf{A} = \begin{pmatrix} 0 & 1 \\ -1 & 0 \end{pmatrix}$, and draw and label the image triangle.

(*b*) Identify this transformation and hence find the matrix $\mathbf{A}^{16}$.

5 A transformation whose matrix is $\begin{pmatrix} 5 & -1 \\ k & 4 \end{pmatrix}$ maps (3, 2) onto (13, 2). Find the value of k and show that (4, 3) is mapped onto (17, 4).

6 The transformation whose matrix is $\begin{pmatrix} 1 & 0 \\ 4 & 2 \end{pmatrix}$ maps (3, 1) onto (*a*, *b*) and (*a*, *b*) onto (*c*, *d*).

(*a*) Show that $a = 3$ and $b = 14$, and find c and d.

(*b*) The matrix $\begin{pmatrix} p & q \\ r & s \end{pmatrix}$ maps the two image points back onto their original points. Show that:

   (i) $3p + 14q = 3$ and $3p + 34q = 3$

   (ii) $3r + 14s = 1$ and $3r + 34s = 14$

(*c*) By solving the pairs of simultaneous equations find the values of p, q, r and s.

(*d*) Find the inverse of $\begin{pmatrix} 1 & 0 \\ 4 & 2 \end{pmatrix}$.

(*e*) Why are the results for (*c*) and (*d*) so related?

Using the unit square to identify transformations

The 2×2 matrix $\begin{pmatrix} a & b \\ c & d \end{pmatrix}$ can represent a transformation of the plane, and the image (x', y') of the point (x, y) can be found by using

$$\begin{pmatrix} a & b \\ c & d \end{pmatrix} \begin{pmatrix} x \\ y \end{pmatrix} = \begin{pmatrix} x' \\ y' \end{pmatrix}$$

As the origin does not move in such a transformation, only transformations in which the origin is an invariant point can be represented by a 2×2 matrix.

The images of the points (1, 0), (0, 1) and (1, 1)

As $\begin{pmatrix} a & b \\ c & d \end{pmatrix} \begin{pmatrix} 1 \\ 0 \end{pmatrix} = \begin{pmatrix} a \\ c \end{pmatrix}$, the image of $(1, 0)$ is (a, c);

$\begin{pmatrix} a & b \\ c & d \end{pmatrix} \begin{pmatrix} 0 \\ 1 \end{pmatrix} = \begin{pmatrix} b \\ d \end{pmatrix}$, the image of $(0, 1)$ is (b, d);

$\begin{pmatrix} a & b \\ c & d \end{pmatrix} \begin{pmatrix} 1 \\ 1 \end{pmatrix} = \begin{pmatrix} a+b \\ c+d \end{pmatrix}$, the image of $(1,1)$ is $(a + b, c + d)$.

The three equations above can be condensed into one equation:

$$\begin{pmatrix} a & b \\ c & d \end{pmatrix} \begin{pmatrix} 1 & 0 & 1 \\ 0 & 1 & 1 \end{pmatrix} = \begin{pmatrix} a & b & a+b \\ c & d & c+d \end{pmatrix}$$

These results show how the **unit square** OABC is transformed under the transformation represented by the matrix $\begin{pmatrix} a & b \\ c & d \end{pmatrix}$. In general, the square becomes a parallelogram; with appropriate values of a, b, c and d it may be a square, a rhombus or a rectangle.

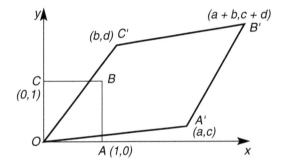

Finding the marix of a given transformation

If we investigate the effect of the transformation on the points $(1, 0)$ and $(0, 1)$ we see from the above that the matrix is known, since the position vectors of the images of these points are the columns of the matrix.

Example 15

Under the transformation, 'reflect in the line $y = -x$', we see from the diagram that

$(1, 0) \rightarrow (0, -1)$ and $(0, 1) \rightarrow (-1, 0)$

and so the matrix of the transformation is $\begin{pmatrix} 0 & -1 \\ -1 & 0 \end{pmatrix}$.

If we consider the effect of this matrix on the general point (x, y), we see that

$\begin{pmatrix} 0 & -1 \\ -1 & 0 \end{pmatrix} \begin{pmatrix} x \\ y \end{pmatrix} = \begin{pmatrix} -y \\ -x \end{pmatrix}$ and so $(x, y) \rightarrow (-y, -x)$

showing that all points in the plane are reflected in the line $y = -x$.

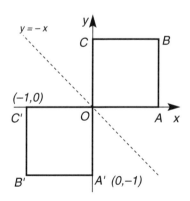

To find the transformation associated with a given matrix

The same technique can be used. The images of the vertices of the unit square OABC can be found using the matrix, and, from a diagram showing OABC and its image OA'B'C', the transformation can be described.

Example 16

To find the transformation whose matrix is $\begin{pmatrix} 0 & -1 \\ 1 & 0 \end{pmatrix}$, we find the images of (1, 0), (0, 1) and (1, 1) to be (0, 1), (−1, 0) and (−1, 1) respectively, using $\begin{pmatrix} 0 & -1 \\ 1 & 0 \end{pmatrix} \begin{pmatrix} 1 & 0 & 1 \\ 0 & 1 & 1 \end{pmatrix} = \begin{pmatrix} 0 & -1 & -1 \\ 1 & 0 & 1 \end{pmatrix}$.

From the diagram we see that the transformation is a rotation of 90° anti-clockwise about the origin.

Combinations of transformations

If matrix $\mathbf{A_m}$ represents transformation **A** and matrix $\mathbf{B_m}$ represents transformation **B**, the matrix of the single transformation equivalent to '**A** followed by **B**' can be found by multiplying the single matrices in the order $\mathbf{B_m} \, \mathbf{A_m}$.

EXERCISE 12.9

1 Describe fully the transformations represented by the following matrices.

(a) $\begin{pmatrix} \frac{1}{2} & 0 \\ 0 & \frac{1}{2} \end{pmatrix}$ (b) $\begin{pmatrix} 0 & 1 \\ 1 & 0 \end{pmatrix}$ (c) $\begin{pmatrix} 0 & -1 \\ 1 & 0 \end{pmatrix}$ (d) $\begin{pmatrix} -1 & 0 \\ 0 & 1 \end{pmatrix}$ (e) $\begin{pmatrix} 5 & 0 \\ 0 & 1 \end{pmatrix}$

2 Find the matrices that represent the following transformations of the plane.

(a) A reflection in the *x*-axis.

(b) An enlargement, centre the origin, of scale factor −3.

(c) A rotation about the origin through an angle of 180° (a half-turn).

3 The diagram shows the effect on the unit square of an anti-clockwise rotation through 30° about the origin.

(a) Show that the coordinates of A' are $(\frac{\sqrt{3}}{2}, \frac{1}{2})$.

(b) Find the coordinates of C'.

(c) Show that the matrix of this transformations is $\begin{pmatrix} \frac{\sqrt{3}}{2} & -\frac{1}{2} \\ \frac{1}{2} & \frac{\sqrt{3}}{2} \end{pmatrix}$.

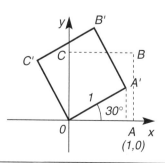

4 Copy the diagram onto graph paper.

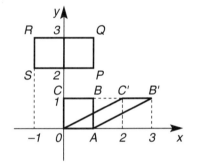

(a) Find the images A', B', C' of the points A, B and C under the transformation **T**, whose matrix is $\begin{pmatrix} -2 & 0 \\ 0 & 2 \end{pmatrix}$ and draw the image triangle A'B'C'.

(b) **T** is a combination of a reflection **R** and an enlargement **E**, centre O.
  (i) Write down the equation of the line of the reflection.
  (ii) Write down the scale factor of the enlargement.

(c) Write down the matrices, $\mathbf{R_m}$ and $\mathbf{E_m}$ representing **R** and **E** and form their product $\mathbf{R_m}\,\mathbf{E_m}$.

(d) Find the images of A, B and C using the matrix found in (c).

5 Copy the diagram shown onto graph paper.
A transformation **S** of the plane maps the square OABC onto the parallelogram OAB'C'.

(a) Write down the matrix $\mathbf{S_m}$ for **S**.

(b) Use this matrix to find the images of the points P, Q, R and S, and add to the diagram the image of this square under **S**.

(c) Find the matrix $\mathbf{S_m^2}$ and deduce that for $\mathbf{S_m^{10}}$.

6 On graph paper draw the triangle ABC where the coordinates of A, B and C are (2, 2), (4, 2) and (3, 5) respectively.

(a) Find the images A', B' and C' of A, B and C under the transformation whose matrix is $\begin{pmatrix} 3 & 1 \\ 2 & 1 \end{pmatrix}$, and draw the image triangle.

(b) Show that the two triangles are equal in area.

(c) Find the matrix of the transformation that maps triangle A'B'C' back onto triangle ABC.

7 On squared paper plot the points A(1, 1), B(3, 1), and C(3, 4). **X** is 'reflection in the x-axis', **R** is 'rotation of 90° clockwise about the origin'.

(a) Draw the image triangle A'B'C' under **X**.

(b) Draw the image triangle A"B"C" of A'B'C' under **R**.

(c) Write down the matrices $\mathbf{X_m}$ for **X** and $\mathbf{R_m}$ for **R** and form the product matrix $\mathbf{R_m X_m}$.

(d) Show that the images of A, B and C using $\mathbf{R_m X_m}$ are A", B" and C".

(e) Describe the single transformation that maps ABC onto A"B"C".

(f) Find the images of A, B and C under the transformation represented by the matrix $\mathbf{X_m R_m}$.

(g) Describe the single transformation having the same effect as 'transformation **R** followed by transformation **X**'.

8 **P** is the matrix representing $\mathbf{T_P}$, the reflection in the line $y = -x$. **Q** is the matrix representing $\mathbf{T_Q}$, the reflection in the x-axis.

(a) Write down the matrices **P** and **Q**.

(b) Without the aid of any calculation explain why $\mathbf{P}^2 = \begin{pmatrix} 1 & 0 \\ 0 & 1 \end{pmatrix}$.

(c) Write down the matrices (i) $\mathbf{P}^{-1}$, (ii) $\mathbf{Q}^7$.

(d) Show that the matrix representing '$\mathbf{T_Q}$ followed by $\mathbf{T_P}$' is $\begin{pmatrix} 0 & 1 \\ -1 & 0 \end{pmatrix}$.

(e) Name the single transformation equivalent to '$\mathbf{T_Q}$ followed by $\mathbf{T_P}$'.

(f) Find the matrix representing '$\mathbf{T_P}$ followed by $\mathbf{T_Q}$'.

(g) Show that $(\mathbf{PQ})^{-1} = \mathbf{Q}^{-1} \mathbf{P}^{-1}$.

Investigation B

In the last exercise the transformation **S** is called a **shear** in which all the points on the x-axis remain fixed and all other points move parallel to the x-axis. Find out more about shears and write notes.

Investigation C

Investigate the effect of the matrix $\begin{pmatrix} \frac{1}{\sqrt{2}} & -\frac{1}{\sqrt{2}} \\ \frac{1}{\sqrt{2}} & \frac{1}{\sqrt{2}} \end{pmatrix}$ on points in the plane.

Find the determinant of this matrix. Write down the matrix that represents an anti-clockwise rotation through $x°$ about O, and deduce that for a clockwise rotation through the same angle.

Investigation D

Investigate the effect of the matrix $\begin{pmatrix} 3 & 2 \\ 6 & 4 \end{pmatrix}$ on points in the plane. Try to include answers to the following questions:
What happens to points (a) on the x-axis, (b) on the y-axis, (c) on the line $x = 2$, (d) on the line $y = x$? What do the images of all the points on the plane have in common?

Investigation E

The figure shows the images of the unit square under a transformation represented by the matrix $\begin{pmatrix} a & b \\ c & d \end{pmatrix}$. Show that the area of OA'B'C' is the value of the determinant, ad-bc. What happens in the case of a singular matrix?

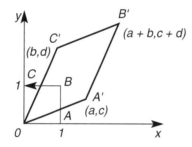

13. Revision exercises

1 A salesman was paid a basic salary of £900 per month, plus $2\frac{1}{2}\%$ commission on the amount by which his sales exceeded £5000.

(a) Calculate his pay for a month in which he sold £13 000 worth of goods.

A new pay deal increased his basic pay by 10%, but his commission was changed to $1\frac{1}{2}\%$, payable on *all* sales.

(b) Calculate his pay under the new pay deal for a month in which he sold £13 000 worth of goods.   (L 1991)

2 (a) Work out $(a + b)(c + d)$.

(b) Jhoti wanted to use her calculator to work out the exact value of 537 142 × 612 304. Work this out on your calculator. Write down the display. Explain why this is not an exact result.

(c) Jhoti then wrote the problem as (537 000 + 142)(612 000 + 304).
   (i) Using the result obtained in part (a), explain how she could find an exact answer to the problem.
   (ii) What is the exact answer?   (N 1992)

3 In a classic experiment to verify Newton's law of gravitation, the mass of a cone-shaped mountain was used to deflect a pendulum. Measured to the nearest 0.1 km, the mountain has a base diameter of 3.4 km and a height of 0.9 km.

(a) Using the formula for the volume of a cone

$$V = \tfrac{1}{3}\pi r^2 h$$

calculate an interval estimate of the volume of the mountain, in km³, giving the bounds to 2 decimal places.

(b) The average density of the mountain is 1.5 tonnes per cubic metre, measured to 1 decimal place. Use your answer in (a) to calculate a lower and an upper bound for the mass of the mountain. Express your answers in standard index form.
           (M 166/5)

4 Which of the following numbers are rational?

(a) 3.14   (b) √3   (c) π^2

(d) $0.\dot{3}$ (e) $\dfrac{53}{107}$ (f) √169   (S, specimen paper)

5 A local authority collects £3.2 × 10⁹ in local taxes. It receives a grant of £8.2 × 10⁸ from Central Government.

(*a*) How much does the local authority receive altogether? Give your answer in standard form.

The Fire Service takes 6% of the total received by the local authority.

(*b*) Calculate the amount of money the Fire Service takes. Give your answer in standard form. (L 1993)

6 The area of a rectangular field is 28 500 square metres and its length is 195 metres, both measurements being correct to 3 significant figures.

(*a*) Find

(i) the greatest possible breadth of the field,
(ii) the smallest possible breadth of the field.

(*b*) What is the breadth of the field correct to 2 significant figures? (N, specimen paper)

7 (*a*) State whether the following numbers are rational or irrational:

$$1.\dot{3}, \qquad \sqrt{3}, \qquad \sqrt{4}, \qquad \sqrt{8}, \qquad \frac{1}{\pi}.$$

(*b*) Give an example of

(i) two irrational numbers whose sum is irrational;
(ii) two irrational numbers whose sum is rational;
(iii) two irrational numbers whose product is rational.

(*c*) Explain what is meant by an irrational number.

(*d*) Prove that the irrational number $\sqrt{2}$ can be represented by a point on an ordinary number scale. (M, specimen paper)

8 When a rod, length L cm, is heated through $T°$C, it expands. Its new length, X cm, is given by the formula

$$X = L + aLT$$

(*a*) Find the new length of a rod when $L = 2$, $a = 0.01$ and $T = 5$.

(*b*) For another rod, $X = 3.1$ when $L = 3$ and $T = 4$. Calculate the value of a.

(*c*) Rearrange the formula $X = L + aLT$ to make T the subject. (S 1992)

9 (a) 1.4 is an approximation for $\sqrt{2}$, correct to 1 decimal place.

Write an approximation for $\sqrt{2}$, correct to 3 decimal places.

(b) What percentage error in the value for 2 does this give when you square it? Show your working.

(c) Tandy finds an approximation for $\sqrt{2}$, correct to n decimal places. She squares it. It gives an error of less than 0.01% in the value for 2. What is the least possible value of n? Show your working. (KS3 1993)

10 Julie swims one length of a pool. The teacher says the length is 27.30 metres.

(a) Using the teacher's measurement of 27.30 metres what are the minimum and maximum lengths the pool can be?

The clock used to time the swimming race adds one to the hundredths digit at the end of each completed hundredth of a second. When the race starts the clock shows 00.00. After one hundredth of a second the clock shows 00.01.

(b) When Julie finishes the length the clock shows 24.37 seconds. What is the shortest possible time Julie took?

(c) What are the minimum and maximum average speeds at which Julie swam the distance 27.30 m in the time the clock showed as 24.37 seconds? Give your answers to 4 decimal places. (KS3 1993)

11 Given the formula:

$$T_n = \tfrac{1}{2}n(n + 1).$$

(a) Copy and complete the table below.

n	T_n	T_{n-1}	$T_n - T_{n-1}$	$T_n + T_{n-1}$	$T_n{}^2 - T_{n-1}{}^2$
1	1	0	1	1	1
2	3	1	2	4	8
3	6	3			
4					
5	15	10	5	25	125

(b) Write down the value of (i) T_6, (ii) $T_7 - T_6$,
    (iii) $T_{11} + T_{10}$, (iv) $T_{100}{}^2 - T_{99}{}^2$.

(c) What is the name given to the sequence of numbers in (i) the second column, (ii) the fifth column, (iii) the sixth column?

(M 1993; 1651/6)

12 (a) Solve the equation

$$x^5 = 0.00243$$

(b) Once a year a scientist measured the mass of a certain piece of a decaying radioactive element. His results are shown.

Time (years)	0	1	2	3
Mass (kg)	20	18	16.2	14.58

    (i) Calculate the annual percentage decrease of the mass.

    (ii) Calculate the mass after 10 years.

    (iii) Estimate the half life of the element (i.e. the time it takes to lose half of its mass). (S, specimen paper)

13 Functions f and g are defined as follows.

    f: $x \mapsto 1 - 2x$,   g: $x \mapsto x^2$.

(a) Write down the values of

    (i) f(2),   (ii) fg(−2).

(b) Write down, in terms of x, the inverse function of f.

(c) Find an expression in terms of x for gf(x) and explain why gf(x) ≥ 0 for all values of x. (N 1990)

14 The costs of raspberries and strawberries at a 'pick your own' farm are x and y pence per pound respectively.

Llinos collects 2 lb of raspberries and 5 lb of strawberries and pays a total of £3.10.

Nazir collects 3 lb of raspberries and 4 lb of strawberries and pays a total of £2.97.

(a) Write down two equations connecting x and y.

(b) Solve the equations to find the cost per pound of

    (i) raspberries,   (ii) strawberries. (W 1993)

15 A cyclist finds that he can save one hour over a distance of 100 km by increasing his usual average speed by 2 km h^{-1}.

Take his usual average speed to be x km h^{-1}. Write down expressions in terms of x for

(*a*) his usual time,

(*b*) his new speed,

(*c*) his new time.

Form an equation and solve it to find his usual average speed in km h^{-1}. (M, specimen paper)

16 The functions f and g are defined by

$$f: x \mapsto 2x + 1$$
$$g: x \mapsto \frac{6}{x} \qquad (x \neq 0)$$

Calculate: (*a*) f(3), (*b*) g(2), (*c*) fg(2), (*d*) gf(2).

(*e*) Find and simplify, but do not solve, the quadratic equation which is equivalent to

$$f(x) = g(x).$$

(*f*) Calculate f^{-1}(2). (L 1992)

17 In the rectangle ABCD, AB $= (3x + 4)$ cm and BC $= (x - 2)$ cm.

(*a*) Explain why AB > 10 cm.

(*b*) (i) Given the AC $= 20$ cm, show that

$$x^2 + 2x - 38 = 0.$$

(ii) Find, correct to 2 decimal places, the two values of x for which

$$x^2 + 2x - 38 = 0.$$

(iii) Hence calculate the length of BC. (M 1992; 1651/6)

Not to scale

18 The velocity, v m/s, of a particle P after t seconds is given by

$$v = 5 + 4t - t^2, t > 0.$$

(*a*) Calculate the value of v after 3 seconds.

(*b*) Calculate the value of t when v becomes zero.

(*c*) Calculate the maximum value of v. (L 1993)

19 The force, **F** Newtons, with which two magnets attract each other is inversely proportional to the square of their distance, *d* cm, apart. When the two magnets are 2.5 cm apart, the attractive force between them is 12 Newtons.

   (i) Obtain an expression for **F** in terms of *d*.

   (ii) Calculate the force between the magnets when their distance apart is 5 cm.

   (iii) Without further calculations, explain the effect of doubling the distance between the magnets on the attractive force between them.   (W 1993)

20   f: $x \mapsto 5x + 4$,
      g: $x \mapsto 4x + 3$.

  (*a*) Find g(2).

  (*b*) Solve, for *x*, the equation $f(x) = g(2)$.

  (*c*) Copy and complete the following, simplifying as appropriate

    (i) $f^{-1}: x \mapsto \ldots$,

    (ii) ff: $x \mapsto \ldots$.

  (*d*) Show that $f(g(x)) = g(f(x))$.

  (*e*) Solve the equation

$$g(x) = \frac{2}{x}$$

    giving your answers to 2 decimal places.   (L 1993)

21 The values of *x* satisfy the inequality

    $3x + 1 \leq 27 \leq 5x - 6$.

  (*a*) (i) Find the largest possible value of *x*.
      (ii) Find the smallest possible value of *x*.

  (*b*) Write down all the possible integer values of *x*.
                         (M 1992; 1651/3)

22 The volume of milk in a full milk bottle is $3d^3 - 3d$.
    The volume of milk in a full glass jug is $3d^3 - (3d - d^2)$.
    d is the thickness in millimetres of the glass.

  (*a*) Which has more milk, the bottle or the jug? Write the volume of the milk in the jug in a different way to help you explain your decision.

The volume of milk in a full glass bowl is $2d^3 + d^2$.

Diana wants to find the value of d for which the volume of milk in the bottle is the same as the volume of milk in the bowl.

This is when $3d^3 - 3d = 2d^3 + d^2$.

She decides to plot the graph of $d \to d^3$.

(b) What other graph should she plot on the same grid to help her find d?

(c) How should Diana use both graphs to find the value of d?

(KS 3)

23 (a) Taking 2 cm to represent 1 unit on each axis, draw the graph of $y = (x - 1)(x + 3)$ for values of x from -4 to $+2$.

(b) Use your graph to find approximate solutions to the equation $(x - 1)(x + 3) = 3$.

(c) By adding a suitable straight line to your graph, estimate the range of values of x for which

$$x^2 + 3x - 1 < 0.$$

(L 1993)

24 $f(x) = x^2$ and $g(x) = x^2 - 2x + 3$.

(a) $g(x) = f(x - a) + b$, where a and b are constants. Find the values of a and b.

(b) Hence sketch the graphs of f and g, indicating clearly the relationship between the two graphs.

(M, specimen paper; 1663/6)

25 The flow chart for a calculation, to be done with a calculator, is shown below.

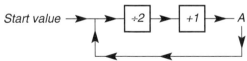

The output number at A is always fed back to provide the next input. The process repeats for ever.

(a) Describe what happens to the value of the number at A as you repeat the process using 5 as the start value.

(b) Try other start values and comment on your findings.

(c) Describe what happens, for various start values, for the new flow chart shown overleaf.

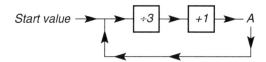

(*d*) For the flow chart shown below, describe what happens when
(i) $p = 4$, (ii) $p = 5$, (iii) $p = n$ (*n* a posiive whole number).

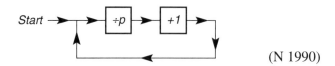

(N 1990)

26 The following table is based on the performance figures for a car
as it accelerates from rest.

Time (seconds) t	0	2	4	6	8	10
Speed (metres per second) v	0	10	18	23.5	27.5	33

(*a*) Draw the graph of v against t.

(*b*) By drawing the tangent to the curve at (4, 18) estimate the
gradient of the curve at this point.

(*c*) What does this value indicate about the motion of the car
after 4 seconds?

(*d*) Describing your method clearly, estimate the area of the
region bounded by the curve, the t-axis and the line $t = 10$.

(*e*) What does this value represent?   (N, specimen paper)

27 The diagram shows the speed-time graph for a train over a
period of 120 seconds. Calculate

(*a*) the total time, in seconds, that the train
is travelling at a speed of 20 m/s,

(*b*) the total distance, in m, travelled,

(*c*) the average speed, in m/s to 3
significant figures, for the total period.

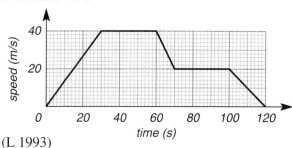

(L 1993)

28 The graph shows the cross-section of a river.
The measurements have been taken under a bridge across
the river.
The width of the river at this point is 80 m.

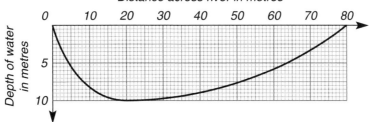

Calculate the approximate area, in m^2, of the cross-section of the river under the bridge.

Use the trapezium rule and take four strips of equal width.

(L 1993)

29 (a) Show that the equation $4 - x^2 = x^3$ can be rearranged to solve each of the following:

(i) $x = \dfrac{4}{x^2} - 1$, (ii) $x = \dfrac{2}{\sqrt{(1 + x)}}$

(b) Using your solutions in (a) as x, determine whether the sequences generated by the iterative formulas below are convergent.

(i) $x_{n+1} = \dfrac{4}{x_n^2} - 1$ (ii) $x_{n+1} = \dfrac{2}{\sqrt{(1 + x_n)}}$

(c) Write down, correct to one decimal place, the positive solution of the equation $4 - x^2 = x^3$. (L, specimen paper)

30 (a) The formula

$$A = 2\pi r^2 + 2\pi rh$$

gives the surface area A of a cylinder in terms of the radius r and the height h. Make h the subject of the formula.

(b) Use your result from part (a) to show that the volume, V, of the cylinder in terms of A and r, can be written

$$V = \tfrac{1}{2} Ar - \pi r^3$$

(c) Copy and complete the table of values below for the function $V = 50r - 3r^3$.

r	0	0.5	1	1.5	2	2.5	3	3.5	4
V	0	24.6	47	64.9					8

(*d*) On graph paper, using a scale of 4 cm to represent 1 unit on the horizontal *r*-axis and a scale of 2 cm to represent 10 units on the vertical *V*-axis, draw a graph of $V = 50r - 3r^3$ for values of *r* between 0 and 4.

(*e*) Use your graph to find the greatest value of *V* in the range $0 \le r \le 4$, and write down the corresponding value of *r*.

(*f*) By comparing the formulae in parts (*b*) and (*c*), explain your answer to part (*e*) in terms of a cylinder.   (M 1993; 1651/6)

31 The diagram shows an open rectangular tank whose base is a square of side *x* metres and whose volume is 8 m³.

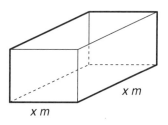

(*a*) Write down an expression in terms of *x* for the height of the tank.

(*b*) Show that the surface area of the tank is

$$(x^2 + \frac{32}{x}) \, \text{m}^2.$$

(*c*) Copy and complete the given table of values for

$$y = x^2 + \frac{32}{x} \, .$$

x	1	2	3	4	5	6
x^2	1			16		36
$\dfrac{32}{x}$	32			8		5.33
y	33			24		41.33

(*d*) On graph paper, using a scale of 2 cm to represent one unit on the *x*-axis and 2 cm to represent 5 units on the *y*-axis, plot the points from your completed table and join them to form a smooth curve.

(*e*) From your graph find the value of *x* for which the tank has a minimum surface area.

Given that the surface area is 27 m²,

(*f*) write down the two possible values of *x*.   (L 1993)

32 A sailing race is over a triangular course, ABC, starting and finishing at A. The first leg of the course, AB, is 5 km on a bearing of 060° to a bouy at B. The third leg, CA, is 6 km, with A due north of C.

(*a*) Calculate the distance and the bearing of the second leg, from B to C.

Support your answer with a clear sketch showing A, B and C and marking relevant angles and distances.

(*b*) If the bearing of B from A, given as 060°, is only accurate to the nearest 10°, what is the greatest possible length of BC? (You may assume that the 5 km and 6 km are still correct.)
(M, specimen paper; 1665)

33 The graph shows how the speed of a car varies with time during a 35 second journey.

(*a*) Describe what happens in the first 20 seconds of the journey.

(*b*) Estimate by drawing a suitable tangent, the acceleration 5 seconds after the start of the journey.

(*c*) Calculate the disance travelled in the last 15 seconds of the journey. (M 1992; 1651/3)

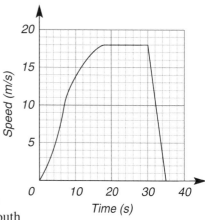

34 The diagram shows the positions of four buildings, on the same horizontal level. A garage G is 8.7 kilometres due south of a hostel H. An inn I is 12.9 kilometres due east of the hostel. A café C is 8.0 kilometres from G on a bearing of 127° (S53°E). Calculate

(*a*) the size, in degrees, of the angle HGI,

(*b*) the distance GI, in kilometres correct to 3 significant figures,

(*c*) the distance IC, in kilometres correct to 3 significant figures,

Given that it is possible to search an area of 6 square kilometres in one hour, calculate

(*d*) how long, to the nearest hour, it would take to search the area inside the quadrilaterial GCIH. (L 1988)

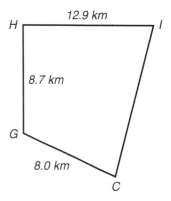

35 (*a*) Find the gradient of the line $4y = 3x + 8$.

(*b*) Draw the graph of $x + y = 3$ on a copy of the axes shown.

(*c*) Indicate clearly on your diagram the region defined by the inequalities

$$4y \geq 3x + 8$$
$$x + y \leq 3$$
$$y \geq 1$$

(M 1993; 1651/3)

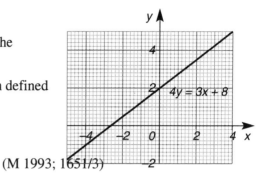

36

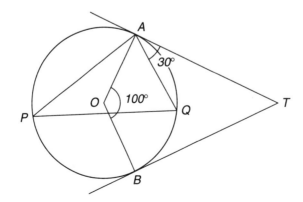

Write down four inequalities which define the shaded region.

(L 1993)

37 $\overrightarrow{OA} = \begin{pmatrix} 4 \\ 3 \end{pmatrix}$ and $\overrightarrow{OB} = \begin{pmatrix} 5 \\ 1 \end{pmatrix}$

OA and OB are sides of a parallelogram OACB.
Find the area of the parallelogram OACB.

(N, specimen paper)

38 The diagram shows a circle, centre O. AT and BT are tangents to the circle and P and Q are points on its circumference.

Angle AOB = 100° and angle QAT = 30°.

Stating your reasons and showing your working, calculate the size of

(i) angle ATB,   (ii) angle BPQ.   (N, specimen paper)

39 (i) The line TS is the tangent at S to the circle PQRS. Given that SP = ST, PR is parallel to TS and angle PTS = 65°, calculate the size of

    (*a*) angle PST,

    (*b*) angle PRS,

    (*c*) angle PSR.

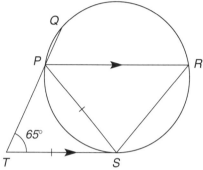

(ii) The point O is the centre of the circle ABECD and angle ADC = 110°. Calculate the size of

    (*a*) angle ABC,

    (*b*) angle AOC,

    (*c*) angle AEC.   (L 1993)

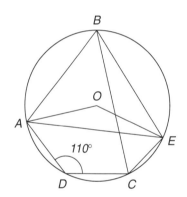

40 Two lightships, A and B, are 30 km apart. The bearing of A from B is 120°. A yachtsman at Y finds that the bearing of A is 140°, and the bearing of B is 246°. Calculate the distance of Y from A.
                                   (S, specimen paper)

41 A wedge of cheese is in the shape of a prism as shown. It is cut into two equal volumes by a single cut, parallel to one face. Calculate the value of *x*.   (N, specimen paper)

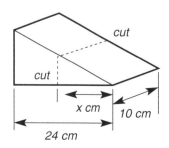

42 A roof is made of wooden beams which form a pyramid.
The base is a horizontal rectangle, ABCD, with AB = 15 m and
BC = 10 m. The vertex E is vertically above the mid-point, O, of
the base. The triangle BEC makes an angle of 35° with the base.

(*a*) Calculate the length of the beam BE.

(*b*) Calculate the angle between triangle AEB and the base.

(S, specimen paper)

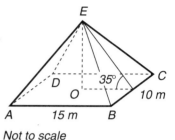

Not to scale

43 (*a*) In the triangle OAB, OA = 3 m, OB = 8 m and
angle AOB = 15°.

Calculate , correct to 2 decimal places,

(i) the length of AB
(ii) the area of triangle OAB.

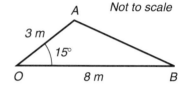

(*b*)

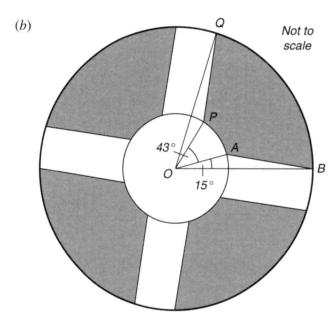

The plan of an ornamental garden shows two circles, centre O,
with radii 3 m and 8 m.

Paths of equal width cut symmetrically across the circles.

The shaded areas represent flower beds.

BQ and AP are arcs of the circles.

Triangle OAB is the same triangle shown in part (*a*) above.

Given that angle POA = 43°, calculate the area of
(i) sector OPA, (ii) sector OQB, (iii) the flower bed PABQ.

(M 1992; 1651/6)

44 Three points A, B and C are on horizontal ground. The distance AB is 60 m. The bearing of B from A is 040° (N40°E). The distance BC is 90 m. The bearing of C from B is 120° (S60°E). D is the point on CB produced which is nearest to A. Calculate

(*a*) the distance AD, in m to 3 significant figures,

(*b*) the distance AC, in m to 3 significant figures,

(*c*) the bearing of C from A, to the nearest degree.　　(L 1993)

45 (*a*) In triangle ABC, AB = 5 cm, BC = 6 cm, AC = 9 cm and angle ABC = x°. Show that cos x° = $-\frac{1}{3}$.

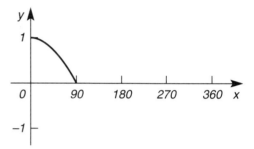

(*b*) (i) The sketch graph is of $y = \cos x$° for $0 \le x \le 90$. Continue this sketch graph for $90 \le x \le 360$.

(ii) The x coordinate of one point, P, on your sketch graph corresponds to the value of angle ABC from part (*a*). Mark the point P on your graph.

(iii) Calculate the x coordinate of P. Give your answer correct to the nearest 0.1°.　　(M 1993; 1651/3)

46 In the diagram, $\overrightarrow{OP} = \mathbf{p}$, $\overrightarrow{OQ} = \mathbf{q}$. Given that M is the mid-point of PQ, find

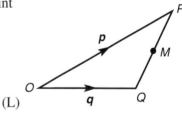

(*a*) the vector $\overrightarrow{QM}$ in terms of $\mathbf{p}$ and $\mathbf{q}$.

(*b*) Find the values of h and k such that

$$(h + 4)\mathbf{p} + (h - k + 2)\mathbf{q} = \mathbf{0}.$$　　(L)

47 **M** is the transformation represented by the matrix $\begin{pmatrix} 1 & 0 \\ 3 & 1 \end{pmatrix}$.

P is the point (*a*, *b*) and **M** maps P to the point (3, 6).

Find the values of *a* and *b*.　　(L)

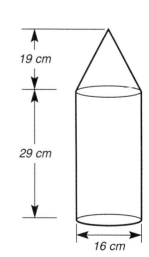

48 The diagram represents a 1 : 50 scale model of a church tower with a spire. The tower is cylindrical and the spire is conical.

On the model, the height of the tower is 29 cm and the height of the spire is 19 cm.

(*a*) Calculate the total volume, in cm³, of the model.

(*b*) Find the ratio of the volume of the scale model to the volume of the real tower and spire.

(*c*) Hence, or otherwise, calculate the total volume of the real tower and spire. Give your answer in m³. (L)

49 The position vector of the point A is $\begin{pmatrix} 3 \\ -1 \end{pmatrix}$, that of the point B is $\begin{pmatrix} 4 \\ 4 \end{pmatrix}$ and O is the origin.

(*a*) Find $\overrightarrow{AB}$.

(*b*) $\overrightarrow{BC} = 3\,\overrightarrow{OA}$. Find the coordinates of C.

(*c*) The point P has coordinates (*x, y*). If BP = 5, find an equation connecting *x* and *y*. (M 1990; 1650/3)

50 A model of a square-based pyramid is to be made with each edge 2 cm long.

(*a*) Calculate the height of E above the plane ABCD.

(*b*) Calculate the angle between the face ABE and the plane ABCD. (N 1988)

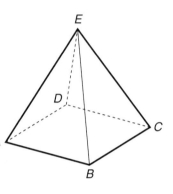

51 The diagram shows a cylindrical metal tube of length 2 m, with an internal radius of 10 cm and an external radius of 18 cm.

(*a*) Calculate the volume of metal, giving your answer in cm³ correct to 3 signficant figures.

The total mass of the tube is 6.3×10^5 g
(*b*) Calculate the mass in grammes of 1 cm³ of metal.

A solid cylinder of radius 8 cm has the same volume as the tube.
(*c*) Find the length of the cylinder. (L 1988)

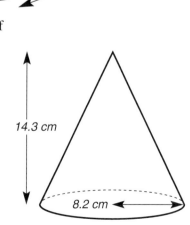

52 A conical firework has a base radius of 8.2 cm and a height of 14.3 cm.

(*a*) Calculate the volume of the firework.

(*b*) The label on the firework covers the entire sloping face. Calculate the surface area of the label. (W 1993)

53 (*a*) Express $\overrightarrow{JL}$ in terms of **a** and **b**.

(*b*) Express $\overrightarrow{JN}$ interms of **a**, **b**, **c** and **d**.

(*c*) The line JL meets the line KN at P and

$$\overrightarrow{KP} = \tfrac{1}{4}\overrightarrow{KN}.$$

Express $\overrightarrow{KP}$ in terms of **b**, **c** and **d**.

(*d*) Given that $\overrightarrow{PL} = \tfrac{1}{2}\overrightarrow{JL}$, and using triangle KPL or otherwise, show that

$$2\mathbf{a} + \mathbf{b} = \mathbf{c} + \mathbf{d}. \qquad\qquad \text{(N 1992)}$$

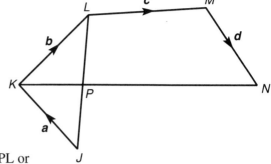

54 A mathematician looking for Christmas presents noticed that the three types of wine glass in a certain store were all similar in shape and that

$$\frac{\text{radius of base of type A}}{\text{radius of base of type B}} = \frac{\text{radius of base of type B}}{\text{radius of base of type C}} = \frac{2}{3}.$$

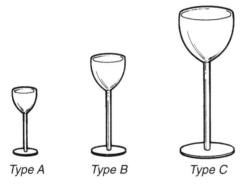

Type A   Type B   Type C

(*a*) Calculate

(i) $\dfrac{\text{perimeter of bowl of glass type C}}{\text{perimeter of bowl of glass type B}}$,

(ii) $\dfrac{\text{radius of base of glass type C}}{\text{radius of base of glass type A}}$,

(iii) $\dfrac{\text{volume of bowl of glass type A}}{\text{volume of bowl of glass type B}}$.

(*b*) If the prices of the wine glasses were in direct proportion to the volume of bowl, and glass type B cost £3.51, what would be the price of glass type A? (N 1988)

55 (*a*) Find the 2 by 2 matrix representing the mapping **Y**, which reflects points in the *y*-axis.

(*b*) By considering the images of the points A (5, 0), B(4, 2) and C(1, 3), find out the mapping represented by the matrix

$$\mathbf{M} = \begin{pmatrix} 0.6 & 0.8 \\ 0.8 & -0.6 \end{pmatrix}$$

(*c*) Investigate the effect of the mapping corresponding to the matrices **YM** and **MY**, describing them as precisely as you can.

(M, specimen paper; 1663/6)

56

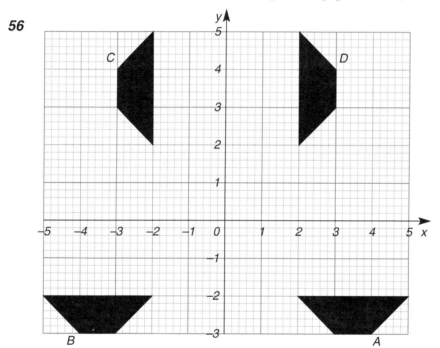

(*a*) Describe fully *two* different single transformations that will each move shape A to shape B.

(*b*) Describe fully the single transformation that moves shape A to shape C.

(*c*) Describe fully the single transformation that moves shape A to shape D. (N 1992)

57 ABCDEFGH is a regular octagon with centre O. Name the triangle onto which triangle AOB is mapped under

(*a*) a reflection in the line GC,

(*b*) a clockwise rotation of 225° about O,

(*c*) an enlargement centre O of scale factor −1. (L 1993)

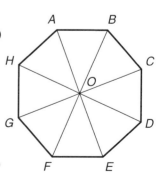

58 The shape A whose corners have coordinates (2, 1), (4, 2), (5, 4), (6, 1) is transformed to the shape B by transformation **P**. The shape B is then transformed to shape C by the transformation **Q**.

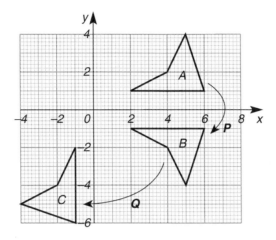

(*a*) Describe clearly the transformation **P**.

(*b*) Describe clearly the transformation **Q**.

(*c*) Find the matrix which represents the transformation **P**.

(*d*) Find the matrix which represents the transformation **Q**.

(*e*) Clearly showing your method, combine your matrices from (*c*) and (*d*) to find the *single* matrix which represents the transformation of shape A to shape C. (L 1992)

59 The activities which are necessary to assemble a piece of furniture are given in the table together with their durations and the preceding activities which must be completed first.

	Activity	Duration (minutes)	Preceding activity
A	Open box	1	–
B	Check parts against list	3	A
C	Check fixings against list	2	A
D	Assemble shell	4	B
E	Cut back to size	4	B
F	Screw shell together	2	C, D
G	Assemble drawers	2	B
H	Glue drawers	1	G
I	Put whole together	3	E, F, H

The furniture is completed when all activities are completed.

(*a*) Draw a network to represent the assembly of the furniture.

(*b*) Obtain the critical path and mark it on your diagram.

(*c*) State the minimum time in which the furniture could be
completed. (L 1993)

60 The activites involved when two workers replace a broken
window pane, and the times taken for each activity, are given in
the table below.

	Activity	Duration in minutes	Preceding activity
A	Remove broken pane	20	–
B	Measure size of pane	15	–
C	Purchase glass and putty	25	B
D	Put putty in frame	10	A, C
E	Put in new pane of glass	5	D
F	Putty outside and smooth	10	E
G	Sweep up broken glass	5	A
H	Clean up	5	F, G

Using a critical path diagram, or otherwise, find how the two
workers should share the activities to complete the replacement
of the broken window pane in the minimum possible time.

State this minimum time. (L, specimen paper)

61 A family decide to decorate the spare room and to have it ready
in time for Grandmother's visit from Australia.

The table lists the tasks that need o be done, which tasks must be
done before others can be started, and the duration of each task.

	Task	Duration (hours)	Tasks that must be completed first
A	Collect tools	1	–
B	Purchase materials	3	–
C	Clear room	2	–
D	Strip walls	3	A, C
E	Repair walls	3	D
F	Redecorate	4	B, E
G	Clean tools	1	F
H	Clean floor	1	F
I	Repair furniture	8	C
J	Replace furniture	1	H

Draw a network to show the order in which the tasks need to be done (assuming that there are as many willing workers as you need, so that several tasks can be progressing simultaneously).

Calculate the shortest time in which the project can be finished.

(M, specimen; 1665)

62 In an investigation, one ball is taken, at random, from the bag, its colour is recorded and it *is replaced*. A second ball is taken, at random, and its colour recorded.

A bag contains 20 balls, of which 3 are green, 5 are red and 12 are brown.

(*a*) Find the probability that a ball taken at random from the bag will be brown.

(*b*) Calculate the probability that
    (i) both balls will be brown,
    (ii) both balls will be the same colour,
    (iii) at least one ball will be brown. (L 1992)

63 On any day during the summer of 1979 the probability that it rained was $\frac{1}{6}$. In 1989, because of climatic changes, the probability that it rained on any day during the summer was only $\frac{1}{10}$.

(*a*) Calculate the probability that any 3 days chosen at random during the summer of 1979 were all wet.

(*b*) Calculate the probability that it rained on a particular date during the summer of 1979 and was dry on the same date in 1989. (S, specimen paper)

64 Each morning a teacher either walks, cycles or drives to school. The probabilities of each of these events are $\frac{1}{2}$, $\frac{1}{3}$ and $\frac{1}{6}$ respectively.

If she walks the probability that she will arrive late is $\frac{1}{6}$. If she cycles the probability that she will arrive late is $\frac{1}{4}$. If she drives the probability that she will arrive late is $\frac{1}{3}$.

(*a*) Copy and complete the tree diagram below, filling in all the probabilities.

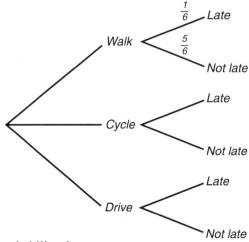

Find the probability that

(*b*) she cycles and is late,

(*c*) she doesn't walk and is not late,

(*d*) she is late.

A term consists of 60 teaching days.

(*e*) Find on how many of these she can expect to be late.

(L 1993)

65 A flour mill produces wholemeal flour.

The weights of the 500 g bags of flour are normally distributed with a mean of 500 g and a standard deviation of 7.5 g.

The graph shows an approximation to a normal distribution.

Estimate the probability that a 500 g bag of flour chosen at random weighs less than 485 g.

Explain your answer. (KS 3)

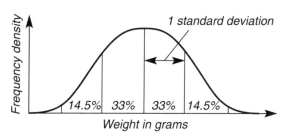

66

Type of medical operation	Frequency	Cost per operation (£)
Varicose veins	50	200
Stomach ulcers	32	450
Knee operations	18	520
Hip replacements	40	780

The table shows the frequency and cost of various medical operations in a hospital over one month.

(*a*) Calculate the mean cost of an operation.

(*b*) Calculate the standard deviation of the cost of an operation. Give your answer to the nearest pound. (L 1993)

67 (*a*) What is the difference between a census and a survey?

A group of 50 people were asked the number of jobs (x) they had applied for in the previous month. The data is presented below.

x	0	1	2	3	4	5
Frequency	3	7	16	13	8	3

(*b*) Calculate the mean and standard deviation of x.

A further group of 100 people were asked the same question and the mean of that sample was 2.0.

(*c*) Calculate the mean of the combined sample of 150 people. (L 1989)

68 A student studied the arrival of cuckoos in Britain by noting the date of the first reported sighting of a cuckoo each year over a period of fifty years. The student recorded the dates by counting x, the number of days after April 30th, so that , for example May 3rd was day 3 and April 28th was day -2. The data are shown in the table.

x	-2	-1	0	1	2	3
Frequency	4	8	12	7	9	10

(*a*) Calculate the mean value of *x*.

(*b*) Calculate the standard deviation of *x*. (L 1991)

69 The weights of babies at birth follow a Normal Distribution with mean 3.1 kilograms and standard deviation 0.5 kilograms.

(*a*) Calculate the probability that a baby will be born with a weight less than 3.7 kilograms.

Babies born with a weight less than 2.2 kilograms require special care.

(*b*) Calculate the number of babies with weights below 2.2 kilograms expected in a sample of 1000 births. Give your answer to the nearest whole number. (L 1993)

70 Caeron is a town with a population of 35 000. The council wants to modernise the town's community centre. It might include these:

youth club, theatre, cinema, art gallery,
bingo hall, disco, nursery.

The councillors are talking about choosing a sample for a survey that represents people's opinions of what the centre should contain.

Some of their comments are sensible and some are not:

1
Don't forget to ask all the community groups we already have in the town.

2
Let's ask everyone who lives near the community centre.

3
We don't need to ask many old people.

4
We only need to ask people who use the centre at the moment.

5
Don't forget the parents with young children…

(*a*) Pick out a comment that would not be sensible to follow up and explain why.

(*b*) Pick out a more sensible comment.

Describe in detail how you would use a **systematic** method for choosing a sample of people which would take account of the issues raised by this comment. (KS3)

71 The weights of a number of potatoes were recorded as follows.

Weight (grams)	Frequency
118–126	8
127–135	13
136–144	21
145–153	27
154–162	13
163–171	11
172–180	7

Calculate the standard deviation for the weights of the potatoes.
(N, specimen paper)

72 The Wellworthy Community Centre is organising a trip to the seaside in a coach.

The coach seats 61 people and costs £220.

It is decided to charge £5 for an adult and £3 for a child.

Adults may only go if they take at least one child.

Enough money must be collected to pay for the coach.

Let x be the number of adults, and let y be the number of children.

(a) Write down three inequalities in x and y which represent the information given.

(b) By graphing the inequalities, or otherwise:

(i) Work out the least number of adults that can go on the trip.

How many children go with them?

(ii) Work out the least number of children that can go on the trip.

How many adults go with them?

Show clearly how you obtain your answers.
(M, specimen paper; 1666)

73 The managing director of the Low-Price supermarket chain is interested in opening a new shop in the vicinity of a large town in the North East of England.

He decides to carry out a survey on a limited budget of £10 000.

Describe how he could organise the survey, taking particular care to show any calculations he might make to help him make decisions.   (N, specimen paper)

74 In a survey, a number of employees were asked how far away they lived from their place of work.

Each employee ticked one of the following responses:

0 km up to but not including 1 km,
1 km up to but not including 5 km,
5 km up to but not including 10 km,
10 km up to but not including 20 km,
20 km up to but not including 40 km,
40 km and over.

Exactly 100 ticked the '5 km up to but not including 10 km' response. No one ticked the '40 km and over' response.

The histogram shows the results of the survey.

Calculate the number of employees who took part in the survey.

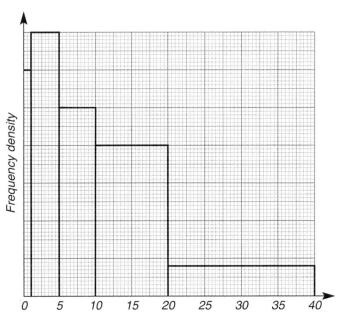

75 The ages of all the 100 employees in a company A are shown.

Age (years)	16–	21–	31–	41–	51–	61–	81–
Frequency	8	12	25	30	20	5	0
Frequency density	1.6	1.2					0

(*a*) (i) Complete the table of frequency densities.

(ii) On graph paper draw a histogram to illustrate the age distribution of the employees in company A.

Company B has the following age distribution of its employees.

Age (years)	16–30	31–40	41–50	51–80
% of employees	8	85	7	0

(*b*) Write down two comparisons about the age distributions of the employees of the two companies.

(S, specimen paper)

76 A fish tank of dimensions 40 cm × 40 cm × 90 cm contained two types of tropical fish; Dwarf Gourami (which have average length of 5 cm) and Climbing Perch (which have average length 20 cm). The Dwarf Gourami require 0.1 g of fish food each day whereas the Climbing Perch need 0.5 g each day.

(*a*) To exist in harmony it is assumed that each fish needs a volume equal to the cube of twice the average length. The number of Dwarf Gourami is x and the number of Climbing Perch is y. Show that x and y satisfy the inequality:

$$x + 64y \leq 144$$

(*b*) Each day 2 g of fish food is available. Show that

$$x + 5y \leq 20$$

(c) (i) Draw the lines $x + 64y = 144$ and $x + 5y = 20$ on graph paper.

(ii) In each case clearly identify which side of the line corresponds to the required inequalities.

(d) There must be at least one of each type of fish in the tank. What is the maximum possible number of fish in the tank?

(S, speciment paper)